D0469921

FAITH UNDONE

*the emerging
church ...
a new
reformation
or an
end-time
deception*

277.3083
O11f

FAITH UNDONE

the emerging church ... a new reformation or an end-time deception

Roger Oakland

Lighthouse Trails Publishing
Silverton, Oregon
San Diego Christian College
Library
Santee, CA

FAITH UNDONE

©2007 Roger Oakland

Published by:
Lighthouse Trails Publishing
P.O. Box 958
Silverton, Oregon 97381
www.lighthousetrails.com

For more information about the author and his ministry see:
Understand the Times
www.understandthetimes.org

All rights reserved. No part of this book may be reproduced, stored in a retrieval system, or transmitted in any form by any means, whether electronic, mechanical, photocopying, recordings, or otherwise without prior written permission from the publisher.

Unless otherwise indicated, Scripture quotations are taken from the King James Version.

Library of Congress Cataloging-in-Publication Data

Oakland, Roger, 1947-
 Faith undone : the emerging church— a new reformation or an end-time deception? / Roger Oakland.
    p. cm.
 Includes bibliographical references and index.
 ISBN-13: 978-0-9791315-1-6 (softbound : alk. paper)
 1. Church. 2. Postmodernism—Religious aspects—Christianity. I. Title.
 BV600.3.O25 2007
 277.3'083—dc22

                              2007011694

Note: Lighthouse Trails Publishing books are available at special quantity discounts. Contact information for publisher in back of book.

Printed in the United States of America

Dedicated to ...

Glen Mc Lean and Lorne Pritchard, who grounded my life in the teaching of the Word of God, to His grace, and to the Gospel of Jesus Christ, according to the Holy Scriptures

Contents

There is a way that seemeth right unto a man,
but the end thereof are the ways of death.
(Proverbs 16:25)

1

A New Kind of Church?

> You see, if we have a new world, we will need a new church. We won't need a new religion per se, but a new framework for our theology. Not a new Spirit, but a new spirituality. Not a new Christ, but a new Christian. Not a new denomination, but a new kind of church in every denomination.[1]—Brian McLaren

It's Saturday night, and inside the old, somewhat dilapidated brick building, in the heart of metropolis downtown, flames from several candles dance on the walls. There's a church service being held, but it's different from any you have seen before. Instead of pews, the congregants (mostly in their twenties) sit on old overstuffed couches and easy chairs spread around the darkened room in a kind of misshapen semicircle. A fellow sits on a bar stool, moderating the *meeting*, but rather than giving a sermon, he asks questions, suggesting several options for answers, and then joins the conversation. This pastor, though that isn't what he is called, sips a cappuccino, as do several others. A sleeping baby lies on a blanket near a young couple. After a while, a young man leans forward and begins playing a song on his guitar. The smell of incense fills the corners of the room.

What's taking place is an emerging church service, and according to some statistics, they are happening all across North America. One source cites over twenty million participants in the United States alone.[2] *Time* magazine named one of its more popular leaders, Brian McLaren, as one of the most influential evangelicals today. This much is for sure, the emerging church is not just some passing fad, and its momentum has caused some to be very concerned.

So what is so bad about overstuffed couches, sweet smelling candles, and sipping cups of hot espresso during a church service? Why are people making such a big deal about changing the atmosphere, returning to a more simplistic style of worship, and asking questions about truth and God?

It is not the ambience (flavor or feel) of the emerging church that causes me to write this book. It is the theological underpinnings. Anyone involved with the emerging church knows it's about a lot more than just candles, incense, and darkened rooms. Listen to the comments made by three different participants who explain what they think the movement is about:

> It's really not a rebellion so much as it's just finding a new set of answers, a different way of being Christians.[3]

> I think it's a new reformation. I think it's a new way of looking at the Bible.[4]

> I think it is a movement that will have an impact on all churches in the United States.[5]

But is this "new reformation" actually the way God has instructed us to go? The Bible warns that in the days before Jesus Christ returns, truth will be abandoned for a wider spiritual road that gives "heed to seducing spirits, and doctrines of devils" (I Timothy 4:1). A new form of Christianity will replace biblical faith with a faith that says man can find his own path to God and create a perfect kingdom of God here on earth. The Word will become secondary to a system of works and rituals driven by ancient mystical experiences.

An ecumenical pattern toward unity with other religions has already become quite apparent. Many people will consider those who refuse to embrace this direction as spiritual oddballs who need to be reprimanded. These resisters who stand up for biblical faith will be seen as obstructions to a one-world spirituality and global peace. Yes, I know these sound like preposterous concerns. Besides, how could a movement such as the emerging church, which seems so unorganized, do so much damage?

A common technique to changing society (or the church) is to repeat an assertion over and over as fact; once people have heard a statement enough times, they come to believe it is true. They even parrot the statement in their own conversations, eager to appear *in the know*. Oh how we need to answer every assertion with, "Says who?" This book examines the underlying spiritual substance of the emerging church movement as Scripture tells us to, "Prove all things; hold fast that which is good" (I Thessalonians 5:21).

Drastic Changes for a Postmodern World

In Ecclesiastes 1:9, King Solomon said: "The thing that hath been, it *is that* which shall be; and that which is done *is* that which shall be done: and *there is* no new *thing* under the sun." But according to emerging church leaders, we now live in a *postmodern* world. They describe it as:

> … a broad, diverse, and often paradoxical emerging culture defined as having passed through modernity and being ready to move to something better beyond it.[6]

It is difficult to define the emerging church. In fact, many say the emerging church is not a church—it's only a dialogue or conversation. One Christian college professor and critic of the movement explains why emergents see the need for their movement:

> Proponents of postmodern ministry believe that
> the modern culture, which began with the
> Enlightenment, has recently been completely
> replaced by a world view which is postmodern.
> These Postmodern ministry proponents insist that
> most evangelical churches are hindered by being
> caught up in the modern era. They will only be
> successful by moving into a postmodern model.[7]

Those in the emerging church suggest these drastic changes because the old ways and old church are no longer effective. We need a new kind of Christianity if we are going to make a difference in people's lives and the world around us. One of the first emerging church books to come on the scene was *The Church on the Other Side* by Brian McLaren. McLaren explains the objective of the movement:

> We are "exploring off the map"—looking into
> mysterious territory beyond our familiar world on
> this side of the river, this side of the ocean, this side
> of the boundary between modern and postmodern
> worlds. We are looking into an exciting, unmapped
> world on the other side of all we know so far.[8]

He is saying that this new postmodern world is much different from anything that has ever existed; emergents see themselves as spiritual Christopher Columbus' exploring "unmapped" spiritual territories. Dan Kimball, who wrote *The Emerging Church*, backs up this idea that the world we live in now is much different from ever before and now includes many different religions:

> In a post-Christian world, pluralism is the norm.
> Buddhism, Wicca, Christianity, Islam, Hinduism, or
> an eclectic blend—it's all part of the soil.[9]

Kimball explains that "the basis for learning has shifted from logic and rational" to "the realm of experience" and the "mystical."[10] And as one commentator in his book suggests, preferences are "constantly changing."[11]

Breaking Away from Tradition

One young pastor who participated in the early stages of the emerging church said the old traditional church is being replaced with an "emerging, missional [church], and bound together by the following traits:"[12]

- The cultural context is postmodern and pluralistic.
- The church accepts that it is marginalized in culture.
- Pastors are local missionaries.
- Church services blend ancient forms and local styles.
- Missions is "glocal" (global and local).[13]

Many of these new "missional" "emerging" leaders want to break away from what they view as a dead, traditional church. One emerging pastor explains:

> In recent decades, every major sphere of life has evolved to become postmodern—movies, literature, art, architecture, business, politics. Everything, that is, except "The Church." In many ways, the church is the last bastion of modernism in our culture.[14]

Leaving their churches and starting new ventures, they put their focus on a new way of doing church. This same pastor states:

> Five years ago, I left the established church. I gave up my job as pastor at one of the largest churches in America to go ... well, nowhere (except my garage-turned office).[15]

A Way That Seems Right

Since Adam and Eve's day until our own, a battle has waged between man's way of doing things and God's way. So often, what may seem to be the right way ends up not being that at all. At the risk of sounding overly simplistic, rebellion is always due to one thing—rejecting God's Word because our own way appeals to us so much more. It is to this scenario I believe the emerging church movement fits.

The Bible is truly an amazing book. If we want to understand man's spiritual journey throughout history, all we need to do is read what God has recorded in His Word. However, while God has provided a way for us to seek after Him and to know Him, God's adversary has a plan of his own. The last thing the devil wants is for man to be obedient to what God has said. Instead, his objective is to lead humanity astray. His greatest goal is to seduce people away from the Savior Jesus Christ with counterfeits; these deadly detours sometimes very closely resemble the real thing … but in reality lead to spiritual disaster. The Bible says as the time before Christ's return shortens, this agenda will only intensify.

When we embrace ideas and philosophies of men rather than the inspired Word of God, it does not take long to be led astray. Following men and their methods can be dangerous if these people are not following Jesus and His Word. Listen to what Jesus said:

> This people draweth nigh unto Me with their mouth, and honoureth Me with their lips; but their heart is far from Me. But in vain they do worship Me, teaching for doctrines the commandments of men. (Matthew 15:8-9)

Here Jesus showed that humans can be misled even in their endeavors to get closer to Him. People can be deceived even though they may believe they are heading down the right road (Matthew 7:21-24).

Emergent leaders say the Christian faith needs to be reinvented or reimagined for the 21st century. They insist that a new faith and a new kind of church must be established in order to reach this generation. If you were to ask most emergent leaders what their primary goal is, they would say—to reach this present

postmodern culture with a faith much different from what current Christianity offers because the present one is not authentic.
They would tell you that today's Christianity is too individualistic
(not communally minded enough), putting too much emphasis on
a heavenly, eternal kingdom and not enough on the kingdom of
God on earth here and now. They would tell you the emerging
church can offer to humanity an authentic, organic, and real faith,
since what we now know is outdated, irrelevant, and ineffective.

Faith Undone challenges the emerging church message, and here
is why: True biblical faith never changes. What Jesus and His disciples offered two thousand years ago is still offered to mankind
today and has been consistently offered to every generation in between. Jude 1:3 exhorts us to contend for the faith once delivered to
the saints. While emergent leaders reject terms like *plan of salvation*
and *asking Jesus to be Lord of your life*, God actually *has* offered man a
plan to be saved.

The Secret Message of the Emerging Church

With obscure language, a seemingly noble cause, and evasive
conversations, the emerging church is mesmerizing many people
(including Christians), receiving the support of established Christian leaders, and leaving a trail of confusion and disarray in its path.

Jesus said, "I am the light of the world: he that followeth me
shall not walk in darkness, but shall have the light of life" (John
8:12). By saying this, Jesus wanted us to know that the world without Him is dark (because of sin). But He has come to dispel the
darkness of sin and give us true life. When we stand in a dark room
with all the lights turned out, we can see nothing. It is the same
spiritually. When we live in sin, we can see nothing (spiritually speaking). When Jesus Christ comes into one's life, His Light releases us
from sin's darkness. Several scriptures back this up:

> Who hath delivered us from the power of darkness,
> and hath translated us into the kingdom of his dear
> Son. (Colossians 1:13)

> For we wrestle not against flesh and blood, but against principalities, against powers, against the rulers of the darkness of this world, against spiritual wickedness in high places. (Ephesians 6:12)

> Ye are all the children of light, and the children of the day: we are not of the night, nor of darkness. (I Thessalonians 5:5)

There are many more. The beautiful thing about the Bible is it was written through the inspiration of God so that even the simplest mind could understand its message. Its message is clear:

> For God so loved the world, that he gave his only begotten Son, that whosoever believeth in him should not perish, but have everlasting life. (John 3:16)

The Bible says we have been given the answer to the mystery of life, which is God coming in the flesh (Jesus) and His Spirit living inside all who accept Him by faith. Contrast this with the message of the emerging church—a message that is not clear at all. One movement leader wrote a book called *The Secret Message of Jesus*. But in truth, there is no secret message of Jesus.

Always Searching, Never Finding

In the beginning of this chapter, we saw a glimpse of an emerging church service. Instead of a pastor preaching from the Bible, a facilitator asks questions, which are followed by more questions by himself or the members of the congregation, some of whom will offer possible answers to these questions. The *salvation* message of the emerging church is not found in doctrine but in dialogue, not in truth but in discussion. In this sense, always searching but never finding is a trademark of the emerging church, because in the endless dialogue (conversation), the truth is never found.

Behind all this is a reconstructed view of God that obliterates the God of the Bible. Laying the revelation of Scripture aside, human understanding much prefers a God too loving to create a place like hell for anyone, particularly for those who are searching. Hence it follows, one can find safety in a congregation of seekers; some emerging church leaders have already said the God who judges and requires penal substitution for sin (i.e., the Cross) does not exist.

Thus, the emerging search for truth continues. As II Timothy 3:7 tells us, they are "ever learning, but never able to come to the knowledge of the truth."

The Scope

While many critiques of the emerging church reach only to the edges of what would be classified as *the* emerging church, I have broadened my scope. *Faith Undone* examines not just the obvious leaders of this movement but will examine the much more encompassing *emerging spirituality*. Through this book, I hope to expose a belief system, rather than just a group of particular leaders. Today, there are x number of emerging church leaders, tomorrow that number will be higher. To write about them all would take volumes, and those volumes would quickly be outdated. But showing you what lies beneath the surface—revealing the energy or force that moves these leaders—will be more beneficial and long lasting.

My intention is not to determine the motives of these individuals but rather to bring to light the truth about the spirituality behind the teachings. Therefore, I will paint a broad picture. At times, I will mention names you would not normally associate with the emerging church in order to show you how this spirituality has a far-reaching effect. If left unchallenged it could soon pervade and warp much of what we know as Christianity.

This book does not attempt to identify every key player in the emerging church movement. There are too many. And even if there weren't, my objective is not to attack individuals but rather to unveil a belief system. Thus, this is not a book out to *get the bad guys*. On the contrary, it is a book that seeks to rescue those involved with the emerging church and countless others heading in that direction.

In the near future, Christians of every denomination will have to decide whether to support or reject the spirituality behind the emerging church. If the emerging church continues unfolding at its present pace, mainstream evangelical Christianity will be restructured so that the biblical Gospel of Jesus Christ will be considered too narrow and too restrictive.

If I believed for one minute that this movement was just another passing whim or the discontent rumblings that so often accompany young people's search for answers to life, I would never have written this book. And if I did not believe that what we are witnessing with this emerging spirituality lines up with biblical end-time prophecy, you would not be reading these pages. But sad to say, the emerging church is far more than a fleeting fad and much more than the complaints of a group of young leaders. It is indeed a "new way of being Christians" and in every conceivable manner, it is striving to bring about a "new reformation." Without a doubt, it will have an "impact on all churches" in the Western world and far beyond. For behind this new kind of church is a well designed strategy and maneuver by the prince of this world, the enemy of our souls, to literally take apart the faith of millions—it will be nothing less than faith undone.

2

The Birth of the Emerging Church

For my thoughts are not your thoughts, neither are your ways my ways, saith the LORD. For as the heavens are higher than the earth, so are my ways higher than your ways, and my thoughts than your thoughts.—Isaiah 55:8-9

You've heard the old saying, "Things are not always as they seem." That adage implies that what appears to be good could very well be quite the opposite. A perfect example of this from Scripture would be Eve in the Garden of Eden. The serpent promised her eternal life and the chance to be like God. His offer came in the form of an appealing, attractive piece of fruit. Eve, even though God had already warned Adam and her, succumbed to what appeared to be so good. And of course, the results were devastating (Genesis 3).

Today, man is still being allured by seemingly wonderful ideas and schemes. But the Lord has made it clear that His ways are so much higher than our ways, and what often appears to be a good thing is not that at all. As we examine the birth of the emerging church in this chapter, I believe you will see that in this case also, things are not as they seem.

While this chapter will lay out the origins of the emerging church, I do not wish to give the impression that this is merely a human endeavor. A distinct spiritual component to it implies a guiding force from the supernatural realm. This movement is very complex, and a short synopsis like this chapter cannot explain all the underlying factors that played a role in its inception.

But my intent is to describe the framework in which this movement sprang and was able to gain the momentum it now enjoys.

Leadership Network

Contrary to what many believe, the current emerging church movement was not initiated by a group of disillusioned young people who were tired of organized religion and could only afford to meet in old coffee houses and run-down basements. In reality, the movement was largely the inspiration of a successful business guru whose ideas of an emerging church were catapulted into existence by *other* successful businessmen, and thus it became the influential religious force it is today. The guru was Peter Drucker, who was writing about the emerging church long before many of today's emerging church leaders were even born. But before we go back to the 1950s and the man Peter Drucker, let's start in the 1990s when the emerging church got its *official* start.

In an article in the *Criswell Theological Review* written by Mark Driscoll of Mars Hill Fellowship, Driscoll recalls the early days:

> In the mid-1990s I was a young church planter trying to establish a church in the city of Seattle when I got a call to speak at my first conference. It was hosted by Leadership Network and focused on the subject of Generation X.... Out of that conference a small team was formed to continue conversing about post-modernism....
>
> By this time Leadership Network hired Doug Pagitt to lead the team and organize the events. He began

growing the team and it soon included Brian McLaren.... Pagitt, McLaren, and others such as Chris Seay, Tony Jones, Dan Kimball, and Andrew Jones stayed together and continued speaking and writing together as friends....

McLaren, a very gifted writer, rose to team leader in part because he had an established family and church, which allowed him to devote a lot of time to the team. That team eventually morphed into what is now known as Emergent.[1]*

To understand the significance of Leadership Network's role in the emerging church, we need to look briefly at the structure and makeup of that organization, which began in 1984 by Bob Buford. At the time, Buford was the owner of a successful cable television company in Texas. With the help of Harold Myra and Paul Robbins of *Christianity Today*, Buford introduced Leadership Network as a "resource broker" to churches, hoping to help leaders of "innovative churches" connect together.[2] However, Leadership Network was not the sole inspiration of Buford. Even before he began the organization, he was consulting with business/management guru, the late Peter Drucker.

Drucker was born in 1909 in Austria and over the course of his life rose to a position of great respect for his contribution to management and business. He died in 2005 at the age of 95, but his influence lives on, not only in the business world but in the religious world as well.

Bob Buford has often publicly expressed his deep admiration for Drucker. Of him, Buford says:

---

*The term Emergent was first used by the group (McLaren, Jones, Kimball, Driscoll, etc.) originally called Young Leaders Network. When they left Leadership Network to go on their own, they became Emergent. Today the terms *emergent* and *emerging* are often used interchangeably.

Peter Drucker is the "intellectual father" of most all that guides my approach to philanthropy. I've long since ceased trying to determine what thoughts are mine and which come from Peter.[3]

In 1988, four years after launching Leadership Network, Buford sought out Drucker, asking him to:

...lend his name, his great mind, and occasionally his presence to establish an operating foundation for the purpose of leading social sector organizations toward excellence in performance.[4]

Buford had a high esteem for the elder mentor, saying Drucker was "the man who formed my mind."[5]

With Drucker's influence and Buford's devotion to Drucker, Leadership Network was bound to succeed. By this time in his life, Drucker had indeed built a "name" for himself and few would argue that his "great mind" and "presence" would be a tremendous asset to any company.

Peter Drucker and Mysticism

If we want to grasp the philosophy and ideologies of Leadership Network, then we need to examine Drucker's beliefs. Remember, Buford said he had "ceased trying to determine what thoughts are mine and which come from Peter." And while Drucker no doubt brought his *business* sense to the Leadership Network table, his spiritual overtones were prevalent as well; and they were passed on to Buford, who in turn passed them on to the emerging church.

Something that would turn out to be extremely significant in the long run was Peter Drucker's attraction to mystics. In particular, he was greatly influenced by existential philosopher and mystic Soren Kierkegaard. According to a *New York Times* article, "A Man's Spiritual Journey from Kierkegaard to General Motors," Drucker was "bowled over" by the writings of Kierkegaard. Drucker called him a "prophet"[6] and being so impressed with

Kierkegaard, he "studied Danish in order to read Kierkegaard's yet-untranslated works."[7] Drucker said Kierkegaard's "religious experience" was "meaningful for the modern world in its agony."[8] In a dissertation at Purdue University, called "Faith and nothingness in Kierkegaard: A mystical reading of the God-relationship," the writer said of Kierkegaard:

> [He] has marked structural similarities to mystics such as Eckhart, who is warmly received by the Japanese philosophical tradition, particularly in the writings of its Zen and Pure Land Buddhist representatives.[9]

Drucker attested to Kierkegaard's mystical affinities, saying he "stands squarely in the great Western tradition of religious experience, the tradition of ... St. John of the Cross,"[10] a mystic in the 1500s.

For those who wonder if Drucker's interest in mysticism and Kierkegaard influenced Bob Buford, we can turn to Buford's autobiography, *Halftime*. In the book, Buford favorably quotes Kierkegaard a number of times and refers to others with mystical persuasions. And on his website, Buford endorses a man named Jim Collins,[11] who took a course by Michael Ray called *Creativity in Business* in 1982. The course (and the book named after the course) takes "much of its inspiration from Eastern philosophies, mysticism, and meditation techniques."[12] The book talks about "your wisdom-keeper or spirit guide—an inner person who can be with you in life" and says, "We meditate to unfold our inner being."[13] The book also presents Tarot cards. Collins calls the course "profoundly life changing" and says he "would not be where I am today, with the wonderful life I've been given, without that course."[14]

Collins was so inspired by Ray's course that he wrote the foreword for Ray's 2004 book, *The Highest Goal*. In the book, Ray tells readers to "practice emptying your mind,"[15] "experience not thinking."[16] and "meditate regularly."[17] Other quotes in the book include those of Eastern religion gurus such as Ram Dass, Jiddu Krishnamurti, and Swami Shantananda.

Buford's website not only carries an endorsement for Jim Collins but also a number of articles by or about those who promote mysticism as well.[18] Clearly, Drucker's interest in mysticism rubbed off on Buford.

The Emerging Society of Peter Drucker

Long before Leadership Network even began, Peter Drucker was writing about emerging spirituality. In his 1957 book *Landmarks of Tomorrow*, the introduction titled "This Post-Modern World" states:

> At some unmarked point during the last twenty years we imperceptibly moved out of the Modern Age and into a new, as yet nameless era. Our view of the world [has] changed.... There is a new spiritual center to human existence.[19]

What Drucker called the "Post-Modern World" had already started, as he saw it. In fact, he was formulating ideas that would be integrated into what would become the emerging church fifty years later. Listen to a few of his statements:

> We thus live in an age of transition, an age of overlap, in which the old "modern" of yesterday no longer acts effectively ... while the new, the "post-modern," ... effectively controls our actions and their impact.[20]

> [W]e still need the great imaginer, the great creative thinker, the great innovator, of a new synthesis, of a new philosophy.[21]

> This is a new view, different alike from the traditional.[22]

Words like "purpose," "emergence," "new frontiers," and "disciplines," fill the pages of *Landmarks of Tomorrow*. These terms (and concepts) are often used by many of today's Christian leaders.

When it states that "we will create a new philosophy—a fresh way of looking at the world,"[23] it sounds very much like what is said today by those in the emerging church.

Drucker felt a strong bond not only with Kierkegaard but also with a panentheist/mystic named Martin Buber (1878-1965), who embraced the teachings of Hasidism (Jewish mysticism).[24] Buber believed that "a divine spark"[25] exists within every human and within everything in creation. He spoke of the relationship, which "must exist between individuals and everything on the planet."[26] In his book *Between Man and Man*, Buber further expresses his views of mysticism:

> Since 1900 I had first been under the influence of
> German mysticism from Meister Eckhart [a mystic]
> … then I had been under the influence of the later
> Kabalah [Jewish mysticism] and of Hasidism.[27]

In *Landmarks of Tomorrow*, Drucker referenced Buber when he stated:

> Mankind needs the return to spiritual values, for it
> needs compassion. It needs the deep experience that
> the Thou and the I [from Buber's book, *I and Thou*]
> are one, which all higher religions share.[28]

In addition, one of Drucker's biographers said that Drucker "[drew] upon the wisdom of the philosopher Martin Buber,"[29] and another writer said that Drucker "was a student of Buber's at the University of Frankfurt."[30]

Drucker's attraction to the mystical did not end with his fascination for Buber and Kierkegaard. In 1990, Drucker established the Leader to Leader Institute, an interspiritual *thought forum*, which to this day includes Buddhist sympathizers, globalists, evangelicals, and New Age sympathizers.[31] Drucker's philosophy of gathering together ideologies from *great thinkers* was not something he saw as contrary to his ideas of religion. He believed that "people's needs" supersede "doctrine" or "institutional structure."[32] This view of minimizing doctrine would become one of the earmarks of the emerging church, which in reality was to be a testing ground for high-tech marketing skills, business management techniques, and an experience-based religion; but its foundation is flawed with a non-biblical, mystical premise.

A "Mega" Paradigm Shift

When Bob Buford gathered the initial group of young emerging leaders, one he chose was Doug Pagitt, a youth pastor from Wooddale Church (a Minneapolis megachurch). Leith Anderson (Pagitt's pastor) had already been helping set the tone for the emerging church. In Anderson's 1992 book *A Church for the 21st Century*, he said a paradigm shift was needed:

> The only way to cope and be effective during this period of structural change in society is to change some of the ways we view our world and the church. It is what some call a paradigm shift—a new way of looking at something. Such a shift will allow us to view our changing world with new perspective. It is like a map. Old maps from 1950 may have sufficed before the construction of interstate highways and the expansion of major cities, but new maps are needed now. Likewise, we need a paradigm shift for the future.[33]

This idea of a paradigm shift would become an integral element of the emerging church. *Webster's Dictionary* defines paradigm as "a philosophical or theoretical framework of any kind."[34] Thus, paradigm *shift* is a shift or change from the present framework. Anderson, Buford, and Drucker all played a role in bringing this about.

While Leadership Network was the catalyst that initially launched the emerging church, many other ministries and organizations have helped to fuel it. One of the major catalysts is Rick Warren. Warren's support for Buford and Leadership Network goes back many years. Warren endorsed Buford's 1994 book, *Halftime*, calling Buford a "rare individual."[35] But perhaps more important is the fact that Warren shared Buford's great admiration for Drucker. At a 2005 Pew Forum on Religion gathering called "Myths of the Modern Mega-Church," Rick Warren stated:

> I did a series of lectures for the faculty in the Kennedy School ... I started with this quote from Peter Drucker: "The most significant sociological phenomenon of the first half of the 20th century was the rise of the corporation. The most significant sociological phenomenon of the second half of the 20th century has been the development of the large pastoral church—of the mega-church. It is the only organization that is actually working in our society."
>
> Now Drucker has said that at least six times. I happen to know because he's *my mentor*. I've spent 20 years under his tutelage learning about leadership from him, and he's written it in two or three books, and he says he thinks it's [the mega-church] the only thing that really works in society.[36]

Incidentally, not only does this quote reveal Warren's devotion to Drucker, but it also shows why Drucker became involved with Leadership Network. Buford's goal was to be a resource to the megachurch, because he saw it as a highly influential instrument for societal changes. Perhaps it was Drucker who convinced Buford to start Leadership Network in the first place.

Warren's view that Buford was a "rare individual" was mutual. Buford reciprocated the admiration when he described Warren and Bill Hybels (Willow Creek) as "change makers" in "the early days of Leadership Network."[37] As for Willow Creek's role with Leadership Network, Buford states:

> The first Foundation conference was held in Dallas and was the beginning of a partnership between

> Bob and Linda, Leadership Network and Willow
> Creek Community Church.[38]

Willow Creek's partnership with Leadership Network has proven to be very helpful for the emerging church shift. Through Willow Creek's various well-attended conferences, and with their endorsements and promotions of books, leaders like Leonard Sweet, Brian McLaren, and Erwin McManus have been able to further propagate the emerging spirituality message.

In this fast moving paradigm, Rick Warren recognizes Leadership Network's role in the success of the emerging church. In one of Warren's e-newsletters, it reveals: "Leadership Network bills itself as the advance scout for the emerging church."[39]

Rick Warren's *Tides of Change*

If Leadership Network was the "advance scout" for the emerging church, Warren's role was also vital to the emerging church's growth. Even before the Young Leaders Network (later becoming Emergent) was launched, Warren was drawn to the Emergent conversation. In 1995, he joined with emerging leader Leonard Sweet to do an audio series titled *Tides of Change*.[40] Sweet is Professor of Evangelism at Drew University, a self-proclaimed futurist, and a popular author and speaker. For 2006, he was voted as one of "The 50 Most Influential Christians in America,"[41] listed as number eight just under Bill Hybels (Willow Creek), Billy Graham, and Joel Osteen, and ranking higher than President Bush, Robert Schuller, and Rick Warren.

In the *Tides of Change* audio series, Sweet and Warren talked about "a new spirituality" that was looming on the horizon. Both Warren and Sweet emulated Drucker in the audio, talking about "new frontiers," "changing times," and letting go of traditions and the old way of doing things. In fact, the similarities between the audio in 1995 and Drucker in 1957 are striking. Of such changes and *new ideas*, Drucker stated:

> We thus live in an age of transition, an age of
> overlap, in which the old "modern" of yesterday
> no longer acts effectively … but what matters most
> for us—the first post-modern generation—is the
> change in *fundamental world-view.*[42]

> In the shift from yesterday's "progress" to today's
> "innovation" … This is a new view.[43]

In a way, Warren and Sweet's audio (subtitled *Riding the Next Wave in Ministry)* sent up an emerging church trial balloon. How would people react to the idea of "new frontiers" and "waves of change"? Sweet had already predicted what the next wave would be in 1991 when he wrote *Quantum Spirituality: A Postmodern Apologetic.* In light of Sweet's role in the emerging church movement, and considering his connections with someone as influential as Rick Warren, we should not ignore what he has to say in *Quantum Spirituality.*

Leonard Sweet's "New Lights"

In the "Acknowledgments" section of Sweet's book, he details that his journey of faith was influenced by a myriad of individuals he calls "New Light leaders." He writes:

> I have followed these "New Light leaders," as I am
> calling them, from varying distances. But it is largely
> because of their writings and lives that I have been
> compelled to join Abraham on the journey. They are
> my personal role models (in an earlier day one could
> get away with "heroes") of the true nature of the
> postmodern apologetic. More than anyone else, they
> have been my teachers on how to translate, without
> compromising content, the gospel into the
> indigenous context of the postmodern vernacular.[44]

When Sweet says these "New Light" leaders have taught him how to translate "the gospel" without compromise, this certainly would sound like the right thing; however, it soon becomes apparent that many of Sweet's "New Light"[45] mentors who led him "into new light" have done Sweet a terrible disservice. His translation of the Christian faith has completely dismantled true biblical faith, as I will show you.

In the "Preface" of *Quantum Spirituality*, Sweet writes:

> The emergence of this New Light apologetic is a harbinger [forerunner] and hope that … the church may now be on the edge of another awakening.…
>
> The New Light movement is characterized by bizarre, sometimes anxious alliances of a ragbag assortment of preachers, theologians, pastors, professors, artists, scientists, business leaders and scholars. What ties their creative piracy together is a radical faith commitment that is willing to dance to a new rhythm.[46]

To understand what Sweet means by dancing to a "new rhythm," it is necessary to look at this "ragbag assortment" of "New Light" leaders he refers to. By his own admission, they have molded and persuaded him in spiritual matters. Thus, if we want to understand what Leonard Sweet believes, it is fair to say we need only look to what his teachers believe as he has given them such a dominant role in his life, saying, "more than anyone else, they have been my teachers."[47]

You may be surprised to learn that Sweet's three pages of acknowledgments of "New Light" teachers is a who's who of the New Age movement. While some names are lesser known, others are quite prolific, such as M. Scott Peck, Matthew Fox, Willis Harman, and Morton Kelsey.[48] Ken Wilber is also named.[49] It is hard to understand how proponents of New Age spirituality can help Sweet "translate, without compromising content, the gospel" message.

The Cosmic Christ Emerges

Sweet's acknowledgment of Matthew Fox is very telling of Sweet's spiritual proclivities. Fox, an Episcopal priest and long-time promoter of New Age spirituality, is the author of *The Coming of the Cosmic Christ*, in which Fox states:

> I foresee a renaissance, "a rebirth based on a spiritual initiative" … This new birth will cut through all cultures and all religions and indeed will draw forth the wisdom common to all vital mystical traditions in a global religious awakening I call "deep ecumenism."[50]

The theme of Fox's book is that the "Cosmic Christ" (as opposed to the historical person of Jesus Christ) resides in all humans. He teaches that Jesus was not *the* Christ but had this *christ-consciousness*, and he was just one of many who did. Gandhi, Moses, Martin Luther King, Jr., and Buddha had it as well, Fox notes.[51]

Equally revealing is Sweet's favorable mention of Ken Wilber and M. Scott Peck, both of whom share Fox's views on spiritual matters.

In *Quantum Spirituality*, Sweet lays the groundwork for the *emerging manifesto* by declaring:

> Mysticism, once cast to the sidelines of the Christian tradition, is now situated in postmodernist culture near the center… Too many people are nothing, as our empty pews are shouting to us, because we give them neither an energy-fire experience of Christ nor the Christ of an energy-fire experience. We may help them apprehend reality through the rudiments of mystical speculations, but not the rapture of flow experiences… Mysticism (which Einstein called "cosmic religiosity") is metaphysics arrived at through mindbody experiences. Mysticism begins in experience; *it ends in theology.* (emphasis added)[52]

It is important to see why Warren and Sweet's alliance is so serious and should not be overlooked. Additionally, neither should Bob Buford's view of Sweet. Seeing Sweet's meaningful role in the emerging church, Buford states:

> I think of Len Sweet as the icebreaker for the 21st-century-church—breaking a path through frozen ideas and methods to the new realities that are shaping the world to come.[53]

Thus, the founder of the emerging church movement welcomes and endorses Leonard Sweet's "New Light movement." Remember, at this time historically, the New Age movement has been radically introducing the world to eastern mysticism. Now a bridge is being built to those who profess to be Christian. The seduction of Christianity has now crossed a line that few would have believed possible a decade or so ago. If highly influential people like Warren, Hybels, Sweet, and Buford are promoting this "new man for the new era" in the name of Christ, it could only be a matter of time before Jesus Christ is replaced by the "Cosmic Christ."

In 2003, Rick Warren gave the emerging church movement a tremendous boost by endorsing and writing the foreword for Dan Kimball's signature book, *The Emerging Church*. Warren made no mistake about his admiration and support for Kimball and the emerging church. (Brian McLaren also wrote a foreword in the book). In Warren's foreword, he states:

> This book is a wonderful, detailed example of what a purpose-driven church can look like in a postmodern world. My friend Dan Kimball writes passionately ... While my book *The Purpose-Driven Church* explained what the church is called to do, Dan's book explains how to do it.[54]

Throughout the book, Warren wrote several sidebar comments and reaffirmed his support for the emerging church.

Warren has consistently promoted the emerging church in both word and deed; he has not only been a proponent through his many book endorsements, but has subscribed to the emerging church mindset in several significant ways. With Rick Warren's help and Leadership Network's resources, the emerging church movement is a sure thing.

Shaping the Minds of the Youth

In the late 1960s, two youth workers in their twenties, Mike Yaconelli and Wayne Rice (who happened to be working for Youth for Christ at the time), wanted to change the way youth ministry was viewed and approached. They self-published a small booklet called *Ideas*, began talking to senior pastors and churches, and in 1970 held their first conference. They called the company Youth Specialties. Interestingly, the late theologian Frances Schaeffer attended their second annual conference.[55] Schaeffer would be very surprised if he had known that thirty years down the road this young sprouting organization would become one of the major catalysts for the emerging church movement.

Just a few years after Youth Specialties was launched, Zondervan publishers took notice of the two men's work:

> Youth Specialties' passion for youth workers caught the attention of Zondervan Publishing House in 1974. Zondervan came to YS and said, "You guys are weird and unpredictable. We want to put your books in bookstores," recalls Mike. Zondervan was very Dutch, very Grand Rapids, very conservative— but hey, they believed in our mission![56]

Zondervan's interest in Youth Specialties would only increase, and over the next thirty years, the two companies would publish over 500 resources for youth workers. It is worth mentioning that Zondervan became the property of Rupert Murdoch's News Corporation in 1988. Murdoch's corporation, also owner of Fox News, has been a major catalyst for *Purpose Driven Life* and now we see for the emerging church through Zondervan. This is significant in light of Rick Warren's relationship with Murdoch. Warren says he is Murdoch's pastor;[57] it is clear that both he and Youth Specialties benefited from a corporation that had a net profit of 21 *billion* dollars for the 2004 fiscal year,[58] and whose founder (Murdoch) received a "papal knighthood" from Pope John Paul II for Murdoch's donation of "large sums of money" to the Catholic church.[59]

In 1984, as Youth Specialties grew and its circle of influence spread across the country, Zondervan signed a co-publishing agreement with Youth Specialties. Eventually, there was the National Youth Workers Convention, the National Pastors Convention, and another 100 seminars throughout the year around the country.

Twelve years later, Youth Specialties partnered with San Francisco Theological Seminary to form the Youth Ministry & Spirituality Project.[60] The following year, the young organization was awarded a grant by the Lilly Endowment.[61]* By this time, Youth Specialties had contacted the new *emergent* leaders and said they wanted to work together. Sharing many of the same spiritual affinities as Emergent, Youth Specialties hoped to help take the movement to the next level with more books, more conferences, and more growth.

In 2006, Zondervan bought Youth Specialties.[62] After the purchase, Zondervan made a commitment that it would continue its support of the emerging leaders.

While Zondervan's role in helping build the emerging church movement cannot be minimized, it is not the only Christian publisher that has added force to the movement. In fact, most major Christian publishing houses have released at least a few books written by emerging church leaders or books that have an emerging spirituality bent to them.

---

* In 2001, the Lilly Endowment awarded Youth Ministry & Spirituality Project another even bigger grant—$691,000.

The secular publishing industry has also played a significant part in the emerging church's tremendous success in getting their message out. In 1996, Leadership Network established a partnership agreement with Jossey-Bass (a large San Francisco-based publishing house), which would turn out to be most beneficial for both parties.[63] Incidentally, Jossey-Bass had a close ongoing relationship with Peter Drucker, who sat on the Jossey-Bass board, and his *Leader to Leader Journal* is to this day published by Jossey-Bass.

Through this strong-arm publishing alliance of Jossey-Bass and Leadership Network, the handful of carefully selected young men (Young Leaders Network) began writing books, and with the Drucker/Buford marketing energies, these young emerging leaders became known world-wide in just a few years, so much so, that in 2005, *Time* magazine named Brian McLaren one of the country's top 25 "Most Influential Evangelicals."[64]

In addition to numerous books being published by the Jossey-Bass Leadership Network series, several conferences have taken place that have further propelled this movement. The secular *Mother Jones* magazine took notice of the young emergent movement and its benefactors, stating:

> Postmoderns receive crucial support—financial and otherwise—from the megachurches. These postmodern ministries are loosely organized by the Leadership Network, a Dallas-based umbrella group for many of the nation's megachurches. It's the Leadership Network that keeps Driscoll's bohemian Mars Hill ministry in touch with the fast-growing, but more traditional, University Baptist Church in Waco by holding conferences and seminars. For the past three years the network has sponsored national conferences that bring together postmodern leaders.[65]

There is little doubt that the emerging church movement would not be what it is today without the zeal, backing, and efforts of Leadership Network, Rupert Murdoch, Jossey-Bass,

Youth Specialties, Willow Creek, Peter Drucker, Rick Warren,
Zondervan publishing, and the Lilly Endowment.

Bob Buford has stated that, "A few men can make a huge
difference," and he adds, "it has become my firm conviction
that the way to affect multitudes is to Focus on the Few."[66] With
such a stealth backing, I can see why this would be true. But if
these "Few" are preaching a different gospel, the "affect" on the
"multitudes" could produce a terrible falling away from the faith.

If such a process does occur, what will it look like? Will it
happen overnight, or will there be a seductive alluring over time?
Will the youth be targeted? And what will happen to those who
warn about this seduction? Will they be considered out of touch
and narrow-minded, holding back *new frontiers* and *tides of change*?

For Christianity to be restructured, a spiritual paradigm shift
of a magnificent strength and clever strategy would have to take
place. It would have to involve all denominations, even ones that
were once biblically based. While humans will carry out this shift,
we know the Bible teaches that the battle we face is not against
flesh and blood and that there is an evil one "which deceiveth the
whole world" (Revelation 12:9). When man turns his back on
what the Lord has said, nothing good can come from it:

> Thus saith the LORD; Cursed be the man that
> trusteth in man, and maketh flesh his arm, and
> whose heart departeth from the LORD. For he shall
> be like the heath in the desert, and shall not see
> when good cometh; but shall inhabit the parched
> places in the wilderness, in a salt land and not
> inhabited. (Jeremiah 17: 5-6)

3

A "New" Faith for the 21st Century

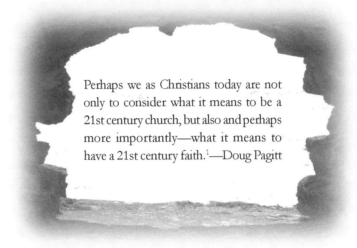

Perhaps we as Christians today are not only to consider what it means to be a 21st century church, but also and perhaps more importantly—what it means to have a 21st century faith.[1]—Doug Pagitt

The Process of Reimagining

Emergent church leaders often provide testimonies explaining how they became involved in their *journey* to *reinvent* Christianity. In his book *Church Re-Imagined*, Doug Pagitt tells how and why his church originated:

> Our attempt at being a church began in January 2000 in a small second-floor loft space in a hip little neighborhood of Minneapolis called Linden Hills. The church was actually birthed much earlier, from conversations between a few friends who shared a desire to be part of a community of faith that not only had a new way of functioning but also generated a different outcome. At that point I had said, on more than one occasion, that I didn't think I would be able to stay

39

Christian in any useful sense over the next 50 years if I
continued with the expression of Christianity I was
currently living—pretty disconcerting stuff for a pastor.[2]

Pagitt explains why he felt he needed to find a new expression of Christianity that was different from what he had been accustomed to previously. He states:

This was not a crisis of faith in the typical sense; I
never doubted God, Jesus, or the Christian faith. And
yet I had a deep sense, which has actually grown deeper
since, that I needed to move into a Christianity that
somehow fit better with the world I lived in, not an
expression reconstituted from another time.[3]

Pagitt goes into more depth at how he views fitting "better with the world" he lives in:

We also understand ourselves as part of a global
community. We are required to live our local
expressions of Christianity in harmony with those
around the world. The beliefs and practices of our
Western church must never override or negate the
equally valid and righteous expressions of faith lived
by Christians around the world. It is essential that
we recognize our own cultural version of
Christianity and make ourselves open to the work
of God's hand in the global community of faith.[4]

Notice the emphasis on a "global community of faith" that
permits all "expressions of faith" by anyone and everyone who
claims to be Christian. As we are going to see, Pagitt bases his
ideas of changing the profile of Christianity on an ecumenical
view that permits beliefs and experiences not found in the Bible.
Not only are they not found in the Bible, the plan can't work
with an intact Bible. In order for the emerging church to succeed,
the Bible has to be looked at through entirely different glasses,

and Christianity needs to be open to a new type of faith. Brian McLaren calls this new faith a "generous orthodoxy."[5] While such an orthodoxy allows a smorgasbord of ideas to be proclaimed in the name of Christ, many of these ideas are actually forbidden and rejected by Scripture.

Pagitt believes that he is part of a cutting-edge response to the new postmodern world. It's a response he and others see as completely unique, never having been tried before in the history of man. Pagitt states:

> It seems to me that our post-industrial times require us to ask new questions—questions that people 100 years ago would have never thought of asking. Could it be that our answers will move us to re-imagine the way of Christianity in our world? Perhaps we as Christians today are not only to consider what it means to be a 21st century church, but also and perhaps more importantly—what it means to have a 21st century faith.[6]

Many people I meet at conferences who come from a wide variety of church backgrounds tell me the church they have been attending for years has radically changed. Their pastor no longer teaches the Bible. Instead, the Sunday morning service is a skit or a series of stories. The Bible seems to have become the forbidden book. While there are pastors who do still teach the Bible, they are becoming the exception rather than the rule.

Emergent leaders often say the message remains the same, but our methods must change if we are going to be relevant to our generation. The measure of success for many pastors today is how many are coming, rather than how many are listening and obeying what God has said in His Word. Let's consider how Doug Pagitt uses the Bible in his own church. He states:

> At Solomon's Porch, sermons are not primarily about my extracting truth from the Bible to apply to people's

lives. In many ways the sermon is less a lecture or
motivational speech than it is an act of poetry—of
putting words around people's experiences to allow
them to find deeper connection in their lives… So
our sermons are not lessons that precisely define
belief so much as they are stories that welcome our
hopes and ideas and participation.[7]

What Pagitt is describing is a *contextual theology*, that is, don't
use the Bible as a means of theology or measuring rod of truth
and standards by which to live; and rather than have the Bible
mold the Christian's life, let the Christian's life mold the Bible.
That's what Pagitt calls "putting words around people's experiences." As this idea is developed, emerging proponents have to
move away from Bible teachings and draw into a dialectic approach. That way, instead of just one person preaching truth or
teaching biblical doctrine, everyone can have a say and thus come
to a consensus of what the Bible *might* be saying. Pagitt explains:

To move beyond this passive approach to faith, we've
tried to create a community that's more like a potluck:
people eat and they also bring something for others.
Our belief is built when all of us engage our hopes,
dreams, ideas and understandings with the story of
God as it unfolds through history and through us.[8]

Contextual Theology

You may not have heard the term before, but contextual
theology is a prominent message from the emerging church.
In his book, *Models of Contextual Theology* (1992), Stephen B. Bevans
defines contextual theology as:

…a way of doing theology in which one takes into
account: the spirit and message of the gospel; the
tradition of the Christian people; the culture in
which one is theologizing; and social change in that
culture, whether brought about by western

technological process or the grass-roots struggle
for equality, justice and liberation.[9]

In other words, the Bible in, and of itself, is not free-standing—other factors (culture, ethnicity, history) must be taken into consideration, and with those factors, the message of the Bible must be adjusted to fit. As one writer puts it, "Contextual theology aims at the humanization of theology."[10] But two questions need to be asked. First, will the contextualizing of Scripture cause such a twisting of its truth that it no longer is the Word of God, and secondly, is Scripture ineffective without this contextualization? To the first, I give a resounding yes! And to the second, an absolute no. The Word of God, which is an inspired work of the living Creator, is far more than any human-inspired book and has been written in such a way that every human being, rich or poor, man or woman, intelligent or challenged will understand the meaning of the Gospel message if it is presented in their native language; and thanks to the tireless work of missionaries for centuries, the Gospel in native languages is becoming a reality in most cultures today.

Dean Flemming is a New Testament teacher at European Nazarene College in Germany and the author of *Contextualization in the New Testament*. In his book, he defends contextual theology:

> Every church in every particular place and time must learn to do theology in a way that makes sense to its audience while challenging it at the deepest level. In fact, some of the *most promising* conversations about contextualization today (whether they are recognized as such or not) are coming from churches in the West that are discovering new ways of embodying the gospel for an emerging postmodern culture. (emphasis added)[11]

These "churches in the West" Flemming considers "most promising" are the emerging churches. He would agree with Bevans' model of theology, but he has an answer to the emerging church's dilemma. He states:

Many sincere Christians are still suspicious that
attempts to contextualize theology and Christian
behavior will lead to the compromising of biblical truth
… we must *look to the New Testament* for mentoring in
the task of doing theology in our various settings.[12]

There's good reason some Christians are suspicious. But it
can seem harmless at first because Flemming suggests the answer
is in the New Testament, which he believes should be used as a
prototype or pattern rather than something for doctrine or theology. New Testament theology is always open for change, he says,
but we can learn how to develop this change by studying New
Testament stories and characters. The premise Flemming presents
of contextualizing Scripture is that since cultures and societies are
always changing, the Word must change with it and be conformed
to these changes. But I would challenge this. The Bible says the
Word is living, active, and powerful:

For the word of God is quick, and powerful, and
sharper than any twoedged sword, piercing even to
the dividing asunder of soul and spirit, and of the
joints and marrow, and is a discerner of the thoughts
and intents of the heart. (Hebrews 4:12)

And if the Word is this powerful, then it is stable and eternal as well. God, in His magnificence, is the Author of Scripture, and He surpasses time, culture, and societies.
Contextualizing says people and cultures change, and therefore
God's Word must change. But, on the contrary, it's people who
need to change to conform to Scripture. If we really believe that
the Bible *is* God's Word, this would be clear to see; but if we
think to ourselves that the Word is not infallible, not inspired,
then contextualization would be the obvious expectation.

While certain parts of the Bible may be read as poetry (as
Pagitt suggests), for indeed the Bible is a beautifully written mas-
terpiece, it is also a living mechanism that is not to be altered—

rather *it* alters the reader's heart and life. It is much more than putting words around people's experiences as emergents suggest. The Bible tells us God is always right; it is man who is so often wrong. When we rely upon human consensus, we will end up with man's perspective and not God's revelation. This is a dangerous way to develop one's spiritual life—the results can lead to terrible deception.

Brian McLaren put it well when he admitted it isn't just the way the message is presented that emerging church proponents want to change … it's the message itself they are changing:

> It has been fashionable among the innovative [emerging] pastors I know to say, "We're not changing the message; we're only changing the medium." This claim is probably less than honest … in the new church we must realize how medium and message are intertwined. When we change the medium, the message that's received is changed, however subtly, as well. We might as well get beyond our naïveté or denial about this.[13]

The Woman at the Well

If you listen to the emergent conversation long enough, you will hear a recurring theme: Christians are wrong to confront unbelievers head on with the Word of God. We should instead lay aside our desire to preach or share the truths from the Word and spend more time developing relationships and friendships with the unchurched (a politically correct name for unsaved). They often use Jesus as an example, saying He did not confront people but always accepted them for who they were.

One example is in Dan Kimball's 2007 book, *They Like Jesus but Not the Church*. In his chapter titled "The Church Arrogantly Claims All Other Religions are Wrong," Kimball refers to the story where Jesus is sitting near a well by Himself (the disciples have gone to the nearby town), and he talks to a Samaritan woman. Kimball alters the story by saying:

He [Jesus] stopped and asked questions of the
Samaritan woman (John 4) and didn't just jump in
and say, "Samaritans are all wrong."[14]

But Kimball is wrong. Jesus did the exact opposite! He didn't
ask her *any* questions, and he confronted her straight on—something Kimball says (throughout his book) is a terrible thing to
do to an unbeliever. Listen to Jesus' words to the woman:

Jesus saith unto her, Woman, believe me, the hour
cometh, when ye shall neither in this mountain, nor
yet at Jerusalem, worship the Father. Ye worship ye
know not what: we know what we worship: for
salvation is of the Jews. But the hour cometh, and
now is, when the true worshippers shall worship the
Father in spirit and in truth: for the Father seeketh
such to worship him. God is a Spirit: and they that
worship him must worship him in spirit and in truth.

The woman saith unto him, I know that Messiah
cometh, which is called Christ: when he is come,
he will tell us all things. Jesus saith unto her, I that
speak unto thee am he. (John 4:21-26)

Kimball largely bases his premise on the reasoning that Christians should not do or say anything that might offend unbelievers, even if that anything is truth and Scripture.

The fact is, Jesus *did* confront people with the truth, as did
His disciples (as well as the Old Testament prophets). And why
did He? He told the woman at the well the reason:

Jesus answered and said unto her, If thou knewest
the gift of God, and who it is that saith to thee, Give
me to drink; thou wouldest have asked of him, and
he would have given thee living water. (John 4:10)

There is no question about it, the Word of God is offensive to the unbeliever just as I Corinthians 1:18 states:

> For the preaching of the cross is to them that perish foolishness; but unto us which are saved it is the power of God.

And again in II Corinthians 2:15-16, when Paul explains the attitude he encountered when witnessing to unbelievers:

> For we are unto God a sweet savour of Christ, in them that are saved, and in them that perish: To the one we are the savour of death unto death; and to the other the savour of life unto life.

If Paul had been adjusting (contextualizing) the Word of God to fit the culture and context of the lives of those he spoke to, he would not have said "the aroma of death leading to death." He took the spiritual state of these people very seriously, and he had full confidence that God's Word, unaltered and unchanged, could reach into the heart and soul of any person who would receive Christ by faith. Whether a person is young, mentally challenged, or of a different culture or ethnic group, the Gospel is *God's* Gospel, and He made it so that all who receive it by faith will understand His love and forgiveness and have eternal life.

Thinking *Out of the Box*

Will Sampson is part of an emergent community in Kentucky called Communality. He also serves on the Coordinating Group of Emergent Village.* In *An Emergent Manifesto of Hope*, Sampson writes:

---

*Emergent Village is the group that formed out of the Young Leaders Network. The organizations website, www.emergentvillage.com, is a strong and influential presence on the Internet.

A rallying cry of the Protestant Reformation was sola scriptura, or Scripture alone. And while this doctrine may have arisen as a necessary corrective to abuses of church leadership in the Reformation period, it is in full effect today. Preachers speak of the Bible as an instruction book or as the only data necessary for spiritual living. But this diminishes some critical elements of theological knowledge. ... Sola scriptura also tends to downplay the role of God's Spirit in shaping the direction of the church.[15]

Sampson says that people who fall into this category "do not take into account the subjectivity of human interpreters." In other words, those men who penned Scripture may not have been that inspired after all. It could have been more a case of their point of view based on their own life experiences. Sampson adds:

Contextual theology is rooted in the notion that God's kingdom is vast and diverse, and it is our task as followers of Jesus to understand the diversity of God's work in the world and join that effort.[16]

Translated, that means that we need to not limit ourselves to Scripture but see God *out of the box*, so to speak. Sampson says that too many "Westerners" look at God scientifically and rationally, and this is a problem for the emerging church mindset. He explains:

Suggesting that God is doing something that may not conform to our previous understandings requires us to *think more broadly*.[17] (emphasis added)

But just how broadly does Sampson believe we should think? Would he suggest we veer from doctrinal truths of the Bible? The answer is yes. He says the "notion of being able to join the work of God simply through belief statements has had a negative impact on the health of the church."[18] He adds:

> [A]nother major delta in the church, the Protestant Reformation, the belief in justification by faith alone caused large parts of the church to split off from what was the global unified church.[19]

Sampson is implying that if it hadn't been for the reformers determination to stick to biblical doctrines, maybe this global unified church could have stayed intact. Sampson takes this line of reasoning a giant step further:

> Some would argue that these splits were necessary to correct false understandings of what it means to be the people of God.… So if by our actions we say that being right is more important than being together, what does that say about the God who formed our communities or how that God wishes to interact with contemporary humanity?[20]

This theological shift is challenging the premise of the 16th century reformation, suggesting that unity and works is more important than the Gospel or justification by faith. Even Rick Warren is talking this way. Regarding what he calls a new reformation, Warren states:

> I'm looking for a second reformation. The first reformation of the church 500 years ago was *about beliefs*. This one is going to be *about behavior*. The first one was *about creeds*. This one is going to be *about deeds*. It is not going to be about what does the church believe, but about what is the church doing. (emphasis added)[21]

A reformation that gives more credence to works and deeds than beliefs and doctrine is flawed right from the get go. With proper beliefs and doctrine, works and deeds will follow. But not so the other way around. Good deeds are not always an indication of true godliness as Scripture states:

> And no marvel; for Satan himself is transformed
> into an angel of light. Therefore it is no great thing
> if his ministers also be transformed as the ministers
> of righteousness. (II Corinthians 11:14-15)

When the Word is Not Heard

> My grandmother had good advice for reading the
> Bible... Reading the Bible is like eating fish. Enjoy
> the meat that's easy to eat first; come back and work
> on the bones later if you're still hungry.—Brian
> McLaren.[22]

Before the 16th century reformation and during the period known as the Dark Ages, the Bible was known as the forbidden book. Thanks to the reformers and the sacrifices they made, the Bible was translated into the language of the common people. The light of God's Word began to shine into the darkness, and people were delivered from the control and corruption of the Catholic Church* and the power of the pope and the priests. God's grace was revealed and people were saved and released from bondage. Once again, people could understand that salvation is a gift of God and that Jesus made the sacrifice once and for all when He died upon the cross.

The point I am making is simple: When leaders who profess to be Christian intentionally or unintentionally hide God's Word from people, the darkness created because of this leads to a desire for spiritual encounters (experiences). In order to convince followers they are being spiritually fed by these Bible-depleted teachings, leaders implement all kinds of experience-based religious rituals and paraphernalia—thus, the reason that icons, candles, incense, liturgy, and the sacraments are deemed necessary for the emerging worship experience.

---

*When this book uses the term "Catholic Church" it is referring to the sacraments, the practices, the church fathers and mystics, and all that encompasses what is known as the Roman Catholic Church.

Now, let's examine something that has happened at Doug Pagitt's church as the literal Word becomes less and less important. In his own words:

> During a recent Life Development Forum we offered a session on Christian practices. In one of the four weeks we introduced the act of making the sign of the cross on ourselves. This gesture has become a very powerful experience for me. It is rich with meaning and history and is such a simple way to proclaim and pray my faith with my body. I hold the fingers on my right hand in the shape of a cross, my index finger lying over the top of my outstretched thumb. I use the Eastern Orthodox pattern of touching first head, then heart, then right lung followed by left. Others in the group follow the Roman Catholic practice with left before right.[23]

Powerful experiences similar to what occurred during the Dark Ages are taking the place of expository Bible teaching. This makes sense in light of what happens when the Bible becomes the *forbidden book*.

Pagitt's statement (at the beginning of this chapter) typifies one of the basic beliefs of the emerging church movement. In a zeal to *reach* this present generation, Christianity must change. This change that requires the Word of God, the very foundation of the Christian faith, to be altered. There is simply no other way of interpreting Pagitt's statement.

However, Pagitt's proposal creates a problem. If faith comes by hearing the Word of God (Romans 10:17), a faith not based *on* the Word is not biblical faith and therefore cannot be the Christian faith.

While reaching today's generation for the cause of Christ is something we as Christians should all desire, we must remember Jesus Christ challenged us to follow Him and be obedient to His Word. Scripture commands us to "be not conformed to this

world: but be ye transformed by the renewing of your mind"
(Romans 12:2). But the emergents are leading followers in the
opposite direction, teaching that the Word of God needs to be
conformed to people and cultures instead of allowing it to conform lives through Jesus Christ. As we are about to see,
reimagining Christianity allows a dangerous kind of freedom;
like cutting the suspension ropes on a hot air balloon, the free
fall may be exhilarating but the results catastrophic.

4

Riding the Emerging Church Wave

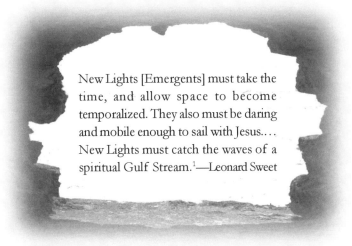

New Lights [Emergents] must take the time, and allow space to become temporalized. They also must be daring and mobile enough to sail with Jesus.... New Lights must catch the waves of a spiritual Gulf Stream.[1]—Leonard Sweet

In the late 1970s, not long after I had become a Christian, I was visiting with an elderly gentleman who had been a Christian most of his life. We were discussing the current wave sweeping Christianity at that time, which was the reintroduction of the 1940s Latter Rain movement.

I will never forget the words this man used to describe what was happening to the body of Christ: "Satan's plan to deceive the world impacts the church just like waves crashing against the shore. He added, "As we get closer and closer to the return of Christ, these waves of deception will be more frequent and influence countless numbers of people."

Then he made a statement that remains etched in my mind: "There is a wave coming before Jesus returns that will sweep the world." But before this final apostasy hits, there will be other significant waves preparing the way for the final wave."

Many years have passed now, and this man's words have proven to be prophetic and true. The waves currently breaking are conditioning the church for the last-days apostasy that Jesus and Paul foretold:

> Now the Spirit speaketh expressly, that in the latter times some shall depart from the faith, giving heed to seducing spirits, and doctrines of devils. (I Timothy 4:1)

I believe the emerging church is one of those deceptive waves. However, emerging church leaders don't see it that way. Leonard Sweet envisions these waves coming across the earth as a great time for humanity:

> God is birthing the greatest spiritual awakening in the history of the church. God is calling you to midwife the birth. Are you going to show up?[2]

According to Sweet, this "spiritual awakening" is impacting the postmodern generation and is characterized by a hunger for experience. He writes:

> A spiritual tsunami has hit postmodern culture. This wave will build without breaking for decades to come. The wave is this: People want to *know* God. They want less to *know about* God or *know about* religion than to *know* God. People want to experience the "Beyond" in the "Within."
>
> Post-moderns want something more than new products; they want new experiences, especially new experiences of the divine.[3]

In Sweet's 1991 book, *Quantum Spirituality*, he describes his view of a new kind of Christian faith that he believes is on the horizon:

Faith is not simply intellectual understanding, or an act of human intention, or following some salvation "how-to" manual, or assent to creedal formulations. Faith is not a matter of doing or even being, but an experience of becoming. Experiencing is faith's most fundamental activity.[4]

As you will see, an experience-based Christianity is the wave of the emerging church, and its leaders are beckoning all to ride.

Experience Over Doctrine

In 1992, Leith Anderson (Doug Pagitt's former pastor), currently the president of the National Association of Evangelicals,* spoke of this new emerging 21st century church. His views eventually became set in stone as the emerging church has chosen experience over doctrine. Anderson reveals:

The old paradigm taught that if you had the right teaching, you will experience God. The new paradigm says that if you experience God, you will have the right teaching. This may be disturbing for many who assume propositional truth must always precede and dictate religious experience. That mindset is the product of systematic theology and has much to contribute ... However, biblical theology looks to the Bible for a pattern of experience followed by proposition. The experience of the Exodus from Egypt preceded the recording of Exodus in the Bible. The experience of the crucifixion, the resurrection and Pentecost all predate the propositional declaration of those events in the New Testament. It is not so much that one is right and the other is wrong: it is more of a matter of the perspective one takes on God's touch and God's truth.[5]

* The National Association of Evangelicals is a religious/political lobbying fellowship representing millions of evangelicals.

Anderson is saying that the Word of God is still being written, and today's experiences can dictate what that Word is. This sounds like Pagitt when he said "putting words around people's experiences to allow them to find deeper connection in their lives."

Experience-Driven Christianity

In his book *The Emerging Church*, Dan Kimball makes the following observation about the world we live in and about what the church must do to reach it. He explains:

> I believe with all my heart that this discussion about the fast-changing culture and the emerging church must take place. While many of us have been preparing sermons and keeping busy with the internal affairs of our churches, something alarming has been happening on the outside. What once was a Christian nation with a Judeo-Christian worldview is quickly becoming a post Christian, un-churched, un-reached nation.... New generations are arising all around us without any Christian influence. So we must rethink virtually everything we are doing in our ministries.[6]

While it is true that the spiritual climate in the Western world has changed radically over the past number of years just as Dan Kimball has stated, we must ask ourselves, what form will this rethinking take? And by what means, if not with biblical doctrine, will this "post-Christian era" be reached? Kimball believes the emerging church and the experiences it provides will be the best way to reach the lost.

One of the arguments for promoting the emerging church in the postmodern era goes something like this: While the seeker-friendly era was successful in bringing a generation of baby boomers to Jesus, that time is past. Now we need to find new innovative methods that will reach the present generation for Jesus. Postmoderns are seeking after experiences that stimulate their senses. The emerging church, they say, can provide these kinds of experiences.

Jim Wilson, in his book *Future Church*, describes the move away from the seeker-friendly, non-offensive style of Christianity towards a mystical-experiential brand:

> In the seeker age, the church tried to make its teachings and its services more user-friendly, practical, and accessible, and to market them to the un-churched. In the post-seeker age Future Churches are not as concerned with marketing services for unbelievers or entertaining believers as they are in ushering people, believers and unbelievers alike, into the presence of God. Intentionally, they do not water down their teachings or ratchet down the intensity of the service to make it more appealing to unbelievers.[7]

In order to appeal to "believers and unbelievers alike" and usher them "into the presence of God," emergent leaders are promoting a number of innovative ideas. Dan Kimball devotes a major portion of his book to these ideas, some of which include the following:

- Overcoming the Fear of Multi-sensory Worship and Teaching[8]
- Creating a Sacred Space for Vintage Worship[9]
- Expecting the Spiritual[10]
- Creating Experiential Multi-sensory Worship Gatherings[11]

Note the terms *multi-sensory*, *sacred space*, and *vintage worship*. What exactly do all these mean and where is this experience-based worship headed?

Ancient-Future Faith

One of the common phrases circulating among emerging church proponents is a concept called *vintage Christianity*. By saying vintage, they mean a spirituality out of the past that Christianity should incorporate to become more effective.

According to this view, mystical experiences practiced centuries ago will attract the postmodern generation. Dan Kimball believes worship must play an important role in this vintage Christianity. In discussing worship, he explains:

> We should be returning to a no-holds-barred approach to worship and teaching so that when we gather, there is no doubt we are in the presence of a Holy God. I believe that both believers and unbelievers in this emerging culture are hungry for this. It isn't about clever apologetics or careful exegetical and expository preaching or great worship bands.... Emerging generations are hungering to experience God in worship.[12]

Rob Redman, author of *The Great Worship Awakening* agrees with Kimball. He has noted that churches which provide a liturgical vintage form of worship are attracting the postmodern generation.[13] Redman says that as the result of this renewed interest in liturgical worship, a "worship awakening" is now underway, and Protestant worship services are beginning to incorporate liturgical worship practices. He states:

> A common approach to the worship awakening among Protestant churches is to create a blended service combining older and newer liturgical elements and musical styles.[14]

One article titled "Ancient New" further backs up the idea that postmoderns are looking for a sensual, experiential worship:

> Post-moderns prefer to encounter Christ by using all their senses. That's part of the appeal of classical liturgical or contemplative worship: the incense and candles, making the sign of the cross, the taste and smell of the bread and wine, touching icons and being anointed with oil.[15]

Leonard Sweet puts it this way:

> Post-moderns want a God they can feel, taste, touch,
> hear and smell—a full sensory immersion in the divine.[16]

An interview with one emerging leader describes the style of worship embraced in the emerging church:

> Evangelicals are using traditions from all liturgical
> churches from Orthodox to Lutheran to Catholic....
> Though they have limited experience using their
> new-found symbols, rituals and traditions, they're
> infusing them with vitality and spirit and life, which
> is reaching people.[17]

In reality, when the emerging church says ancient future, they are saying we need to go back to former practices, but not as far back as the disciples and Jesus' teachings in the Bible. They say we need only look back to Catholicism and early century monks and mystics.

The Impact of Imagery

The Bible says that "faith cometh by hearing, and hearing by the word of God [i.e., an intellectual or cognitive approach]" (Romans 10:17). Not so in the emerging church. Faith comes by seeing images, touching icons, smelling incense, and hearing chants and liturgical recitations; then the "word" follows. Leonard Sweet calls it "EPIC culture: Experiential, Participatory, Image-Driven, Connected."[18] Images of Jesus hanging on the cross are very common. So are icons of Mary and baby Jesus.

An article written by *Worship Leader Magazine* editor Chuck Fromm provides interesting background information with regard to the significance of imagery to our present generation. Fromm states:

We are now living in a "post *Passion of the Christ*
world." The extraordinary success of Mel Gibson's
landmark film, and the controversy that surrounded
it, underscores in no uncertain terms how imagery
shapes our cultural consciousness. The implications
for the church and its service of worship, have been
both profound and ambiguous.[19]

While Gibson's use of vivid imagery may have had effects
on the emotions, I wonder how truly effective watching graphic
depictions and images is in changing the human heart? In addition, while the emerging church and many Christian authors promote the view that *mystical encounters and sensory engagements* are a
more effective tool for evangelism, they are not supported by
Scripture; however, these ideas *can* be found in *church tradition* as
Chuck Fromm comments in his article:

In many ways, the Church is seeking a way back to
its oldest and most sacred traditions: those in which
all the senses are fully engaged in the act of worship
from incense and bells to icons and vestments.[20]

Apparently, justification for the return of these *ancient traditional practices* is based on the idea that our present generation is
looking for such experiences. Fromm states:

The power of the preached word is being augmented,
and occasionally outpaced, by the impact of the
visual. The primacy of music as an essential
expression of worship is being challenged by
congregations hungry for more direct means of
engagement.[21]

What is tragic is that the Word of God is being replaced
with a sensual spirituality, and that means that millions of lost
souls will miss the chance to hear the Word of God but will

think they are getting truth because it makes them feel good. And without that hearing of the Word, faith cannot come:

> For whosoever shall call upon the name of the Lord shall be saved. How then shall they call on him in whom they have not believed? and how shall they believe in him of whom they have not heard? and how shall they hear without a preacher? And how shall they preach, except they be sent? as it is written, How beautiful are the feet of them that preach the gospel of peace, and bring glad tidings of good things! But they have not all obeyed the gospel. For Esaias saith, Lord, who hath believed our report? So then faith cometh by hearing, and hearing by the word of God. (Romans 10:13-17)

5

Ancient-Future Worship

> In the emerging culture, darkness represents spirituality. We see this in Buddhist temples, as well as Catholic and Orthodox churches. Darkness communicates that something serious is happening.[1]—Dan Kimball

On October 12, 1998 in Glorieta, New Mexico, over 500 young leaders came together in what was called The National Reevaluation Forum. The objective was to train and listen to "leaders of the new millennium's emerging church."[2] A Young Leaders Network article on the event described it as a time to "discuss everything from restoring arts in the church" to dialoguing about "worship, the use of story and the mystical, and the experiential aspects of faith."[3] Plenary speakers included Stanley Grenz, Leonard Sweet, Brian McLaren, and Sally Morgenthaler. According to the article, Sweet told the group: "The primary challenge in this Postmodern transition is navigational tools."[4]

Over the years, since that 1998 meeting in New Mexico, the emerging church has defined many of these "navigational tools," and has implemented them within the structure of emerging *worship*.

The late Robert Webber is recognized by many as one of the foremost authorities on *worship renewal*. He regularly conducted workshops for almost every major denomination in North America through the Institute of Worship Studies, which he founded in 1995. Before his appointment to his position at Northern Baptist Theological Seminary, Webber taught at Wheaton College for 32 years as Professor of Theology. He authored over forty books and was also a regular contributor to numerous magazines and newspapers including *Worship Leader*.

I first came across Webber's views when I read an article he had written titled "Wanted: Ancient Future Talent." In that article, Webber states::

> I am personally most gratified to see the shift toward a recovery of the ancient. While many good choruses have been produced over the past forty years, the rejection of the sources of hymnody and worship by the contemporary church has resulted in a faith that is an inch deep.[5]

Webber listed a number of things he believed were necessary for "talented workers" to become a successful part of this new movement. Some of these he listed are:

- Rediscovering how God acts through the *sacred signs of water, bread and wine*, oil and laying on of hands.

- Rediscovering the central nature of the table of the Lord in the Lord's Supper, breaking of bread, communion and Eucharist.

- Rediscovering *congregational spirituality* through the Christian celebration in Advent, Christmas, Epiphany, Lent, Holy Week, Easter and Pentecost.[6]

Unfortunately, Webber's hope to return to "the ancient" is not limited to reintroducing the great hymns of the past. In fact, many of the practices he includes in this call to "ancient-future worship talent" cannot be found in the Bible.

Mystics from the Past

Like his emerging church colleagues, Robert Webber was convinced that Christianity needs to be revised for this new century. But in order to go ahead, we must go back (thus the term ancient-future) to the mystics and learn from them. While he acknowledged the Bible is an important book for the Christian faith, he also believed that it needed to be supplemented by the teachings of spiritual mystics from the past. He writes:

> The primary source of spiritual reading is the Bible. But we now recognize that in our love of Scripture we dare not avoid the mystics and the activists. Exposure to the great devotional literature of the church is essential. More and more people are turning to the great work of the mystics. Richard Foster has called us to recover Augustine's *Confessions*, Bernard of Clairvaux's *The Steps of Humility*, [etc.].[7]

Webber's list of recommended books written by mystics includes: Thomas a Kempis, Meister Eckhart, Teresa of Avila, John of the Cross, Thomas Aquinas, Thomas Merton and numerous others.[8] You may not be familiar with all these names, but they all have something in common—they are Catholic mystics. Webber makes the following statement about them:

> To immerse ourselves in these great works is to allow our vision to be expanded by a great treasure of spirituality.[9]

Webber was enamored by the writings of Catholic mystics, and he admonishes his readers to embrace them as well:

> The value of all these books as well as many not

mentioned are indispensable to spirituality. Those who neglect these works do so to their harm, and those who read them do so for their inspiration and spiritual growth.[10]

This statement by Webber is quite strong: without the teachings of these former mystics, our spiritual lives will suffer. Webber explains that those willing to adhere to these ancient-future teachers do not have to leave their own religious tradition. He explains:

A goal for evangelicals in the postmodern world is to accept diversity as a historical reality, but to seek unity in the midst of it. This perspective will allow us to see Catholic, Orthodox, and Protestant churches as various forms of *the one true church*— all based on apostolic teaching and authority, finding common ground in the faith expressed by *classical* Christianity. (emphasis added)[11]

Several of the mystics that Webber lists as those we should be gleaning from have something else in common—they had visions of an apparitional woman they believed to be Mary, the mother of Jesus. In a book titled *Saints Who Saw Mary*, the author documents these visitations. Some of those whom she lists as having seen Mary are Francis of Assisi,[12] Catherine of Siena,[13] Theresa of Avila,[14] John of the Cross,[15] Ignatius of Loyola,[16] and Bernard of Clairvaux.[17] Could this indicate where the fascination for the mystics will possibly lead?

Multi-Sensory Worship

Stimulating images that provide spiritual experiences are an essential element of the emerging church. While many are bewildered why their churches are darkening their sanctuaries and setting up prayer stations with candles, incense, and icons, promoters of the emerging church movement say they know exactly what they are doing. Mark Driscoll of Mars Hill Fellowship explains:

> Everything in the service needs to preach—
> architecture, lighting, songs, prayers, fellowship, the
> smell—it all preaches. All five senses must be
> engaged to experience God.[18]

Often, Christians who have been attending church all their lives find the changes their pastors are implementing disconcerting, as they see the trend away from Bible teaching to multisensory stimulation. Dan Kimball quotes an older gentleman who had expressed his concerns about the implementation of an emerging style of mystical worship:

> Dan, why did you use incense? I am not sure I like
> walking over to those prayer stations with all those
> props; can't we just pray from our seats? Why aren't
> you just preaching just the Bible? I wasn't too
> comfortable when you had those times of silence,
> and it's a little too dark in there for me.[19]

The comment by this gentleman in his seventies is typical of the comments I hear from many as I travel and speak at conferences around North America. But comments like this not only come from the elderly; many younger people are saying the same things. Both young and old are becoming concerned as they see multi-sensory mystical worship replace the preaching and teaching of the Word.

Nevertheless, Kimball and many others are convinced they are on the right path based on their view that emerging generations desire a multi-sensory worship experience. For example, in a chapter of Kimball's book titled "Creating a Sacred Space for Vintage Worship" Kimball states:

> [A]esthetics is not an end in itself. But in our culture,
> which is becoming more multi-sensory and less
> respectful of God, we have a responsibility to pay
> attention to the design of the space where we

assemble regularly. In the emerging culture, darkness represents spirituality. We see this in Buddhist temples, as well as Catholic and Orthodox churches. Darkness communicates that something serious is happening.[20]

Kimball further states:

How ironic that returning to a raw and ancient form of worship is now seen as new and even cutting edge. We are simply going back to a vintage form of worship which has been around for as long as the church has been in existence.[21]

Of course, that is not really true. There is no evidence in the Bible that the disciples or the early church turned to a "raw" form of worship, especially one that needed darkness to feel more spiritual. If the early believers were in darkness, it would have been because they were meeting in secret to avoid arrest. To insinuate they were thinking about multi-sensory practices is an insult to their courage and devotion to God. Nowhere in Scripture is there even a hint of this.

The Labyrinth

The labyrinth is a maze-like structure that is growing in popularity, used during times of contemplative prayer. The participant walks through this structure until he comes to the center, then back out again. Unlike a maze, which has several paths, the labyrinth has one path. Often *prayer stations* (with candles, icons, pictures, etc.) can be visited along the way. The labyrinth originated in early pagan societies. The usual scenario calls for the *pray*-er to do some sort of meditation practice, enabling him or her to *center down* (i.e., reach God's presence), while reaching the center of the labyrinth.

In a *Christianity Today* article (written by Dan Kimball) titled "A-maze-ing Prayer," Kimball describes when he and his wife went through a labyrinth at the National Pastors Convention:

Meditative prayer like that we experienced in the labyrinth resonates with hearts of emerging generations. If we had the room, we would set up a permanent labyrinth to promote deeper prayer. Until then, however, Graceland will continue to incorporate experiential prayer and encourage our people to stop, quiet themselves, and pray.[22]

After Kimball and his wife experienced the labyrinth at the convention, they put up a temporary labyrinth at their own church. He explains how they "hung art on the walls, draped fabric, and lit candles all around the room to create a visual sense of sacred space."[23] Describing how "more than 100 people" went through the makeshift labyrinth, Kimball said, "It was a joy to see so many people on their knees communing with God through the experiential prayer elements."[24]

Having some understanding of how the current interest in the labyrinth began and the nature of this practice will give us some further insight into the emerging church and its use of multi-sensory worship practices.

Lauren Artress, canon of Grace Cathedral in San Francisco, is considered the modern-day catalyst for the labyrinth. One article explains:

For her [Artress], the labyrinth is for the "transformation of human personality in progress" that can accomplish a "shift in consciousness as we seek spiritual maturity as a species." Artress says she walked her first labyrinth at a seminar in 1991 with psychologist and mystic/channeler Jean Houston, who several years ago famously assisted First Lady Hillary Clinton in trying to contact the departed spirit of Eleanor Roosevelt.... She calls her discovery of the labyrinth ... one of the "most astonishing events of my life." For her, the labyrinth is a "spiritual tool meant to awaken us to the deep

rhythm that unites us to ourselves and to the Light
that calls from within."[25]

Artress says the "sacred geometry [of the labyrinth] is based
on ancient, sacred knowledge," and she sees the labyrinth as is a
way to connect with the "divine feminine."[26] While Artress is not
considered part of the emerging church, she has a strong tie to it,
and her spirituality is similar. The Reverend Alan Jones (who I
will discuss in a later chapter) is Artress' pastoral overseer at Grace
Cathedral. It is safe to say that Jones resonates with Brian McLaren,
who endorsed the back cover of Jones' book, *Reimagining Christianity*. This book has all the flavor of any emergent book.

Doug Pagitt also has found use for the labyrinth. He explains:

> The first day of Lent this year brought the first
> Ash Wednesday gathering in our church's history
> and in mine. The evening began with people walking
> a candlelit labyrinth… The experience of walking
> the labyrinth invites the body into a rhythm of
> moving around and moving toward the center, then
> back out. Dozens of people may walk the labyrinth
> together, some walking in, some walking out.[27]

Pagitt proceeds to say that after people completed the labyrinth, they participated in a Lent service in which ashes were
applied to those confessing. It seems that Pagitt's experiences
with the labyrinth led to other unbiblical practices supported by
Rome. This willingness of emergent leaders to experiment with
mystical practices like the labyrinth can only lead to trouble.

Drumming Up "Jesus"

The *drumming circle* at Church of the Holy Comforter in the west
end of Richmond (VA) was founded by Regena Stith. In an
interview, she states:

> A drum circle really is what it says it is…. It's a

gathering of people in a circle with drums…. It's really a very ancient form of expression…. You move out of your head.[28]

Stith first experienced the power of drums in the late 1990s during a yoga retreat in Massachusetts. She came home and announced to her husband, "I need to get a drum."[29]

One organization held an event in which an advertisement for the meeting read:

> [W]e are uniting people around the world in 1 hour of drumming in unison! Getting together in a true global village of drumming! It's the first time the drumming event is this big in our country. To imagine the whole world beating the drums at the same hour, for one hour![30]

This shamanistic-type drumming is promoted as a way to enter a mystical state. While tuning one's brain into a hypnotic state, the beat of a drum may "speak directly to the intelligence of the body."[31]

Even though some in the emerging church might consider the drumming at the Church of the Holy Comforter in Richmond a bit extreme, it is growing in popularity and use in the postmodern religious scene. And according to proponents, drumming is a doorway for ecumenical harmony:

> [Drumming] also speaks to the simplicity of a good beat—and the way something as simple as a hand brushed against the skin of a conga drum can transcend denominational and cultural boundaries.[32]

Professor Johan Malan from the University of Limpopo in South Africa and a believer in Christ explains what is behind this drumming sensation. He says, "The interest in African drumming has exploded into a modern fad in many countries of the

Western World."[33] Malan explains that we can not separate African drumming from its "cultural context." He adds:

> Its wide range of functions include the promotion
> of harmony with your inner self, with other people
> and with nature, relaxation and healing from stress,
> the invoking of spirit guides and the promotion of
> cosmic energy flow, an aid to meditation and the
> attaining of trances, and also, in more aggressive
> styles of drumming, the arousing of various wild
> passions. The latter may even take the form of
> revolt against society and its norms.[34]

Perhaps drumming is still cutting edge, but it is gaining momentum. An article at Calvin Institute of Christian Worship refers to drumming. Speaking favorably of the practice, the author states:

> It would be to our advantage as worshippers to
> harness this resource that we see in secular world
> culture and adapt it and bring it into the church,
> not only to attract a diverse congregation but to
> communicate to the congregation the universality
> of the church and the diversity of humanity.[35]

But as Professor Malan so carefully warns:

> Only people who are not truly committed to biblical
> Christianity would dare to venture on the wicked ways
> of pagan cultures. But in doing so, strong delusion
> will come upon them, which will blind them to the
> light of the gospel (II Corinthians. 4:3-4).[36]

Old is "New" Again

Dale Dirksen is Associate Professor of Worship and Church Ministry at Briercrest Seminary in Saskatchewan. In an article he wrote titled "Old is 'New' Again: the Emergent Church,"

Dirksen says that emergent people are "questioning" things like "the power of human reason" and "have a lot of interest in ancient ideas." He says they are "hungry for mystery and searching for God."[37] Dirksen explains what he sees as advantages for the changes the emergent church hopes to bring. He explains:

> Cultural change requires careful and thoughtful response.... It is often in change that we refine, or even rediscover the major things and set aside the ones that do not matter so much. We have the chance to do that now. [38]

Similar to most emergent church advocates, Dirksen is looking for a new kind of Christianity. He asks:

> If we are going to get serious about following the command of Christ to make disciples, it will mean adopting a new kind of attitude, a new sense of mission. How can we learn about this new culture in which we find ourselves? What is its language? What are its practices? What are its gods?[39]

Dirksen provides his readers with insights that can be used for evangelizing the postmodern generation. He offers a suggestion to understanding emergent language and culture:

> [The emergent language] is more than a verbal language. It involves pictures, symbols, actions, even smells. To speak "emergent" the church will need to use more than just words. The good news is that we can find this emergent language in our own faith. But we will have to *look back a long way. (emphasis* added)[40]

Just how far back does Dirksen think we need to look? He answers that when he states:

> To connect with emergent people, however, we will
> need to look back much further than the twentieth
> century or even the Reformation. Ancient practices
> that seem to have spiritual significance for emergent
> people are often found in the third century, the turn
> of the first millennium, or the drama of worship in
> the Middle Ages.[41]

Going back to ancient teachings is necessary, according to
Dirksen, but only as far back as the mystics of the third century.

"Roman" Catholic or Just Catholic?

Going back to the past to find experiences that will attract
the postmodern generation is one goal of the emerging
church movement. However, a serious question needs to be asked
at this point. Why only go back to the Middle Ages, the turn of
the first millennium or the third century? Wouldn't this open the
door for some devious doctrines that may have crept into the
church? Why not just stay with Scripture in order to remain in
the truth?

> All scripture is given by inspiration of God, and is
> profitable for doctrine, for reproof, for correction,
> for instruction in righteousness. (II Timothy 3:16)

Those convinced that great spiritual insight can be gleaned
from church fathers and mystics often overlook such definitive,
God-inspired instruction. The Bible is stable and eternal; thus
the truths in it centuries ago are still relevant today. I propose it
isn't biblical truths that emergents say we need to go hunting for
in previous historical periods, but rather unscriptural methods,
rituals, and mystical experiences to be gathered and brought into
the present time.

Vintage spirituality proponents have an apologetic for those
who question leaving Scriptural doctrine behind for post-New
Testament extra-biblical revelation. Robert Webber writes:

> I once believed that the church became apostate at the close of the first century and hadn't emerged again until the Reformation. I jokingly say to my students, "We Protestants act as though Pentecost occurred October 31, 1517, when Martin Luther tacked his 95 Theses on the door of the Wittenburg church." This attitude results in a negative view of the early church fathers and Christianity prior to the Reformation. The fact is that God's church has existed from the Pentecost described in Acts. We belong to the whole church and need, for our own spiritual health, to affirm every part of it.[42]

Webber recognized some are suspicious about taking instruction from the church fathers, especially when the church fathers are the fathers of the Catholic Church. In order to answer this concern, he writes:

> Because evangelicals fear that a respect for early church fathers will turn them into Roman Catholics, a distinction needs to be made between *catholic* and *Roman Catholic*. The early Fathers are catholic in the sense that they defined the classical Christian tradition for the whole church. This is a tradition, as I have been presenting, common *to every branch of the church*. Roman Catholicism, as such, is a tradition that has added to the common tradition. I believe in the common tradition and share that tradition with my Catholic brothers and sisters. But I do not believe in some of the added traditions of the Romanization of the church in the medieval era.[43]

Webber, like many emergents leaders, was trying to differentiate between Roman Catholicism and Catholicism (as a universal body). However, the Roman Catholic Church does not make this distinction because they claim an apostolic succession of papacy (popes) beginning with the apostle Peter. Therefore, all of Catholicism is Roman Catholicism. Some in the emerging church do not show an attachment to the authority of the papacy but embrace the practices and early history of the Catholic Church as described above by Webber. But many Protestants who began by attaching themselves to the history, teachings, and practices of the early Catholic Church have now taken the natural next step of becoming *Roman Catholic*.

Webber's statement may convince some there is no danger in embracing the Catholic Church fathers from the first to third centuries who promoted many ideas without biblical basis. However, before you are convinced, consider another statement Webber makes:

> The early Fathers can bring us back to what is common and help us get behind our various traditions, not in a sense that we deny our own tradition, but that we give a priority to the common teaching of the church. Here is where our unity lies. To summarize, the words *One, Holy, Catholic, and Apostolic* point to the oneness of the church, as a matter of faith. Christians do not believe something *about* the oneness of the church; they believe *in* the oneness of the church. Consequently, evangelicals need to go beyond talk about the unity of the church to experience it through *an attitude of acceptance of the whole church* and an entrance into dialogue with the Orthodox, Catholic, and other Protestant bodies. (emphasis added)[44]

A Catholic Perspective of the Church Fathers

By Webber's estimation, listening to the Catholic Church fathers is as safe as mother's milk. He and other emerging church teachers insist there are so many spiritual insights to gain by studying the church fathers that we can only benefit from them.

This of course would be true if the church fathers point us to God's Word. But what if that is not the case? The unsuspecting could actually be led away from biblical doctrine toward the doctrines made up by man and even inspired by demons when trusted leaders and professors espouse these mystics as safe and equal to Scripture. If it can be shown that heretical teachings had already entered in through many of these early church fathers, shouldn't we be leery, to say the least?

With this in mind, let's look at these early Catholic Church fathers. The following is an excerpt from a lecture by the International Catholic University titled "Importance of Studying the Church Fathers." The author states:

> But why do we study them? The Holy Father has given us the basic reasons. They are the framers of the structure of the Church built upon Christ Jesus as the cornerstone and the Apostles as the foundation. Specifically, they are the privileged witnesses to traditions. Founders, whether they be founders of institutions or founders of religious societies, always have a privileged position.... They were the closest to the sources; the early Fathers, referred to as Apostolic Fathers, personally knew the Apostles and the Disciples. They had access to the purity of the sources of the living tradition, the very teachings of those closest to Christ, and they were the ones that developed the first structures of the Church.[45]

If we embrace the teachings of these early church fathers, where will it lead us? Well, according to the author of this lecture, right into the arms of the Catholic Church:

> The Church Fathers are the guarantors of an authentic Catholic tradition.... Many great Christian men and women have found their way either back to, or into, the Catholic Church through meditating and reflecting upon the writings of the

Church Fathers. John Henry Cardinal Newman, a great nineteenth century English Cardinal who in his younger years was a member of the Church of England, fell in love with the writings and thought and spirit of the Church Fathers. And in his *Apologia pro vita sua*, he points out that he saw in them the true Church, the universal Church, the Catholic Church, and they became very instrumental in his acceptance and embrace of the Roman Catholic Church.[46]

Journeys Home

For John Henry Cardinal Newman, his conversion to the Catholic Church took place after he began "meditating and reflecting" on the writings of the Catholic Church fathers. This same story can be repeated thousands and thousands of times now that we are in the 21st century.

Journeys Home edited by Marcus C. Grodi is a book that documents many of these conversions. In the introduction of the book, we read the following:

> Many of these men and women came from Protestant faiths.... From an early age they had been taught all kinds of things about Catholics and their beliefs, sometimes horrifying, repulsive things, that made them wonder whether Catholics could be saved. Yet in each case, and in uniquely different ways, the Holy Spirit opened their hearts to realize that much of what they had been taught about the Catholic Church was never true.[47]

Sharon M. Mann, in a section of *Journeys Home*, provides personal testimony as one of many who have made the journey home to Rome. She testified that the church fathers played an important role to start her on her journey to Catholicism. In her own words:

I started reading the early Church Fathers and realized that whatever they believed, they surely were not Protestant. Catholic themes peppered the landscape of Church history. I couldn't deny it— nor could I accept it. Surely they were misguided! The Church was floundering in the first centuries and tons of crazy ideas were floating around—so I thought! When I began reading St. Augustine, however, I was stunned how Catholic he was.[48]

Like many others who have read the writings of Augustine and other Catholic Church fathers, Sharon wanted to know more about the Catholic tradition. She went to a chapel where Eucharistic adoration was under way, and like many others, she had an experience that changed her life. This is how Sharon described her encounter:

Finally, Saturday night, at the Eucharistic adoration, I saw 1000+ people kneeling on a hard, concrete floor giving adoration to the Sacrament. I found tears streaming down my face. I knelt, too, not knowing if this was real or whether the people were just crazy! But every time the Sacrament came near me, my throat tightened and I couldn't swallow. I was being torn apart by my convictions. If the Lord was truly passing by, then I wanted to adore and worship Him, but if He wasn't, I was afraid to be idolatrous. The weekend left a very powerful imprint on my heart, and I found myself running out of good arguments to stay Protestant. My heart was longing to be Catholic and be restored to the unity with all Christendom.[49]

The Eucharistic experience drew Sharon to Catholicism. Her journey began with an interest in the Catholic Church fathers and led her right into a Catholic *conversion*. The emerging church, through its emphasis on the teachings of the church fathers (the mystics), based upon a foundation that ancient-future faith is the answer to reaching the postmodern generation, has the potential to open the same door that Sharon walked through. This ancient-future path of worship is leading possibly millions into the arms of Rome.

Do you recall what Paul prophesied would happen to the early Christian church? He stated:

> Take heed therefore unto yourselves, and to all the flock, over which the Holy Ghost hath made you overseers, to feed the church of God, which He hath purchased with His own blood. For I know this, that after my departing shall grievous wolves enter in among you, not sparing the flock. Also of your own selves shall men arise, speaking perverse things, to draw away disciples after them. (Acts 20:28-30)

Paul actually warned the church that after he was gone, "grievous wolves" would enter the church and hurt believers. A look at church history validates Paul's prophetic warning. He said it would happen, and then it happened. Numerous church leaders emerged during the first to the third centuries. Scriptural principles were ignored, and many followed the experiential teachings of men who claimed they had discovered new and innovative methods to get in touch with God.

The reason why this happened is simple. We know God's Word is light. When we replace the Word of God with the words of man, which are considered to bring enlightenment, we have a perfect formula for returning to darkness. The early mystics added ideas to Christianity that cannot be found in the Bible—a recipe for spiritual detriment. Jude also warned about the coming apostasy in the early church:

> For there are certain men crept in unawares, who were before of old ordained to this condemnation, ungodly men, turning the grace of our God into lasciviousness, and denying the only Lord God, and our Lord Jesus Christ. (Jude 4)

Many emerging church leaders are suggesting the need to study the ideas and beliefs of church leaders of the post-disciple era. They say if pastors and church leaders reintroduce these teachings from the past, we will have spiritual transformation and successful churches in the 21st century.

But wait a minute! If the church that emerged from the New Testament church was based on ideas and beliefs foreign to Scripture, why would we want to emulate a previous error? When doctrines of men replace the doctrine of Scripture, many are led astray. It has happened in the past, and it is happening now. Following doctrine not based on the Word of God always results in the undoing of faith.

6

When West Meets East

Spiritual disciplines, both East and West, are based on the hypothesis that there is something that we can do to enter upon the journey to divine union once we have been touched by the realization that such a state exists. Centering prayer is a discipline designed to reduce the obstacles ... choose a sacred word [to repeat] ... Twenty to thirty minutes is the minimum amount of time necessary for most people to establish interior silence.[1]—Thomas Keating

Contemplative spirituality* is a vital element of the emerging church. In fact, wind is to a sail boat what contemplative prayer is to the emerging church. Without it, there is no momentum—it is woven into the very fabric of the emerging church's ambience. In order to understand why this is so important, it is first necessary to understand the dynamics of contemplative spirituality. One proponent defines it like this:

> To help the mind become quiet, we can follow our breathing. Or we can repeat silently a chosen prayer phrase or a word.[2]

---

*Contemplative Spirituality: A belief system that uses ancient mystical meditation practices to induce altered states of consciousness (the silence).

That may sound beneficial at first glance, to quiet ourselves in the midst of a busy and hectic world. What Christian doesn't want to find peace and rest? But let's take a closer look at the infrastructure of this type of prayer and the belief system behind it. One practitioner explains that those who learn to perfect this type of meditation actually can enter a "deep trance state" much like a hypnotic condition.[3]

Most Christians would say they would never do a spiritual practice that took them into a deep hypnotic trance. That's just for New Agers, right? But it may surprise many to learn that this meditative state (brought on by either repeating a word or phrase or focusing on the breath or an object) has become entrenched within mainstream Christianity. Often referred to as *going into the silence* or *sacred space*, New Agers and Catholic monks have taught the practice for a long time. Thomas Keating, a Catholic monk, has this to say about contemplative prayer and the silence:

> Contemplative prayer is not so much the absence of thoughts as detachment from them. It is the opening of mind and heart, body and emotions— our whole being—to God, the Ultimate Mystery, beyond words, thoughts and emotions.[4]

When Keating speaks of "interior silence," he is differentiating between solitude or outer quietness (i.e., sitting by a creek, turning off the phones and radio, etc.) and an inner stillness or stilling of the mind. One contemplative critic says stilling the mind is like "putting it in the equivalent of pause or neutral."[5]

While outer quietness is legitimate, inner stillness of the mind is not. In order to have this "interior silence," the mind must be rid of thoughts and distractions, and this can only be done through a hypnotic, repetitive practice.

In order to comprehend this more fully, let's look at the history of contemplative prayer. The *desert fathers* from the early centuries of the church initially practiced it. A former New Ager suggests where these desert mystics adopted the practice:

Perhaps the Desert Fathers either came into contact
with someone from the East who shared these practices
with them, or maybe they stumbled across it themselves.[6]

The practice remained obscure for many centuries and never
became mainstream practice until just a few decades ago, when a
Catholic monk named Thomas Merton brought it out of the con-
vents and monasteries and presented it to a much broader audience. Catholic priest and mystic Henri Nouwen further expanded
this interest to Protestant and even evangelical circles. Others who
played a vital role in the propagation of mystical prayer were Matthew Fox, Basil Pennington, and Thomas Keating. Pennington's
book alone, *Centering Prayer*, sold over a million copies.

Pope John Paul II also showed interest in the practice and
encouraged its use:

> Pope John Paul has urged people to take to prayer,
> especially a contemplative type of prayer.[7]

And the Second Vatican Council validated contemplative prayer as
is evident in the following statement (taken from a Catholic source):

> [The Second Vatican Council] gave both religious and
> lay people a new sense of freedom and a desire for
> spiritual renewal…. Centering Prayer and meditation
> groups following the teaching of John Main have
> helped introduce large numbers of Christians to a
> deeper life of prayer.[8]

A mystical prayer movement endorsed and actually initiated
by Catholic monks (and accepted by Catholic leadership) should
be alarming to any discerning Christian. Blanking out one's mind
to arrive at a meditative state has long been practiced as a means
of contacting the spirit world. While it is common to Eastern
religion, it is foreign to Scripture; any references in Scripture to
praying a mantra or going into self-induced altered states of

consciousness are condemned (Matthew 6:7, Deuteronomy 18:9-14).

In the next chapter of this book, I will document the coupling together of mysticism and the emerging church, but for now let's further examine contemplative spirituality, which I believe has its roots in what the Bible refers to as divination:

> There shall not be found among you any one that maketh his son or his daughter to pass through the fire, or that useth divination, or an observer of times, or an enchanter, or a witch. Or a charmer, or a consulter with familiar spirits, or a wizard, or a necromancer. For all that do these things are an abomination unto the LORD: and because of these abominations the LORD thy God doth drive them out from before thee. (Deuteronomy 18: 10-12)

Thomas Merton - God in Everybody

Thomas Merton was a world-renowned Trappist monk who lived at the Abbey of Gethsemani in Kentucky from 1941 until he died in 1968. His interest in mysticism led him on a journey that eventually caused him to say, "I'm deeply impregnated with Sufism"[9] and also the following:

> Asia, Zen, Islam, etc., all these things come together in my life. It would be madness for me to attempt to create a monastic life for myself by excluding all these. I would be less a monk.[10]

Merton said these things because he came to appreciate the mystical element that these other religions had, in particular Buddhism. At one point of his life, he thought he would have to leave Christianity to become a true mystic. But when he met a Hindu swami named Dr. Bramachari, Bramachari "left a deep influence on Thomas Merton" for whom Merton had "great respect and deep reverence."[11] Bramachari told Merton he could find this same mysticism within the confines of *Christian* mystics.[12] Merton found if he had an "openness to Buddhism, to Hinduism and to these great Asian [mystical] traditions"[13] he would be able to incorporate these into his own Christian tradition.

Merton came to believe, much through Bramachari's influence, that the realm reached during meditation is the same no matter what religion you are. So the question is, what exactly is being reached? If people of these different religions are reaching God during meditation, then the Gospel of Jesus Christ would be unnecessary. And if that were the case, then Scripture would not be true when it says:

> For there is one God and one mediator between God and men, the man Christ Jesus, who gave himself as a ransom for all men—the testimony given in its proper time. (I Timothy 2: 5-6)

The underlying premise of contemplative spirituality is the belief that God is in all things and in all people, virtually in all of creation (panentheism). When studying Thomas Merton, it becomes apparent he believed this:

> It is a glorious destiny to be a member of the human race, ... If only they [people] could all see themselves as they really are ... I suppose the big problem would be that we would fall down and worship each other.... At the center of our being is a point of nothingness which is untouched by sin and by illusions, a point of pure truth.... This little point ... is the pure glory of God in us. It is in everybody.[14]

So since all things are connected to God, and since you reach God (or divinity) in meditative states, you are connected to all things. You do not have to be a Bible scholar to see the error in Merton's theology. Merton has been credited with rediscovering contemplative prayer. If he wanted to become a good Buddhist and he saw no contradiction between Buddhism and Christianity, shouldn't that be a warning to those who believe contemplative prayer is a modern-day *hotline* to God?

Celebration of Discipline

One of the most influential and well-known *evangelical* Christians in support of contemplative prayer is Richard Foster, author of the best-selling and highly acclaimed *Celebration of Discipline*. First published in 1978, it is still going strong today. It has sold more than two million copies,[15] and *Christianity Today* named it number eleven in the "Top 50 Books That Have Shaped Evangelicals."[16] Many Christian seminaries and colleges use it in their classes, and countless ministries and organizations promote it.

In *Celebration of Discipline*, Foster voices his support for contemplative prayer when he says, "[W]e should all without shame enroll as apprentices in the school of contemplative prayer."[17] In the back of the book, Foster recommends to readers a book by Tilden Edwards. His recommendation is really quite revealing. Edwards, founder of the Shalem Institute in Washington, DC, says that contemplative prayer is what bridges Eastern religions with Christianity.[18] Edwards is referring to mysticism when he speaks of this bridge between the two:

> [T]he more popular Eastern impact in the West through transcendental meditation, Hatha Yoga, the martial arts, and through many available courses on Eastern religions in universities, has aided a recent rediscovery of Christian apophatic mystical tradition.[19]

Like Edwards, Foster too embraced this bridge between the East and the West. Perhaps the greatest evidence of this is Foster's embracing of Thomas Merton. In Foster's book, *Devotional Classics*, he has compiled the writings of 52 people, at least half of whom are mystics. Foster defends Merton, saying that even in his "attempts to bridge the gap between Eastern and Western spirituality" Merton "never surrendered his belief in the importance of a relationship with God through Jesus Christ."[20] What Foster doesn't understand—or doesn't say—is that Merton became convinced by Bramachari that he didn't *have* to let go of one to have the other. That is because they believed all paths reach God. Nevertheless, Foster's admiration for Merton is obvious. In *Devotional Classics*, Foster says of Merton:

> I am constantly pleased at how applicable Merton's writings are to the nonmonastic world in which most of us live. The guidance he gives on meditative prayer is practical and "bite-sized."[21]

Foster believes that Merton's contribution to modern-day spirituality may surpass anyone else's and that even "Zen masters from Asia" saw him as an authority on meditative prayer.[22] Foster recognized Merton's hope "to make the gift of contemplation more accessible to all."[23]

Why would someone who claims to be a Christian as Foster does, after reading and understanding Merton's position on Eastern religion, promote his ideas? Foster knows the kind of prayer Merton stood for was different from biblical prayer. He admits that Merton's prayer lined up with that of Zen masters and Buddhist monks. And yet he said, "Merton continues to inspire countless men and women."[24]

The fact that Foster resonates with the spirituality of mystics can also be seen in his companion book, *Spiritual Classics*, where once again he has compiled over fifty devotional writers. But when we take a look at these writers, they include a list of mystics like Merton, Henri Nouwen, Julian of Norwich, Richard Rolle, and Ignatius of Loyola. When Foster told readers (in *Celebration of Discipline*) that contemplative prayer was for everyone, he was referring to the prayer of these mystics. Research analyst Ray Yungen explains:

Foster openly quotes Merton on the virtues and benefits of contemplative prayer putting forth the view that through it God "offers you an understanding and light, which are like nothing you ever found in books or heard in sermons." But when one digs deeper and finds what exactly this "understanding" is, it casts a very dubious light on Foster's judgment.[25]

Foster has a consistent history of favorably referencing mystics as those we should admire. One of them, John Main, a Benedictine monk, was known for "the way of the mantra."[26] In *Spiritual Classics*, Foster said Main "understood well the value of both silence and solitude" and that he "rediscovered meditation" from the "Far East," believing that "[s]ilence is a path into the reality of the universe."[27] This reality he speaks of, though, is the altered state acquired through meditation. *Spiritual Classics* dedicates a section to Main and offers a recommended reading list of other books by Main, certainly a hearty dose of contemplative for the reader who takes Foster's advice.

Main explains his "way of the mantra":

Listen to the mantra as you say it, gently but continuously.... If thoughts or images come these are distractions at the time of meditation, so return simply to saying your word. Simply ignore it and the way to ignore it is to say your mantra. Return with fidelity to meditation each morning and evening for between twenty and thirty minutes.[28]

When Foster says Main understands the value of contemplative prayer, Foster is speaking as one who sees value in it himself; otherwise he would not have said that. Clearly, Foster shares a mutual adherence to the inner silence sought after by the mystics. And yet, so many view Foster as a trustworthy teacher of evangelical Christian doctrine through spiritual formation.

Enamored by Mysticism

Henri Nouwen was probably even more influential than Richard Foster in his role to bring contemplative spirituality to mainstream Christendom. Nouwen was enamored with both Merton and mysticism. And yet his books, *In the Name of Jesus* and *Way of the Heart*, both of which clearly demonstrate Nouwen's contemplative sympathies, are used in countless seminaries and Christian colleges, and are endorsed or quoted frequently by evangelical leaders. One of these is Rick Warren, who says his wife, Kay, recommends *In the Name of Jesus*. Kay Warren loved the book so much she said, "I highlighted almost every word."[29] Warren shares his wife's admiration for Nouwen, as can be seen on his website, which has several positive references to Nouwen.

Nouwen devotes an entire chapter in that book to contemplative prayer, saying that leaders of the future must move from the *moral to the mystical*.[30] In *The Way of the Heart* he says, "The quiet repetition of a single word can help us to descend with the mind into the heart."[31] When Nouwen says things like moving from the moral to the mystical and the mind to the heart, he sounds very much like those in the emerging reformation who say we must move from theology and doctrine to experience.

When Nouwen met mystic Andrew Harvey at a lecture, he wrote that he'd found a "soul-friend" in Harvey. Nouwen said it was Harvey's mystical propensities that attracted him to Harvey.[32]

It is very common for those who consistently practice contemplative prayer to eventually embrace eastern spiritual persuasions. This was evident in Nouwen's life when in *Sabbatical Journey*, he said:

> Today I personally believe that while Jesus came to open the door to God's house, all human beings can walk through that door, whether they know about Jesus or not. Today I see it as my call to help every person claim his or her own way to God.[33]

And in his book, *Here and Now*, he stated:

The God who dwells in our inner sanctuary is also
the God who dwells in the inner sanctuary of each
human being.[34]

The list of those who have paved the way for contemplative prayer to enter the evangelical church is expansive: Merton, Nouwen, Keating, and Foster—these are certainly some of the forerunners, but there are many others who laid hold of their teachings and began preaching this mystical spirituality, which has spread to the point where today the Christian authors who have at least some contemplative element are the norm rather than the exception. And that's not to mention the overwhelming number of authors in the emerging church camp, nearly all of whom write and teach Merton's universal prayer.

In this one chapter in *Faith Undone*, I cannot give a full discourse of how mysticism has come into the Christian church through contemplative spirituality (i.e., spiritual formation.) If you have not read *A Time of Departing* or *Running Against the Wind*, I encourage you to do so. Both books show how extensive contemplative has entered the church. Without a good understanding of this belief system, you may miss the signs of the apostasy that are quickly overtaking so much of mainstream Christianity today.

Spiritual Formation and Transformation

When I first began writing in the field in the late 70s and early 80s the term "Spiritual Formation" was hardly known, except for highly specialized references in relation to the Catholic orders. Today it is a rare person who has not heard the term. Seminary courses in Spiritual Formation proliferate like baby rabbits. Huge numbers are seeking to become certified as Spiritual Directors to answer the cry of multiplied thousands for spiritual direction.[35]—Richard Foster

A move away from the truth of God's Word to a mystical form of Christianity has infiltrated, to some degree, nearly all evangelical denominations. Few Bible teachers saw this avalanche coming. Now that it is underway, most do not realize it has even happened.

The best way to understand this process is to recall what happened during the Dark Ages when the Bible became the *forbidden book*. Until the Reformers translated the Bible into the language of the common people, the great masses were in darkness. When the light of God's Word became available, the Gospel was once again understood.

I believe history is repeating itself. As the Word of God becomes less and less important, the rise in mystical experiences escalates, and these experiences are presented to convince the unsuspecting that Christianity is about feeling, touching, smelling, and *seeing* God. The postmodern mindset is the perfect environment for fostering *spiritual formation*. This term suggests there are various ways and means to get closer to God and to emulate him. Thus the idea that if you do certain practices, you can be more *like* Jesus. Proponents of spiritual formation erroneously teach that *anyone* can practice these mystical rituals and find *God within*. Having a relationship with Jesus Christ is not a prerequisite. In a DVD called *Be Still*, which promotes contemplative prayer, Richard Foster said that contemplative prayer was for anyone and that by practicing it, one becomes "a portable sanctuary" for "the presence of God."[36]

Rather than having the indwelling of the person of Jesus Christ and the Holy Spirit, spiritual formation through the spiritual disciplines supposedly transforms the seeker by entering an altered realm of consciousness.

The spiritual formation movement is widely promoted at colleges and seminaries as the latest and the greatest way to become a spiritual leader. It teaches people that this is how they can become more intimate with God and truly hear His voice. Even Christian leaders with longstanding reputations of teaching God's word seem to be succumbing. In so doing, many

Christian leaders are frivolously playing with fire, and the result will be thousands, probably millions, getting burned.

It isn't going into the silence that transforms a person's life. It is in accepting Jesus Christ as Lord and allowing Him to change us, that transformation occurs.

> And you, that were sometime alienated and enemies in your mind by wicked works, yet now hath he reconciled in the body of his flesh through death, to present you holy and unblameable and unreproveable in his sight: If ye continue in the faith grounded and settled, and be not moved away from the hope of the gospel. (Colossians 1:21-23)

We are reconciled to God only through his "death" (the atonement for sin), and we are presented "holy and unblamable and unreproveable" when we belong to Him through rebirth. It has nothing to do with works, rituals, or mystical experiences. It is Christ's life in the converted believer that transforms him.

A New Age Christianity

Time has a way of bringing about change. Gradual indoctrination takes place over time and eventually brings about a significant shift. Unfortunately, it has happened to Christianity too. For those of us who have lived on this planet for a half a century or more, the changes we've experienced are phenomenal. Yet we wonder how our world could have changed so much without many noticing.

I became a Christian in the late '70s. For me, it was like a light coming on in a dark room. I could see reality for the first time. As an unbeliever, I had been locked into a world of materialism, evolutionism, and secularism. When the grace of God drew me to the Word of God, I experienced an awakening. From the moment I was converted, I was able to see God's plan to save mankind in contrast to Satan's plan to deceive the world.

In the early '80s, I became aware of a major shift in thinking that was sweeping the Western world. Religious pagan practices of the past, once relegated to a world of darkness, were now being embraced as the ways and means of ushering in an age of enlightenment. Instead of physics, it was metaphysics. Rather than believing in God, people were following men who said they *were* gods. Instead of worshipping the one true God who created everything, they were worshipping everything the Creator had made. All was God, and even man could become god. Every method and therapy imaginable imported from Hinduism, Buddhism and every form of Eastern mysticism suddenly was in vogue. The age of enlightenment had arrived, we were told.

So now that we are well into the third millennium, it is interesting to look back. What happened, how did it happen, and what might lie ahead? These are questions that Scripture can answer. Reading through the Old Testament, a pattern emerges. In short, when human beings turn away from God, they will worship anything and everything as God, even themselves. Satan has a master plan to lead man away from God.

There are many verses that can help us understand why Eastern mysticism is gaining a stronghold worldwide. Pay attention to God's warning to Israel through the prophet Isaiah:

> O house of Jacob, come ye, and let us walk in the light of the LORD. Therefore thou hast forsaken thy people the house of Jacob, because they be replenished from the east, and are soothsayers like the Philistines, and they please themselves in the children of strangers. (Isaiah 2:5-6)

The Bible explains how God's chosen people were seduced into darkness by embracing doctrines of demons from the "east" in the past.

In the early '80s, it became apparent to me that Eastern religion was being widely promoted in the West as something new. While New Agers were enthusiastically advocating yoga, meditation, crystals, spirit guides, and chanting mantras as the ways and means to achieve global consciousness and enlightenment, professing Christians that I knew could see Satan's strategy. No Bible-believing Christian would ever fall for such deception!

At least that was the way it was twenty-five years ago. Today it is becoming increasingly common to hear about churches promoting *Christian* yoga or *Christian* leaders suggesting the best way to enhance one's prayer life is by getting in tune with God through repeating a mantra. What was once described as New Age and occultic is acceptable now in some Christian circles.

What has happened? Has God changed His Word, or has the Christian departed from it? Or is it possible that Satan has duped Christians and lulled them to sleep? Anyone who cares to do the research will find that yoga and its connection to Eastern religion remains the same. Linking oneself with the universal energy is still its goal. A Christian can believe that yoga is for health and well being if he or she wants, but the facts have not changed.

The amazing thing to me is how quickly Christianity has changed in such a short period of time. Why has this happened? Does it have something to do with the undermining of the Word of God? Christians seem to have joined hands with the New Age, and we now have a *New Age* Christianity the Bible has always warned us about.

Straying away from the God of Scripture to follow other gods is an abomination unto the Lord, and it will be judged. There is not one verse in the Bible that supports a New Age Christianity.

"Christian" Yoga

"Yes to Yoga: Can a Christian breathe air that has been offered to idols?"[37] The title caught my attention in a *Christianity Today* article. The author begins:

> It's 7:45 p.m. on a weekday and for the first time today, I consciously slow down my breathing. I send the air deep down into my belly, letting it rise and fall like a wave.

> In … Out … Along with a group of 30 people …
> I use the unhurried cadences of the air filling and
> leaving my lungs to lull my muscles and joints into
> daring postures.…
>
> Finally—my favorite pose that comes at the end of
> each workout—a corpse, during which I lay down
> and relax every muscle.[38]

Now, you may be asking the question, why would *Christianity Today* publish an article promoting Eastern religion? Yet, the author of the article claims to be an evangelical born-again Christian. She says yoga draws her closer to Jesus. In her own words:

> [Y]oga has never had any negative influence on me,
> and it doesn't trigger any harmful religious impulses.
> Just the opposite is true. The three hours a week I
> spend doing yoga … draw[s] me closer to Christ.[39]

The woman sees yoga as a way to connect with the Holy Spirit, and the breathe in, breathe out repetition is essential:

> Holy Spirit in. Anything that's not from God out.
> Come Holy Spirit. Renew my mind. In. Out.[40]

Christian yoga practitioners often claim they cannot be deceived, even though they know what yoga is and where it comes from. The author of the article states:

> Now, my enthusiasm for yoga doesn't mean I'm in denial
> about its Hindu roots.… I know that hard-core yogis
> believe that yoga is more than exercise or a relaxation
> technique. To them, it's a religious ritual. But the Hindu
> gods don't make it onto my mat. Yoga purists don't
> lead classes at mainstream American gyms.[41]

In other words, it's OK to do yoga if you only do it halfway. But the problem is, you cannot disobey God just halfway—and the demons know it. So what would Jesus say? Can a Christian incorporate Hindu spiritual practices in order to get closer to the Jesus of the Bible? I have a strong suspicion the "Hindu gods" have an agenda to introduce unsuspecting yoga practitioners to a different Jesus.

A most insightful article on this topic comes from a surprising source. The article, titled "There is No Christian Yoga," is written by Yogi Baba Prem, a Hindu Yogi, a Vedavisharada trained in the traditional gurukural system. Listen to what he has to say about Christian yoga:

> It was quite astonishing to see on the flyer "Christian Yoga! This Thursday night...." I could feel the wheels spinning in my brain. "Christian Yoga," I thought. Now while Christians can practice yoga, I am not aware of any Christian teachings about yoga. Yoga is not a Judeo/Christian word! ... It is a Hindu word, or more correctly a Sanskrit word from the Vedic civilization. So how did we get "Christian Yoga"?...
>
> Hinduism should reclaim its full heritage and not allow other groups to rename its sacred teachings under their banner, especially when they have no history of those teaching within their own system. If they wish to 'borrow' and say this comes from our brothers and sisters in Hinduism, then that is another thing.... Hinduism should guard against its sacred traditions becoming distorted and taken away.[42]

This Hindu yogi resents Christians grabbing Hinduism's spiritual practice and calling it Christian. His resentment is understandable. How would we feel if there was suddenly a new craze called Hindu communion. We'd say, "Communion is about Jesus Christ. It can't possibly be called Hindu." How tragic that a Hindu guru sees the problem, but Christian leaders don't. In 2006, the same year this article came out, Thomas Nelson, the largest Christian publisher, published a book titled *Yoga for Christians*. And incredibly enough, many ministries and Christian organizations are selling the book in their bookstores!

From the New Age to Jesus Christtt

Brian Flynn, author of *Running Against the Wind*, is a former New Age medium. Today, he travels around the country speaking about his experience and warning believers about the New Age. I met Brian at a conference in 2006 and found his story to be fascinating and very relevant. After he became a Christian, he became alarmed when he learned that some of the same practices he had done as a medium were being utilized within Christendom, disguised as biblical practices (often referred to as spiritual formation). When Brian tried to warn about what was happening, even in the megachurch he attended at the time, he was met with opposition, which further alarmed him. Brian explains how he discovered the contemplative prayer movement within Christianity:

> One day I received an e-mail from a West Coast publisher asking if I would be willing to review a book. I accepted the offer and when the book arrived, I started reading *A Time of Departing* by Ray Yungen.
>
> The book described a style of praying I had never heard of before called *contemplative prayer*. As I continued to read I was struck by the similarities between an Eastern style of meditation like Transcendental Meditation and this contemplative prayer. The author wrote the book because he believed this style of prayer was infiltrating the church. I initially found that hard to believe.[43]

As a born-again Christian, he encountered a warning by another Christian that the New Age techniques he had turned his back on were infiltrating the church. At first, he thought this must be just some fringe group and not all that significant. Later he discovered that Christians were promoting contemplative prayer, using the same New Age methods he had escaped:

> What a shock it was to learn how this style of prayer [contemplative prayer] had become a standard practice in many churches across the nation. But it was even more disturbing that pastoral leadership was welcoming it. Many were actually defending it! I soon began to realize that many pastors had little knowledge of Eastern thought or its practices.[44]

Flynn's comments are accurate. The Christian church is embracing Hindu-style practices. However, when concerned believers point this out, they are often scoffed at, ridiculed, and put down as divisive. This was the case with Flynn. When he realized his own church, which coincidentally happened to be megachurch Wooddale in Minneapolis (Doug Pagitt's former church), was promoting contemplative, he tried to warn the leadership. For several years, Brian had been presenting a seminar at Wooddale to interested members. But when he began incorporating the warning against contemplative into the seminar, he was told to stop:

> [T]he pastors insisted that if I was going to continue my seminar there, I was forbidden to name names, and in fact, the pastors did not even want me mentioning the practice of contemplative prayer.... I learned that Ray Yungen's book, which had been purchased by our church bookstore, had suddenly been banned from the store....
>
> Within a few weeks, I was called into a special meeting. Those present were furious with me—explaining to me that the church's policy was to never name names.... I respectfully told them I was compelled to share the truth—I would not be able

to comply with their wishes. Thus, it became clear to everyone in the room that day that I no longer had a place in that church..…

[M]y initial reaction to *A Time of Departing* was tepid as I did not believe this practice could possibly be epidemic. At the time, I was unaware that not only was it being promoted in my own home town, it had spread throughout America's churches.[45]

How true that is! Contemplative spirituality has literally taken the church by storm. However, we are living in a time when many believe that Christians cannot be deceived. And in fact the topic of *spiritual deception* is rarely heard in most pulpits anymore.

Contemplative Prayer or Terror?

Proponents of contemplative prayer say the purpose of contemplative prayer is to tune in with God and hear His voice. However, Richard Foster claims that practitioners must use caution. He admits that in contemplative prayer "we are entering deeply into the spiritual realm" and that sometimes it is not the realm of God even though it is "supernatural." He admits there are spiritual beings and that a prayer of protection should be said beforehand something to the effect of "All dark and evil spirits must now leave."[46] Where in Scripture do we find such a prayer? Where in witchcraft?

I wonder if all these Christians who now practice contemplative prayer are following Foster's advice. Whether they are or not, they have put themselves in spiritual harm's way. Nowhere in Scripture are we required to pray a prayer of protection *before we pray*. The fact that Foster recognizes contemplative prayer is dangerous and opens the door to the fallen spirit world is very revealing. What is this—praying to the God of the Bible but instead reaching demons? Maybe contemplative prayer should be renamed *contemplative terror*.

While Foster has said repeatedly that contemplative prayer is for everyone, he contradicts himself when he says it is only for a select group and not for the "novice."[47] He says not everyone is ready and equipped to listen to God's voice through the "all embracing silence."[48]

This is amazing. Foster admits that contemplative prayer is dangerous and will possibly take the participant into demonic realms, but he gives a disclaimer saying not everyone is ready for it. My question is, *who* is ready, and how will they know they *are* ready? What about all the young people in the emerging church movement? Are they ready? Or are they going into demonic altered states of consciousness completely unaware? Given Foster's admission of the danger, he does great damage when he says: "We should all, without shame, enroll in the school of contemplative prayer."[49]

Foster's implication that *some* contemplative prayer is safe is terribly mistaken. *No* contemplative prayer is biblical *or* safe—even the most *mature* of the Christian mystical leaders proved susceptible to its demonic pull. Thomas Merton at the end of his life said he wanted to be the best Buddhist he could be. Henri Nouwen at the end of his life said all paths lead to God. This was the spiritual fruit of their lives after years of practicing mystical prayer.

In concluding this chapter on mysticism and contemplative spirituality, the real question is whether or not the realm of the *silence* is God's realm or Satan's—light or darkness. The Bible tells us that Satan is very deceptive, and what can often look good is not good at all:

> And no marvel; for Satan himself is transformed into an angel of light. Therefore it is no great thing if his ministers also be transformed as the ministers of righteousness. (II Corinthians 11:14-15)

The word occultism means hidden or secret. There are two connotations to this. The first level involves employment of these practices themselves. Throughout human history, mystical techniques were used by only a small number of persons. The terms esoteric and arcane are often used to signify the fact that these practices have been traditionally concealed. Occult methods almost always employ the use of altered states of consciousness induced by prolonged focus and repetition—a practice that has largely been unknown to many … until now!

A second and perhaps more important concept agrees that behind the physical world lies a hidden reality, and we can interact and have a relationship with this hidden spiritual realm. Occult practitioners in every age and every country agree that all of creation is connected together and God is *in* all of creation—thus, all is God. These two definitions sum up occultism succinctly. The contemplative prayer movement conforms to these aspects of occultism to the letter.

It is for this very reason I have devoted an entire chapter of *Faith Undone* to contemplative spirituality. Mystical practices have entered the church through these ancient *Christian* mystics (*ancient wisdom*), and they have become the driving force of the emerging church.

7

Monks, Mystics, and the Ancient Wisdom

> I stopped reading from the approved evangelical reading list.... I discovered new authors and new voices at the bookstore—Thomas Merton, Henri Nouwen and St. Teresa of Avila. The more I read, the more intrigued I became. Contemplative spirituality seemed to open up a whole new way for me to understand and experience God.[1]—
> Spencer Burke, The Ooze

A lmost without exception, leaders in the emergent conversation embrace mysticism (i.e., contemplative spirituality) in their theological playgrounds; it is the element that binds the movement together. While those who promote these ideas are convinced they are doing no harm, the danger of this is paramount as I described in the last chapter. When one traces the origin of these ideas to their roots, one thing becomes certain—the Bible is not the source. In truth, this mystical formation, also known as *ancient wisdom*, is occultic by its very nature. And through the emerging church, this occult wisdom is overtaking the spirituality of countless lives.

While various Christian media, apologists, and others write criticisms and discuss concerns about the emerging church, there is often an unexplainable and alarming failure to discuss the mystical element. It is alarming because mysticism is rooted in panentheism (God is *in* all things) and pantheism (*all* is God). Since mysticism is the very steam that drives the emerging church, to exclude it from critique is to side-step the real danger of this movement.

As discussed in chapter 2, Peter Drucker was formulating the emerging church in the 1950s and was influenced by those with mystical persuasions. He attended Martin Buber's course and embraced his views. And interestingly, today's evangelical leaders often quote and refer to Buber. In his book *Cure for the Common Life*, Max Lucado quotes Buber's statement that "a divine spark lives in every being and thing."[2] This quote is from Buber's 1950 book *The Way of Man* where Buber also says that "All men have access to God, but each man has a different access."[3] He clarifies his interspiritual beliefs when he adds:

> God does not say: "This way leads to me and that does not," but he says: "Whatever you do may be a way to me."[4]

Buber's mysticism led him to believe that God is in all things and all things are God, that all paths lead to God because ultimately all *is* God. I bring up Buber because it is his mystical orientation that attracted Drucker, and it is that same appeal attracting so many within Christianity today, including the emerging church. In actuality, mysticism is not just attracting the emerging church—it *is* the emerging church.

In Buber's book *Ecstatic Confessions: The Heart of Mysticism*, it states:

> There is no God apart from the world, nor a world apart from God ... In the highest mystical ecstasy the Ego experiences that it has become God.... Why not? ... there ceases to be a difference between the world and myself. "That I became God." Why not?[5]

In the introduction of Buber's book, the following further solidifies his spirituality:

The fruit of mysticism is interspirituality. And in that realm where all things are unified and supposedly no separation between man, God, or creation exists, all is welcome ... except the Cross of Jesus Christ. Rejection of the atonement is where interspirituality ultimately leads. This is where the emerging church is going. We will look more at this later in the book, but first let's examine the emerging church's embracing of the *ancient wisdom*.

The Sacred Way

Tony Jones, one of the original emergent leaders from Bob Buford's Young Leaders Network wrote a book called *The Sacred Way: Spiritual Practices for Everyday Life*. Phyllis Tickle, who wrote the foreword to the book says Jones, after spending several years as a Protestant youth pastor "yearned for the passion and clarity that were the church of the first century; who wanted to go, not home, but to what Robert Webber called 'the ancient-future.'" She adds:

> Now as an academic and doctoral candidate at Princeton Theological Seminary, Jones spends himself by shifting through the intervening and obfuscating centuries to ferret out those treasures of the early church's practices that formed the first of us and that, pray God, will form the ancient future that more and more of us long to call home.[7]

After growing up in a traditional Midwestern church-going family, Jones became disillusioned. He took a three-month sabbatical from his job to travel to Europe where he visited a prayer center for young people. Known as the Reading Boiler Room, the center hosted a 24 hours-a-day, seven days-a-week prayer vigil and called themselves a "Generation X monastery."[8] Jones also traveled to Dublin, Ireland, where he met with Catholic priest Alan McGuckian and the staff at the Jesuit Communication Center. He then spent time at Taize, a contemplative ecumenical community in southern France. Jones explains how this physical journey set him on a spiritual journey that revolutionized his thinking and spiritual beliefs:

I voraciously read authors and books they didn't assign in seminary: St. John of the Cross, St Theresa of Avila, and *Pilgrim's Way*. I met with other Protestants, with Roman Catholics, and with Eastern Orthodox Christians. I took a long hike in the Red Mountains of Utah with a shaman [a guru-type leader who practices altered states of consciousness].[9]

According to Jones, this journey led him out of the darkness into the light. He now desires to be an evangelist for his new-found spirituality. He says, "there is incredible richness in the spiritual practices of ancient and modern Christian communities from around the world."[10]

Jones said he found new ways of praying and meditating. One of those ways is the *Jesus Prayer*. Jones explains how this is done:

[S]eated comfortably in a dimly lit room with the head bowed, attend to your breathing, and then begin the prayer in rhythm with your breathing. Breathe in: "Lord Jesus Christ, Son of God;" breathe out: "have mercy on me a sinner." Guarding the mind against all distractions, the pray-er focuses during every repetition on the meaning of the words, praying them from the heart and in the heart... In order to keep track of my repetitions, I use a prayer rope.[11]

Jones says that monasteries in Greece make these prayer ropes. Each one has one hundred knots in it, and each knot holds nine crosses. Another meditation practice Jones encourages is *centering prayer*. He states:

Like the Jesus Prayer, Centering Prayer grew out of the reflections and writings of the Desert Fathers... Unlike the Jesus Prayer, a repetitive prayer is not used. The pray-er is encouraged to choose a simple, monosyllabic word, like "love" or "God."[12]

When the mind is distracted, this word is used to bring the mind back to focus on God.[13]

Tony Jones' spiritual journey is typical of many others who are headed down the same road. Jones is convinced these mystical practices provide a way for him to get closer to God. He expresses his attraction to the mystical:

> Maybe it's that there's something mystical and mysterious about these ancient rites, like we're tapping into some pre-technological, pre-industrial treasury of the Spirit.[14]

Such a pragmatic approach to spirituality is a recipe for spiritual deception. Jones, whether he realizes it or not, has become an evangelist for the ancient wisdom. Going into altered states of consciousness through repetitive chants and focusing on the breath have become part of his *gospel* message.

The Alpha State

As we have already seen, Youth Specialties has been a pioneer in the emerging church movement, teaming up with both Emergent and Zondervan to help usher in this emerging spirituality. An article by one Youth Specialties freelance writer gives a clear illustration of the movement's adherence to mysticism. The article, titled "Disciplines, Mystics and the Contemplative Life," is written by Mike Perschon, a Canadian Mennonite associate pastor in Alberta.

His article provides another example of how Emerging leaders are introduced to mystical ideas and then pass them on to others. Perschon explains how he became an ancient-future supporter and promoter:

> I bumped into the classic spiritual disciplines … in my second year of Bible school. One of our textbooks

was *The Spirit of the Disciplines* by Dallas Willard. The
course and textbook only touched on the actual
disciplines, but the concept captivated me. The
following spring, I found a copy of Richard Foster's
spiritual classic *Celebration of Discipline* in a used
bookstore. Opening it and discovering each discipline
detailed chapter by chapter, I felt a profound sense of
joy and excitement. I'd found a real treasure.[15]

After reading these two books on spiritual formation (i.e.,
contemplative), Perschon continued his spiritual journey, where
he was led to more mystical sources that revolutionized his thinking. He writes:

My church history class introduced me to the word
"mystic" in the Christian tradition, and after looking
further into the history of Christian mysticism, I
found overlap between the disciplines I so wanted to
practice and the teachings of these Christian fathers
and mothers. I read the writings of Meister Eckhart,
St. John of the Cross, and Teresa of Avila.[16]

Perschon has been active in transferring his newfound spirituality which he gained from monks and Catholic mystics to the
young people he teaches at youth retreats and summer camp
settings. Describing some of these activities, he writes:

At soul labs we used ... multiple rooms for different
music to create a number of prayer stations, where
people could try various approaches to
contemplative prayer.[17]

Perschon built a "sanctuary" in a basement closet that
contained candles, incense, rosaries, tapes of Benedictine monks
and books on meditation. Sometimes his meditation took him
into what he referred to as the "alpha" state.[18]

Researcher Ray Yungen says that "alpha brain patterns" can open the door to the occult. He explains:

> When I hear a Christian talking like this, it creates a very deep concern within me for that person because I know what is meant by "alpha."[19]

Yungen gives as an example of witch Laurie Cabot. Cabot's book, *Power of the Witch*, uses the term "alpha" when talking about meditation and the silence. Cabot explains:

> It is my belief that all information ... comes to us in alpha because all information in the universe consists of light energy. Light enters the pineal gland, or Third Eye, located in the center of the head between the eyebrows, where many psychics say they experience physical sensations when they receive extrasensory information.[20]

Cabot says that the alpha state is "the heart of Witchcraft."[21] Occultist Aldous Huxley talked about this altered state, saying that mysticism is "the highest common factor" among the world's religions?[22] Liberal evangelical Tony Campolo, a prolific writer and author who often speaks at emerging church events, suggests the same thing in his book, *Speaking My Mind*, when he says:

> Beyond these models of reconciliation, a theology of mysticism provides some hope for common ground between Christianity and Islam. Both religions have within their histories examples of ecstatic union with God ... I do not know what to make of the Muslim mystics, especially those who have come to be known as the Sufis. What do they experience in their mystical experiences? Could they have encountered the same God we do in our Christian mysticism?[23]

If Cabot's alpha state is indeed the same as Perschon's and Tony Jones' alpha state and the Celtic thin place, then what we are seeing is an entire movement walking right into occultic realms, and taking millions with them.

"The Next Billy Graham?"

In a Chicago Sun-Times article, the headline reads, "The Next Billy Graham?" At first glance, someone like Rick Warren or Luis Palau might come to mind. But neither of those were who the reporter had in mind. Instead, Rob Bell, pastor of Mars Hill (Michigan), is named as a possible *successor*. While that may seem unlikely to many, the article quotes Brian McLaren as saying it "very well could be true."[24] And in January 2007, Bell was named number ten in the "50 Most Influential Christians in America," coming in as more "influential" than Rick Warren (#16) and Luis Palau (#15).[25]

Bell, a graduate of Wheaton College (the same as Billy Graham), is the producer for short films called Noomas (derived from the word Pneuma, meaning breath or spirit.) In his Nooma film called *Breathe*, Bells states: "Each day we take around 26,000 breaths ... Our breathing should come from our stomach, not our chest."[26]

This sounds fairly benign at first glance. But in a 2004 *Christianity Today* article titled "Emergent Mystique," Bell says, "We're rediscovering Christianity as an Eastern religion, as a way of life."[27] Is Bell just trying to sound *postmodern* and *culturally-relevant* when he says this, or does he really believe that Christianity is an Eastern religion? The answer to that question can be found in two people with whom Bell strongly resonates.

In Bell's *Velvet Elvis*, in the "Endnotes" section, Bell recommends Ken Wilber (whom I mentioned in chapter two as one of Leonard Sweet's "New Light" teachers). Of Wilber, Bell states:

> For a mind-blowing introduction to emergence theory and divine creativity, set aside three months and read Ken Wilber's *A Brief History of Everything*.[28]

Ken Wilber was raised in a conservative Christian church, but at some point he left that faith and is now a major proponent of Buddhist mysticism. His book that Bell recommends, *A Brief History of Everything,* is published by Shambhala Publications, named after the term, which in Buddhism means the mystical abode of spirit beings. Wilber is one of the most respected and highly regarded theoreticians in the New Age movement today.

Wilber is perhaps best known for what he calls *integral theory.* On his website, he has a chart called the Integral Life Practice Matrix, which lists several activities one can practice "to authentically exercise all aspects or dimensions of your own being-in-the-world."[29] Here are a few of these spiritual activities that Wilber promotes: yoga, Zen, centering prayer, kabbalah (Jewish mysticism), TM, tantra (Hindu-based sexuality), and kundalini yoga. There are others of this nature, as well. *A Brief History of Everything* discusses these practices (in a favorable light) as well.

For Rob Bell to say that Wilber's book is "mind-blowing" and readers should spend three months in it leaves no room for doubt regarding Rob Bell's spiritual sympathies. What is alarming is that so many Christian venues, such as Christian junior high and high schools, are using Velvet Elvis and the Noomas.

Wilber's integral theory (history of everything) is the same as Leonard Sweet's Theory of Everything,[30] which in essence is God in everything. And that is what Rob Bell means when he says "emergence theory and divine creativity." In the section of his book where he footnotes Wilber, Bell says the following:

> Then God said, "Let the land produce vegetation:
> seed-bearing plants and trees on the land that bear
> fruit with seed in it, according to their various kinds."
> And it was so. The next verse is significant: "The land
> produced vegetation." Notice that it doesn't say, "God
> produced vegetation." God empowers the land to do
> something. He gives it the capacity to produce trees
> and shrubs and plants and bushes that produce fruit
> and seeds. God empowers creation to make more.[31]

While that might sound a little obscure, this is an example of "divine creativity" that Bell mentions in his book—creation (including man) is co-creating with God, and the reason is because all creation is divine. Everything is God. Of course, we know from Scripture that this is not true. As you read on in *Faith Undone*, the significance of this will unfold.

On March 19, 2006, Bell unveiled a little more about his spiritual beliefs. He invited a Dominican sister to speak at his church. He said as he introduced her, "I have a friend who has taught me so much about resting in the presence of God."[32] During the service, Bell and the sister led the congregation in various meditative exercises.

The sister who spoke at Mars Hill during that service is from the Dominican Center at Marywood in Michigan where a wide variety of contemplative/mystical practices are used and taught.[33] One of the practices at the Center is Reiki (similar to therapeutic touch). The belief behind Reiki is that everything in the universe is united together through energy. In Japan, the word Reiki is the standard term for the occult (or ghost energy). It is ghost energy because when Reiki is practiced, spirit guides are reached. William Lee Rand, the head of the International Center for Reiki Training, states:

> There are higher sources of help you can call on. Angels, beings of light and Reiki spirit guides as well as your own enlightened self are available to help you.... The more you can open to the true nature of Reiki which is to have an unselfish heart centered desire to help others, then the more the Reiki spirit guides can help you.[34]

Reiki is becoming very popular in the Western world. In the United States alone, there are now over one million Reiki practitioners.[35] If Reiki gains a foothold into Christianity, Rob Bell's statement "We're rediscovering Christianity as an Eastern religion" could be very accurate in the sense that Eastern religion (i.e., mysticism) is quickly becoming a qualifier for mainstream Christianity.

Coming to Christ Through Mysticism

The spiritual formation movement teaches that if people practice certain spiritual disciplines, they can become *like* Jesus and model their lives after him. But being born again and having the indwelling of Christ is not a prerequisite. Neither is receiving Him as Lord and absolute Savior. What spiritual formation offers is an alternative to God's plan of salvation revealed in Scripture.

Here is the problem: The spiritual seeker is looking for something to make him feel close to God. If he does not have the indwelling of the Lord, perhaps has never heard the message of repentance and rebirth, he will seek something to help him feel intimate with God. When he is introduced to meditation, which produces a feeling of euphoria and well-being, he mistakes this for the presence of God. And thus the foundation of his faith is not on Christ or the Word of God but rather on this feeling. This would explain why so many teachers of contemplative and spiritual formation begin dropping the emphasis on biblical truth and distort the doctrines of the faith.

Tony Campolo, professor emeritus of sociology of Eastern University in St. David's, Pennsylvania, is founder of the Evangelical Association for the Promotion of Education. His own testimony is an example of someone who has not only embraced mysticism, it is the avenue through which he considers himself born again.

In his book *Letters to a Young Evangelical,* Campolo shares his own personal testimony in a chapter called "The Gospel According to Us." He begins the chapter the following way:

> As you may know, most Evangelicals at some point make a decision to trust in Jesus for salvation and commit to becoming the kind of people he wants us to be.[36]

Campolo presents the details of his conversion experience. He begins by stating:

When I was a boy growing up in a lower-middle-class neighborhood in West Philadelphia, my mother, a convert to Evangelical Christianity from a Catholic Italian immigrant family, hoped I would have one of those dramatic "born-again" experiences. That was the way she had come into a personal relationship with Christ. She took me to hear one evangelist after another, praying that I would go to the altar and come away "converted." But it never worked for me. I would go down the aisle as the people around me sang … "the invitation hymn," but I just didn't feel as if anything happened to me. For a while I despaired, wondering if I would ever get "saved." It took me quite some time to realize that entering into a personal relationship with Christ does not always happen that way.[37]

Now, it is certainly true that not all conversions are experienced by coming to Christ at an evangelistic crusade. However, it's important to carefully consider how Campolo describes in this same chapter his personal conversion experience in light of Scripture. He continues:

In my case intimacy with Christ has developed gradually over the years, primarily through what Catholic mystics call "centering prayer." Each morning, as soon as I wake up, I take time—sometimes as much as a half hour—to center myself on Jesus. I say his name over and over again to drive back the 101 things that begin to clutter up my mind the minute I open my eyes. Jesus is my mantra, as some would say.[38]

The purpose of repeating a mantra or focusing on an object or the breath is to remove distractions with the hopeful outcome of hearing God's voice. Buddhists and Hindus practice the repetition of a word or phrase in their attempts to empty their minds and reach higher states of consciousness that *reveal their own divinity*. But nowhere in Scripture is such a practice recommended. In fact, Jesus says in Matthew 6:7, "But when ye pray, use not vain repetitions, as the heathen *do*: for they think that they shall be heard for their much speaking."

Thin Places of "Oneness"

Mantra-style meditation is actually divination, where practitioners perform rituals or meditation exercises in order to go into trances and then receive information from spiritual entities. Campolo elaborates on the fruit of mysticism, an atmosphere he calls "the thin place":

> The constant repetition of his name clears my head of everything but the awareness of his presence. By driving back all other concerns, I am able to create what the ancient Celtic Christians called "the thin place." The thin place is that spiritual condition wherein the separation between the self and God becomes so thin that God is able to break through and envelop the soul.[39]

This term "thin place" originated with Celtic spirituality (i.e., contemplative) and is in line with panentheism. Listen to one meditator:

> I experienced a shift deep within me, a calmness I never knew possible. I was also graced with a sense of "oneness" with nature around me and with everyone else in the human family. It was strangely wonderful to experience God in silence, no-thingness.[40]

This "oneness" with all things is the essence of the ancient wisdom. Marcus Borg, a professor at Oregon State University and a pro-emergent author, also speaks of "thin places." One commentator discusses Borg's ideas on this:

In *The Heart of Christianity*, Borg writes of "thin places," places where, to use Eliade's terminology, the division between the sacred and the profane becomes thin. Borg writes that he owes this metaphor of "thin places" to Celtic Christianity and the recent recovery of Celtic spirituality. As the following passage reveals, his understanding of "thin places" is deeply connected to his panentheism, his articulation of God as "the More," and his—like Eliade—division of the world into layers of reality.[41]

Borg says these thin places (reached through meditation) are "[d]eeply rooted in the Bible and the Christian tradition,"[42] but he, like others, is unable to show biblical evidence that God mandates meditation. In a later chapter we will see, however, that Borg *does* deny such basic biblical essentials as the virgin birth and Jesus being the Son of God. Thin places imply that God is in all things, and the gap between God, evil, man, everything thins out and ultimately disappears in meditation:

God is a nonmaterial layer of reality all around us, "right here" as well as "more than right here." This way of thinking thus affirms that there are minimally two layers or dimensions of reality, the visible world of our ordinary experience and God, the sacred, Spirit.[43]

Mike Perschon also found these thin places as he went into the silence:

We held "thin place" services in reference to a belief that in prayer, the veil between us and God becomes thinner. Entire nights were devoted to guided meditations, drum circles, and "soul labs."[44]

I believe that Campolo, Borg, and Perschon each experienced the same realm in their *thin places*, but the question is, what *is* that realm? In another letter Campolo wrote in his book *Letters to a Young Evangelical,* he gives further instructions regarding how to have a "born-again experience":

> I learned about this way of having a born-again experience from reading the Catholic mystics, especially *The Spiritual Exercises of Ignatius of Loyola....* Like most Catholic mystics, he developed an intense desire to experience a "oneness" with God.[45]

Campolo's belief that you can be born again by experiencing a "'oneness' with God" while embracing the teachings of Ignatius of Loyola is preposterous. Ignatius founded the Jesuits with a goal to bring the *separated brethren* back to the Catholic Church.[46] He and his band of ruthless men would do everything possible to accomplish this goal. Several centuries have passed. Now that we are in the twenty-first century, his plan is becoming a reality.

Campolo calls Henri Nouwen "one of the great Christians of our time."[47] He obviously is very moved by mysticism as was Nouwen, and he attributes this treasure to the Catholic Church. He explains:

> After the Reformation, we Protestants left behind much that was troubling about Roman Catholicism of the fifteenth century. I am convinced that we left too much behind. The methods of praying employed by the likes of Ignatius have become precious to me. With the help of some Catholic saints, my prayer life has deepened.[48]

Spiritual Disciplines

> Many Christian leaders started searching for a new approach under the banner of "spiritual formation." This new search has led many of them back to Catholic contemplative practices and medieval monastic disciplines.[49]—Brian McLaren

Promoters of the emergent conversation say we are on the verge of an era that promises renewed spiritual awareness. *Spiritual disciplines* are being touted as the avenue to a spiritual formation that will take Christianity to a new and higher level of spirituality, drawing participants closer to God.

Books published by major Christian publishers and written by well-known authors are plentiful on this topic. For example, in 2006, NavPress published a book co-authored by J.P. Moreland and Klaus Issler titled *The Lost Virtue of Happiness: Discovering the Disciplines of the Good Life*. Both authors are professors at Talbot School of Theology at Biola University in southern California. Moreland is professor of philosophy, and Issler is professor of Christian education and theology. On the back cover of their book, the following statement is made:

> [W]e are happy only when we pursue a transcendent purpose—something larger than ourselves.... *The Lost Virtue of Happiness* takes a fresh look at the spiritual disciplines, offering concrete examples of ways you can make them practical and life transforming.[50]

Moreland and Issler believe they have rediscovered important spiritual principles that have been lost. Two of the spiritual disciplines the authors have recovered are "Solitude and Silence."[51] The book says that these two disciplines are "absolutely fundamental to the Christian life."[52]

While it is true, getting away to be alone is often the best way to concentrate and evaluate life's most important decisions, the isolation and solitude Moreland and Issler promote have definite eastern mystical overtones. The authors attempt to add credibility to this *rediscovered* spiritual discipline by quoting Henri Nouwen, who said:

> A man or woman who has developed this solitude of heart is no longer pulled apart by the most

divergent stimuli of the surrounding world but is able to perceive and understand this world from a quiet inner center.[53]

This "quiet inner center" Nouwen wrote about is suspect, especially in light of spiritual disciplines practiced by those involved in the Buddhist and Hindu faiths. Continuing to develop the idea of the lost art of finding the "quiet inner center," Moreland and Issler state:

> In our experience, Catholic retreat centers are usually ideal for solitude retreats… We also recommend that you bring photos of your loved ones and a picture of Jesus… Or gaze at a statue of Jesus. Or let some pleasant thought, feeling, or memory run through your mind over and over again.[54]

I have searched the Scriptures. Gazing at a picture or statue of Jesus or concentrating on a thought or feeling in order to establish "a quiet inner center" just isn't there! But that isn't all they recommend. For example, Moreland and Issler provide tips for developing a prayer life. Here are some of the recommendations they make:

> [W]e recommend that you begin by saying the Jesus Prayer about three hundred times a day.[55]

> When you first awaken, say the Jesus Prayer twenty to thirty times. As you do, something will begin to happen to you. God will begin to slowly begin to occupy the center of your attention.[56]

> Repetitive use of the Jesus Prayer while doing more focused things allows God to be on the boundaries of your mind and forms the habit of being gently in contact with him all day long.[57]

Moreland and Issler try to present what they consider a scriptural case that repetitive prayers are OK with God. But they never do it! They say the Jesus Prayer is derived from Luke 18:38 where the blind man cries out, "Jesus, thou son of David, have mercy on me"[58] but nowhere in that section of the Bible (or any other section for that matter) does it instruct people to repeat a rendition of Luke 18:38 over and over.

I have been to the country of Myanmar (formerly called Burma) twice. On both occasions, I observed and videotaped both Catholics and Buddhists practicing repetitive prayer. By the way, in both cases they were chanting these prayers over and over again while counting beads. Yes, Catholics and Buddhists both have a *rosary* technique to keep track of how many times they have chanted a prayer.

I have also interviewed Catholics and Buddhists praying in Myanmar. I have asked them what they are doing and why they are doing it. Each time I asked this question, I have been told the same thing. It is a way to concentrate and focus their thoughts and get in tune with the spirit world. Chanting repetitive phrases to get closer to God is not biblical; it is Satanic.

It is interesting, yet very sad, that so many people today, like Tony Campolo, have spiritual lives grounded in mysticism. When a true relationship with Jesus Christ is non-existent in a person's life, mystical experiences appear to fill that spiritual void. The euphoria and bliss that meditation creates is thought to be the voice and presence of God. But in reality, these practices are tied to Buddhism, Hinduism, and Catholicism rather than to biblical Christianity. The Bible makes it clear the only way to be born again is through receiving Jesus Christ as Lord and Savior by faith. While being called Christian, these doctrines of ancient wisdom are anything but Christian. Let us remember Paul's stern exhortation and not exchange a true and wonderful relationship with Jesus Christ for one that can only lead to darkness:

Ye are all the children of light, and the children of
the day: we are not of the night, nor of darkness.
Therefore let us not sleep, as do others; but let us
watch and be sober. For they that sleep sleep in the
night; and they that be drunken are drunken in the
night. But let us, who are of the day, be sober,
putting on the breastplate of faith and love; and
for an helmet, the hope of salvation. For God hath
not appointed us to wrath, but to obtain salvation
by our Lord Jesus Christ, Who died for us, that,
whether we wake or sleep, we should live together
with him. (I Thessalonians 5: 5-10)

A Third Jesus

In *A Generous Orthodoxy*, McLaren describes his spiritual journey,
which took him from a conservative Christian upbringing to
a Pentecostal Jesus and eventually led him to say, "About that
time, quite by accident, I met a third Jesus."[59] This following account gives important insight that we should pay attention to—
because many are following this same path. McLaren describes:

[B]y my mid-20s, I had met the conservative
Protestant Jesus, the Pentecostal Jesus, and the
Roman Catholic Jesus.[60]

McLaren found that the Protestant Jesus was too limiting.
His dissatisfaction led him on a quest for something more.
McLaren found what he was looking for in the mystics:

I discovered other Roman Catholic writers—
twentieth-century writers such as Flannery
O'Connor, Thomas Merton, Henri Nouwen,
Romano Guardini, and Gabriel Marcel, as well as
the medieval mystics and others.[61]

From these mystics, McLaren's whole attitude toward salvation and spirituality changed. He began to emulate Thomas Mer-

ton and Henri Nouwen as illustrated when he states:

> I didn't think of them as different saviors ... But I
> was still unsatisfied, especially because I sensed that
> if Jesus were truly the Savior, he wasn't just my
> personal Savior, but was the Savior of the whole
> cosmos.[62]

This third Jesus McLaren discovered was the same Jesus Thomas Merton and Henri Nouwen had found, who both came to believe that God dwelled in all persons and that all paths lead to God. This third mystical Jesus is very much in tune with the New Age version of Jesus. McLaren's journey on the path that Merton and Nouwen had traveled led him to the same conclusions as the mystics he discovered. Contemplative prayer, spiritual formation, the interspiritual path—they inevitably lead all who follow them to the same non-biblical conclusions, and if not repented of—ultimate spiritual destruction.

8

The Second Coming of the Eucharistic Christ

I remember the first time I heard the term *emerging church*. I had just returned from South Africa where I had been speaking on the topic of the *New Evangelization*—the Catholic program to win the world to the Catholic Eucharistic Christ.[1] A lady who had heard me speak sent me an e-mail with an attached article about the emerging church. She asked, "Do you think the emerging church could be the bridge to the Catholic New Evangelization program you were telling us about?" At the time, I had no idea just how much of a bridge there really was.

Eucharistic Evangelization

For those who are not aware of the Catholic Church's New Evangelization program, let me provide a brief overview. The Catholic Church plans to establish the kingdom of God on earth and win the world to the Catholic Jesus (i.e., the Eucharistic Christ). This will be accomplished when the world (including the *separated brethren**) comes under the rule and reign of Rome and this Eucharistic Jesus.

The Eucharistic Jesus is supposedly Christ's presence that a Catholic priest summons through the power of *transubstantiation*,

---

*The name the Catholic Church gives to Protestants, those who are separate from the *One True Church*

the focal point of the Mass.

Many Christians believe the Christian tradition of communion is the same as the Catholic tradition of the Eucharist. But this is not so. The Eucharist (i.e., transubstantiation) is a Catholic term for communion when the bread and the wine are said to be transformed into the very body and blood of Jesus Christ. The Catholic Catechism states:

> In the most blessed sacrament of the Eucharist "the body and blood, together with the soul and divinity, of our Lord Jesus Christ and, therefore, the whole Christ is truly, really, and substantially contained."[2]

The host is then placed in what is called a monstrance and can then be worshiped as if worshiping Jesus Himself. The implications are tied directly to salvation itself. With the Eucharist, salvation becomes sacramental (participation in a ritual) as opposed to justification by faith in Christ alone, described in Galatians 2:16. While this mystical experience is a form of idolatry (as well as the very heart of Catholicism), there is a growing interest by evangelical Christians in this practice, particularly by the emerging church.

The Catholic Church leadership, concerned with apathy for the Eucharist within the Catholic ranks, is hoping to "rekindle the amazement"[3] of the Eucharist through what is called their "New Evangelization program."[4] With a two-fold purpose—to keep present Catholics and to bring evangelicals into the Catholic Church—church leadership has a plan to re-emphasize the Eucharist as the focus of the Catholic faith. By saying "rekindle the amazement," they mean bring out the mystical, supernatural element of the Eucharist.

All Catholics are expected to worship the host (Eucharistic Adoration of the transformed wafer), and church leadership says it is *anathema* (to be accursed) to reject this teaching. At the Council of Trent, the official Catholic position was:

> If anyone denies that in the sacrament of the most
> Holy Eucharist are contained truly, really and
> substantially the body and blood together with the
> soul and divinity of our Lord Jesus Christ, and
> consequently the whole Christ, but says that He is
> in it only as in a sign, or figure or force, let him be
> anathema.[5]

> If anyone says that Christ received in the Eucharist
> is received spiritually only and not also sacramentally
> and really, let him be anathema.[6]

While it is true that during the Reformation and Counter
Reformation, many who refused to believe in transubstantiation
were tortured and executed for their faith in the Gospel, time
has a way of forgetting the facts of history.

In April of 2003, the pope wrote an encyclical promoting
the "New Evangelization" program for the purpose of "rekin-
dling amazement" for the Eucharist.[7]

Then in October of 2004, John Paul II initiated "The Year
of the Eucharist" as part of his evangelistic plan to bring the
world to the Eucharistic Christ. Following his death in April of
2005, Pope Benedict XVI picked up Pope John Paul's mission
immediately. He called the "faithful to intensify" devotion to
the Eucharistic Jesus, and said the Eucharist is the "heart of
Christian life."[8]

Benedict hopes to perpetuate his pontificate where the previous
pope left off. The article states:

> Pope Benedict asked the faithful to "intensify in
> coming months love and devotion to the Eucharistic
> Jesus and to express in a courageous and clear way
> the real presence of the Lord."[9]

Pope Benedict XVI suggested that praying to Mary would
help "all Christians" draw closer to the Eucharistic Christ:

Mary is the "Eucharistic woman".... Let us pray to the Virgin that all Christians may deepen their faith in the Eucharistic mystery, so that they live in constant communion with Jesus and are his valid witnesses.[10]

It is important to note here that the entire premise of the Catholic Mass is critically flawed. During each Mass, the Eucharistic *Jesus* is offered as an unbloody sacrifice. This repeated offering is in contradiction to the one-time *new covenant* offering of Hebrews 9:28:

> So Christ was once offered to bear the sins of many; and unto them that look for him shall he appear the second time without sin unto salvation.

Notice the verse indicates *one* offering, not numerous ones. The reason for this is apparent—in the essence of any sacrifice, there has to be some element of suffering, pain, or loss. Christ suffered for our sins, and God accepted this as a one-time offering for sin. Isaiah 53:10 explains: "Yet it pleased the LORD [the Father] to bruise him," and "he hath put him to grief: when thou shalt make his soul an offering for sin." It also says that when God, the Father sees "the travail of his [Christ's] soul," He "shall be satisfied" (vs. 11).

Calvary was the only offering that was or ever could be accepted by God—for it was the only one that contained the "travail of his soul." If the Mass, which Catholic apologists openly acknowledge, does not contain the suffering of Christ (which it doesn't), then it cannot be presented as an offering, because it does not fit the Isaiah 53 context.

Further, Hebrews 12:2 says Christ "endured the cross, despising the shame." Thus, the Mass cannot be the same as the Cross, for Jesus would constantly be in a state of shame. Therefore, the Mass is empty. It cannot atone for sins.

Rekindling Amazement

The New Evangelization program plans to revitalize the Catholic faith by reigniting strong interest in the Eucharistic Jesus. It is not just the pope who is enthusiastic about this—cardinals, bishops, and priests all over the world are joining in to help with the mission. Something very significant is happening. Eucharistic adoration is becoming the foundation for the new evangelization of the Catholic Church.

For example, in one New York Catholic cathedral, where special events were held in honor of the Eucharist, the presiding Cardinal stated:

> Our God is present on that altar—body, blood, soul and divinity.... the flesh and blood of Jesus Christ.[11]

The Cardinal said that Christ was "'fiercely clear' in offering followers 'his flesh to eat and his blood to drink.'"[12]

So, while leaders in Rome are calling for a renewed devotion to the Eucharistic Jesus, a cardinal in the USA echoes the same message in order to re-educate "the faithful" about the true meaning of "one of the Church's central rituals."[13]

Interestingly, I happened to be in Rome at the time an article came out about the New York event on the Eucharist. While there, I witnessed the feast of Corpus Christi firsthand. This is a Catholic celebration that was started by a nun who was inspired by gazing at the moon. As a colleague and I stood patiently awaiting the arrival of Pope Benedict XVI, we were eventually corralled behind a steel fence barrier erected to separate the common people from the Church authorities, which included hundreds of secret service men and women.

Finally, after almost three hours of standing and waiting, the pope and his entourage arrived. The pope was carrying the Eucharistic *Jesus* in a monstrance. Earlier that day during a mass at St. Peter's, this Eucharistic Jesus had been *created* from a wafer that had been *consecrated*. Later in the day, the same *Jesus* was transported to St. John's for another ceremony. Finally, for a finale, the pope transported *Jesus* to the Major Church of Mary.

The pope took the monstrance, ascended the stairs of the church, and held *Jesus* up for the masses to see. Then this Jesus was placed on an altar temporarily erected at the top of the steps. A cardinal then opened the glass window of the monstrance, removed the consecrated wafer (*Jesus*), and hustled him inside the church where he placed *Jesus* in a tabernacle. This experience gave me a sobering reminder of this terrible apostasy.

The World's Greatest Secret Revealed

The Catholic Church has made its program to evangelize the world to the Eucharistic Christ public for all to see. Catholic authors have written a number of books, revealing what is happening and where the New Evangelization program will be headed in the future. For example, Thomas W. Petrisko has written a book titled *Mother of the Secret: From Eucharistic Miracles to Marian Apparitions Heaven Has Sought to Illuminate and Defend What Was Once the Church's Greatest Secret*. Petrisko, who believes the *presence of Christ* in the Eucharist has always been a sacred belief of the Catholic Church, says the time is soon coming when the entire world will witness Christ's Eucharistic reign.

A statement on the back cover of Petrisko's book is quite revealing:

> Petrisko traces for us the exciting history of this important part of our faith. And he reveals how what was once the Church's *greatest secret* is about to become the cornerstone of a *glorious new era*, an era in which Jesus Christ will soon come to reign throughout the world in the sacrament of the Holy Eucharist. (emphasis added)[14]

To clarify what Petrisko means by the "glorious new era," he states in his book:

Visionaries foretell that mankind will move from a secular, agnostic, practically atheistic realm into a world that basks in the reality of God and belief in the presence of the supernatural. The prophets say that mankind will then thrive on secure faith and confidence in this reality, for true peace will rule and the Church will reign supreme. Most notably, many Catholic visionaries insist that the world will at last come to deeply understand the power, the mercy and the grace that is available in the miraculous True Presence of Jesus Christ in the Sacrament of the Holy Eucharist.[15]

Petrisko believes that Mary, Jesus' mother, will play a crucial role in the conversion process that must occur if the world is going to embrace the Eucharistic Reign of Christ. This apparitional woman has been announcing the coming of a new era in which the Eucharistic Christ will bring peace to the world. Petrisko states:

According to the Virgin Mary, it is particularly the faith in this Eucharistic nourishment which will effect the greatest changes in the new era. Mary says that much of the world will not only come to believe this mystery, but also will partake in it. Indeed, it is said that the Triumph of the Immaculate Heart of Mary during our times will gloriously lead the world into a new era of true peace. At that time, the Holy Eucharist will be better known, appreciated and treasured. It will be a reign not just within the Church and individual lives, but in whole nations. Thus, the infinite power and grace available in the Eucharist will no longer be the world's greatest secret![16]

Second Coming Catholic Style

Ted and Maureen Flynn, authors of *The Thunder of Justice*, investigate the prophetic side of messages coming from the *Queen of Heaven*. In their book, they state:

As John the Baptist prepared the way for the first coming of Jesus, Mary prepares the way for His Second Coming. Mary proclaims that a new world and era is upon us, and the triumph of Her Immaculate Heart and the Second Pentecost (the outpouring of the Holy Spirit) will usher in the Reign of the Sacred Heart of Jesus.[17]

According to the Flynns, the "Blessed Mother" prophesied:

The glorious reign of Christ, which will be established in your midst and the Second Coming of Jesus into the world is close at hand…. That which is being prepared is so great that its equal has never existed since the creation of the world.[18]

One person who documents this *new era* is Dwight Longenecker, a former evangelical Protestant and author of *The Road to Rome: Modern Journeys to the Catholic Church*. In his biography, Longenecker tells how he was raised in an evangelical home and later attended a conservative Christian university. In 1995 he and his wife "were received into the Catholic Church."[19]

Longenecker's book is a collection of stories of people who converted to Catholicism. A statement on the back cover calling the book a "glimpse of a possible future for the church" says:

As we enter the third millennium, Catholicism, Evangelicalism, and Orthodoxy will continue to converge…. old cultural, national and doctrinal controversies [will] become increasingly irrelevant. Then as the Age of Reform draws to a close and the millennium of division gives way to a "Second Spring," the Church may once more speak with a united voice.[20]

In speaking of the pope's view on the Eucharist, Protestant-turned Catholic Scott Hahn states:

The coming of Jesus Christ—what the Greek New Testament calls his "parousia"—is not simply some far-off event. It is his presence in the Eucharist. Fundamentalists reduce the meaning of "parousia" to Christ's coming at the end of time; but for the first century Greek speakers the word meant "presence." Catholic theology holds on to that original meaning.[21]

The presence of *Christ* in the Eucharist is the Second Coming Catholic style. Unfortunately, many evangelical Protestants are not even aware of this. And as I will soon be showing you, the emerging church is one of the more significant bridges that has been established to bring the separated brethren back to the Mother of All Churches. The prophetic significance of this is of paramount importance. But first let's take a glimpse of how the evangelical church has fared when it comes to the Eucharistic Christ.

The Eucharist and the Evangelical Church

While Eucharistic adoration contradicts biblical Christianity, a growing number of popular evangelicals (especially those leaning toward emerging spiritualities) seem to find no offense in such a doctrine. And with the increased acceptance of mysticism and an attraction to imagery within evangelical circles, it only makes sense that many evangelical Christians find nothing wrong with the Eucharist and Eucharistic adoration. Such acceptance, however, is neutralizing former evangelical resistance to all things Catholic.

In 1992, Prison Fellowship's Chuck Colson helped to draft a document called *Evangelicals & Catholics Together*—it would end up playing a significant role in desensitizing Christians into finding common ground and unity with Catholicism. The document quotes Pope John Paul II as stating that we are in "a springtime of world missions."[22] The document says we all serve the same Christ and expresses the need to eradicate the tension and gap between Catholics and Evangelicals. It explains:

> The two communities in world Christianity that are most evangelistically assertive and most rapidly growing are Evangelicals and Catholics…. in many places around the world, the scandal of conflict between Christians [Catholics and Evangelicals] obscures the scandal of the cross, thus crippling the one mission of the one Christ.[23]

It cannot be possible that we serve the same Christ—the Catholic Eucharistic Christ is much different than the Jesus Christ in the Bible. This notion presents a serious dilemma. And yet well-respected and trusted evangelical leaders (like Richard Land of the Southern Baptist Convention) participated in the drafting of this project.[24]

Other Christian leaders have openly shown their willingness to lessen the gap between Catholicism and biblical Christianity as well. Rick Warren, author of *The Purpose Driven Life*, has made the following statements:

- The small group structure is the structure of renewal in every facet of Christianity—including Catholicism.[25]

- I would encourage you to look at this evolving alliance between evangelical Protestants and Catholics, particularly in the evangelical wing of Catholicism.[26]

- Now when you get 25 percent of America, which is basically Catholic, and you get 28 to 29 percent of America, which is evangelical, together, that's called a majority. And it is a very powerful bloc, if they happen to stay together on particular issues.[27]

Warren has also developed a Catholic *Purpose Driven Life* program,[28] and on his pastors.com website, EFCA pastor Larry Osborne says the following:

[C]hurches that place a greater emphasis on the sermon and the personality of the preacher, *rather than the Eucharist* and the office of minister, will have a harder time adjusting to an equal or nearly equal interchange of preachers.[29]

United Methodist Keith Howard McIlwain believes that incorporating the Eucharist is essential to what he refers to as the renewal of the church:

[T]he faithful administration of the Eucharist is a certain key to renewal in the Church.... If the United Methodist Church and its smaller partners are to experience renewal, we must also allow the Holy Spirit proper place in worship, ministry, and pastoral care. Done with theological integrity, this must be done by re-examining the Eucharist ...Then, and only then, will we be able to once again effectively lead the way to transformation for the sake of Jesus Christ.[30]

Another well-known Protestant figure who apparently has no problem joining hands with Rome for the purpose of evangelization is Nicky Gumbel, founder and head of the Holy Trinity Brompton based Alpha course. During an audience with Pope John Paul II in Rome in February 2004, Gumbel held the pope's hands and later declared:

It was a great honor to be presented to Pope John Paul II, who has done so much to promote evangelization around the world ... We can be united and proclaim this Jesus to a desperately needy world.[31]

While some may believe the Alpha course will evangelize Catholics to the biblical Gospel, I can assure you the Vatican's idea of evangelism is quite the opposite—to win converts to Rome.

Catholic priest Raniero Cantalamessa (also called pastor to the pope) would be more than willing to introduce the Catholic Eucharistic Jesus to the separated brethren. On several occasions, he has been keynote speaker for Nicky Gumbel's Alpha program. It is at these meetings that Cantalamessa has introduced Alpha leaders and participants to the Catholic view of the sacraments, the saints, and Mary the Queen of Heaven.[32]

Is it possible that unsuspecting evangelical Protestants will soon be the target of the New Evangelization program? I am often amazed that so few people understand the Catholic vision. What is worse, many well-known Christian leaders and teachers who promote the emerging church are now advocating the Catholic view of the presence of Jesus in the Eucharist.

Eucharistic Adoration and the Emerging Church

When Christians begin to chase after powerful mystical experiences that supposedly bring them closer to Christ, this becomes like a slippery slope that will have disastrous results. The emerging church is already on this slope.

When I do a series of radio programs or write commentaries for our website warning people about the dangers of ecumenism, I know ahead of time what the response will be. It is not popular to stand up for biblical truth these days. The message we often hear is *unity at any cost*. I experienced this firsthand not too long ago, when I was a speaker at a regional pastors conference. I was to speak on Catholicism in the morning. Then in the afternoon, I would show how the emerging church movement was going in that direction. When I finished my morning talk and had left the podium, the organizer of the event came up to me, notably upset. "These pastors didn't come here to hear this sort of thing," he began. "You aren't going to talk about the emerging church this afternoon." He conveyed to me that the topic was unnecessary. Thus, I was forbidden to issue my warning to this group of Christian pastors.

An article titled "Returning to the rituals: Some evangelicals are exploring high liturgy" explains the paradigm shift that is occurring:

> New Hope, a nondenominational church of about 60 members, is one of a small but growing number of evangelical congregations that are beginning to experiment with worship elements more commonly associated with such highly liturgical traditions as Roman Catholicism, Orthodox Christianity and Anglicanism.[33]

Matthew Hay Brown, the author of the article, notes that this movement is headed in a particular direction. He writes:

> [O]bservers inside and outside the movement have noted a greater evangelical interest in the Eucharist, the liturgical seasons of Advent and Lent, and monastic life. Many of the practices can be traced to the early church.[34]

In Doug Pagitt's 2003 book *Church Re-imagined*, he describes his initial attraction to rituals associated with the Eucharist:

> The first day of Lent this year brought the first Ash Wednesday gathering in our church's history and in mine.... Until this point, Ash Wednesday had not been part of my Christian faith experience. Not only had I never applied ashes to anyone's forehead, but I had also never had them applied to mine. After this experience I wondered how I could have celebrated 19 Easters as a Christian without this tremendous experience.[35]

Scot McKnight, another emerging church influencer, is professor of religious studies at North Park University and on the Coordinating Group for Emergent Village. Of the emerging church, he states:

As a theologian, I have studied the movement and interacted with its key leaders for years—even more, I happily consider myself part of this movement or "conversation." As an evangelical, I've had my concerns, but overall I think what emerging Christians bring to the table is vital for the overall health of the church.[36]

McKnight is the author of *The Real Mary* and *The Jesus Creed*. In referring to an Anglican service, McKnight speaks of the Eucharistic focus. He states:

[T]he point of an Anglican gathering on a Sunday morning is not to hear a sermon but to worship the Lord through the celebration of the Eucharist.... First some scripture readings and then the sermon and then some announcements and then the Eucharist liturgy— with everyone coming forward to kneel and participate—publicly—in the body and blood.[37]

McKnight says that "the Eucharist profoundly enables the grace of God to be received with all its glories and blessings."[38] No doubt, McKnight will have an impact on those in the emerging church movement, and his views on the Eucharist will rub off. He is a popular speaker at many events including Willow Creek's Small Group Conference and the National Pastors Convention. Both of these events reach the postmodern generation.

The late Robert Webber was very influential in closing the gap between Eucharistic adoration and the evangelical church. A document he authored called "A Call to an Ancient Evangelical Future" states: "We call for a renewed consideration of how God ministers to us in ... Eucharist."[39] Two well-known evangelical publishers, Baker Books and InterVarsity Press (both of which now publish emerging church authors) sponsored the document as did *Christianity Today*. The AEF, which the document is called, is endorsed by various emerging church leaders such as Brian

McLaren who calls it "a preaching resource" that "emphasize[s] the importance ... of Advent or Lent."[40] Participants of the AEF include numerous Christian seminaries like Bethel Seminary in Minnesota, Dallas Theological Seminary, and pastors from many different denominations including Nazarene, Wesleyan, Mennonite, Reformed, and Baptist.

The new reformation is supposed to bring enlightenment through spiritual insights gleaned from the mystics. Unfortunately, participants are not being drawn into the light of God's Word but rather toward the authority and practices of the Catholic and Orthodox Churches. Robert Webber said that postmoderns are looking for "an encounter with God, they were looking for mystery, they were looking for more Eucharist."[41]

If the current *road to Rome* through mysticism continues, we can expect Webber's prediction to come true. Webber's insights may well have been based on his own personal experience. There is reason to believe this is the case. For example, in an interview, Webber was asked the question, "What do you think the North American evangelical church is going to look like twenty-five years from now?" He answered:

> Biblical symbols such as baptismal identity and Eucharistic thanksgiving will take on new meaning. The church will be less concerned about having an eschatology and more committed to being an eschatological community.[42]

Over the past several years, Webber's estimation of the future of the church has turned out to be quite accurate. Many who were once anticipating the soon and imminent return of Jesus are now asleep. Some are saying: "The Lord has delayed His coming." Others are saying: "We have been misled by pastors and teachers who taught us the second coming is a literal return of Jesus to set up His kingdom."

Experiencing the Eucharist

One might ask the following legitimate question: How do evangelical Protestants like Robert Webber become supporters of Catholic views? In order to find out more about Webber's background and his conversion experience, I read his testimony in a book titled *Signs of Wonder*. Webber explains that his "most memorable encounter with a style of worship"[43] different from his own happened at an ecumenical weekend retreat. He says:

> The group consisted of Catholics, Lutherans, Presbyterians and evangelicals who met monthly to read and discuss Scripture, to pray together, to talk, and to just have fun. When the time came for many of us to graduate and move on to new places, we decided to bring our two-year fellowship to an end with a weekend retreat at a local Catholic conference center. It was there we faced an issue we had never even discussed. Could we take Communion together? Could a Catholic priest give the bread and wine to an evangelical? Could an evangelical receive the bread and wine from a Catholic priest?[44]

Webber says the priest who was present shared his dilemma as to whether non-Catholics could partake in the Catholic communion service. He stated to the group:

> As a rule we Catholics only allow other Catholics to receive the body and blood of the Lord. But I have agonized over this separation of our churches, as I know you have.[45]

The priest then decided to "break with Catholic tradition" and offer each person in the group the bread and wine. He explained:

Why? Because it is my experience that all of you are true Christians devoted to our Lord. But I cannot tell any of you what to do. You may not feel comfortable receiving the bread and the wine. You must make that decision for yourself. If you don't come to receive, your decision will be respected, and if you do come, you will be welcomed.[46]

At this point in Webber's story, he began to question his own beliefs and what he called his "prejudices." He states:

> I considered the spiritually rich times I'd shared with these people.... Those memories said, "*Go ahead. After all,* there is only one Lord, one church, one faith, one baptism, one Holy Communion."

> In that moment, God broke through the walls I had allowed to separate me from my brothers and sisters of different denominations. I am convinced the prejudices we hold and the walls we build between ourselves and other communities of Christians actually block our experience of God's presence in our lives.... rejecting a part of God's church keeps us from experiencing what the creed calls "the communion of the Saints."[47]

After Webber participated in the communion service, he was dramatically affected. He goes on to describe how his beliefs changed. He explains:

> You might say I was surprised by joy! ... I had never had an experience like that in my life. In that Catholic chapel, a new worship experience had bumped up against that old prejudice of mine, and a new attitude was born. I had taken into myself the experience of another tradition, I had been in dialogue with another worship tradition, and I was surely the richer for it.[48]

This experience obviously revolutionized Webber's thinking. His books and articles thereafter portray this repeatedly and have played a significant role in the shift many are taking toward the path to Rome and a new reformation.

The Eucharistic Jesus is Mystical

To those who traditionally haven't had much ritual in their lives (i.e., Protestants), the ambience of the Mass would have great appeal because of its religious novelty—thus the interest in the Eucharist by those who promote contemplative spirituality. And for many Catholics, the Mass (where the Eucharist is presented), in, and of itself, is not a mystical experience. However if the contemplative dimension is added, one actually can enter the mystical realm. On the surface, this phenomenon seems complex, but once we begin to understand mysticism, it all makes sense. Within the contemplative prayer realm, the meditator is actually getting in touch with a spiritual power or force. Combining the tradition of the Eucharist, which appeals to many raised in the Catholic Church, with the relatively recent explosion of contemplative practice, the Catholic Church sees this as a way to recover its robust state of previous decades.

Father Raniero Cantalamessa, preacher to the Pontifical Household, discusses the Eucharistic mystery:

> I believe that the most necessary thing to do on the feast of Corpus Christi is not to explain some aspect of the Eucharist, but to *revive* wonder and marvel *before the mystery*. (emphasis added)[49]

This willingness to place mystery and mystical experience as the foundation of the Christian faith has the potential to win the world to a Jesus that is not the Jesus of the Bible, especially if this Jesus receives credit for supernatural healings.

Think about this: What if the Eucharistic Jesus that Catholics worship and adore miraculously started healing those who adored his presence? Wouldn't this be a strong draw to those yet outside the Catholic Church? And as Boston College professor and meditation proponent Peter Kreeft predicted in his book *Ecumenical Jihad*, Eucharistic adoration will have a powerful ecumenical, interspiritual effect. He says "the power that will reunite the Church and win the world is Eucharistic adoration."[50]

Right now, some may be asking, is the physical presence of Jesus held inside the elements of the Eucharist? Or as some evangelicals and emergents have suggested, is there a special presence and power in the Eucharist? The answer to both is a resounding no! Jesus Christ indwells the heart of every person who is born again and who belongs to Him by faith through grace. He promises never to leave or forsake us, meaning that His presence is in our lives at all times. We are not required to partake in a ritual to experience His presence, nor is He confined in benign, lifeless wafers and wine (or juice). As Jesus said:

> It is the spirit that quickeneth; *the flesh profits nothing*; the words that I speak unto you, they are spirit [spiritual as opposed to physical], and they are life. (John 6:63, emphasis added)

Jesus said this in response to his disciples' confusion over His statement "my flesh is meat indeed" (vs. 55). Paul adds further clarity in writing to the Romans that all we need to do is call upon the true Jesus, and He is there:

> But what saith it? The word is nigh thee, even in thy mouth, and in thy heart: that is, the word of faith, which we preach; That if thou shalt confess with thy mouth the Lord Jesus, and shalt believe in thine heart that God hath raised him from the dead, thou shalt be saved. For with the heart man believeth unto righteousness; and with the mouth confession is made unto salvation. For the scripture saith, Whosoever believeth on him shall not be ashamed.

> For there is no difference between the Jew and the Greek: for the same Lord over all is rich unto all that call upon him. For whosoever shall call upon the name of the Lord shall be saved. (Romans 10:8-13)

At this point, we see the great chasm that separates Catholicism from the light of the Gospel—a light the reformers saw, for which many of them gave their lives. They recognized that participation in the sacraments is not what saves people.

We see then that our concern for the Catholic's New Evangelization is no small issue. Darkness has crept over the Christian church the same way an avalanche sweeps down a mountain. Every day new unsuspecting victims are being swept away and buried. And the role the emerging church plays in bringing this about is something that should alarm every discerning Christian.

For an in-depth look at the evangelization of Eucharistic Adoration and the Eucharistic Christ, see *Another Jesus*, Lighthouse Trails, Summer 2007.

9

The Kingdom of God on Earth

> The Kingdom of God is a central conversation in emerging communities. ... And let me tell you "Kingdom of God" language is really big in the emerging church.[1]—Doug Pagitt

The Bible says that Jesus Christ will establish His kingdom when He returns to the earth. Until then, we will never establish a utopia here on earth, but on the contrary, we will continue to have wars and rumors of wars; and the conflict between good and evil will remain until Jesus returns, as we find in John's description of the human heart in the last days:

> He that is unjust, let him be unjust still: and he which is filthy, let him be filthy still: and he that is righteous, let him be righteous still: and he that is holy, let him be holy still. (Revelation 22:11)

From the context of John's prophetic statement, it is clear that this is how conditions will be until Jesus returns. But today a theology called Kingdom Now or Dominionism is permeating Christian thinking, and the emerging church movement is taking this theology full speed into the next generation. With the idea that the church can establish the kingdom of God *before* Christ returns and essentially turn our world into a *Christian world*, this belief system has literally changed the way countless Christians view the world and go about their Christian living. What most of these Christians don't realize is this kingdom of God on earth mindset is an all out effort by Satan to distort the message of the true kingdom of God and thus negate the Gospel message of Jesus Christ.

An Emergent View on the Future of Planet Earth

By examining the eschatology (study of the last days) beliefs of emerging church proponents, we can better understand their beliefs of the kingdom of God.

In Brian McLaren's book, *A Generous Orthodoxy*, McLaren lays the foundation for his view of the future, one that many other emergent leaders support. Under the subheading "The eschatology of abandonment is being succeeded by an engaging gospel of the kingdom," he writes:

> Evangelical-dispensational "left-behind" eschatology (the doctrine of last things or end times that expects the world to be destroyed in just over seven years or one thousand and seven years, depending on the fine print) makes perfect sense in the modern world.[2]

Condemning the warning and message in the Book of Revelation and the teaching of the return of Jesus Christ, McLaren adds:

> Christians in the power centers of modernity (England in the 1800s, the United States in the 1900s) saw nothing ahead in the secular story of industrial modernity... nothing but spiritual decline and global destruction. Their only hope? A skyhook

Second Coming, wrapping up the whole of creation like an empty candy wrapper and throwing it in the cosmic dumpster so God can finally bring our souls to heaven.… There is virtually no continuity between this creation and the new heavenly creation in this model; this creation is erased like a mistake, discarded like a non-recyclable milk carton. Why care for creation? Why get sentimental about a container that's served its purpose and is about to be discarded into the cosmic trash compactor of nothingness?[3]

McLaren does not read the Scriptures from an apocalyptic mindset, and in fact, implies that such ideas are relatively new, not originating in the Bible at all. He claims that those who believe in a last-days scenario have seriously miscalculated:

This pop-Evangelical eschatology made an understandable but serious mistake: it wrongly assumed that modernity was all there was or ever would be, while it rightly assessed how hopeless the future would be if modernity-without-end was indeed upon us. Just as early Christians could not imagine the gospel outlasting the Roman Empire … nineteenth and twentieth century Evangelicals couldn't imagine the gospel outlasting modernity, the empire of Scientism, consumerism and individualism.[4]

McLaren attempts to convince readers that eschatological views of Christ's return, apocalypse, tribulation, etc. are up for grabs in the ever-changing world we live in. And of course, if these theologies are not found in the Bible, then McLaren is right. However, the modern world is not the author—God is, and the Bible backs this up!

McLaren reworks many Scriptures in order to support his belief that the kingdom of God will be established here on earth sometime in the future by human effort. He writes:

For pop-Evangelical eschatology to proliferate, it had to ignore or, better reinterpret much written by the Old Testament prophets. Prophetic visions of reconciliation and shalom *within* history (metaphorically conveyed via lions and lambs, children and serpents, swords and plowshares, spears and pruning hooks) had to be pushed *beyond* history, either into a spiritual heaven or a millennial middle ground—a post-historic time zone between history and eternity, so to speak. They also had to marginalize Jesus with all his talk of the kingdom of God coming on earth, being among us now, and being accessible today.[5]

McLaren misses the whole point of Jesus' talk about the kingdom of God. Jesus said, "My kingdom is not of this world" (John 18:36), and "the kingdom of God is within you" (Luke 17:21). He was referring to the Holy Spirit living inside those who receive Him by faith. McLaren is referring to a communal kingdom established on the earth (prior to Christ's return when He said He would establish this physical kingdom) that focuses on social justice as opposed to individual personal relationships with Jesus Christ. McLaren is not the only one who sees the kingdom of God this way—the same concept is the foundation of Rick Warren's Purpose Driven church growth model.

The Purpose Driven *Inclusive* Church

Rick Warren has an ambitious plan called the P. E. A. C.E. Plan, which he hopes will usher in the kingdom of God here on earth. The acronym stands for Planting (and Partnering) churches, Equipping leaders, Assisting the poor, Caring for the sick, and Educating the next generation.[6]

While political leaders and economic leaders from around the world have previously discussed similar social programs in order to rid the world of its problems, thus far, all have failed. Warren believes he has uncovered the missing component for success—an all *inclusive* church.

This inclusive church is the third leg of what Warren calls a "three-legged stool." In an interview, he explains what he means by that:

> These problems are so big, everybody has failed [to solve them]. The United States has failed, the United Nations has failed. Nobody has solved these five problems because [the solution needs] a three-legged stool. For the stability of a nation, you must have strong healthy government, strong healthy businesses, and strong healthy churches.
>
> A three-legged stool will have stability. So I'm going from country to country teaching business its role, teaching church its role, and teaching government leaders their role—you've got to work together! We cannot solve the problem in your country or in the world if we won't work together.[7]

Most likely Peter Drucker spawned this idea in Warren. Drucker spoke of the political, economic, and spiritual legs of society and the need for them to work synergistically so the world can be transformed into a peaceful and orderly society.

Part of Warren's process is for the church to lay down its differences with other religions and secular entities so that a more powerful and effective body can be developed. In an interview with PBS interviewer Charlie Rose, Warren defines this idea. He states:

> When I go out and I start telling people, "Do you want to work with us on poverty, disease, AIDS, illiteracy, injustice?" I often find people are more unwilling to work with us than we are willing to work with them. In other words, we're saying, "You don't have to change your beliefs for us to work with you." If you can only work with people that you agree with, then most of the world, you're ruling out. Okay. I don't insist that a Muslim change his

belief for me to work on poverty. I don't even insist
that a gay person has to change their beliefs. They're
not going to accept my belief, or I'm not going to
accept theirs.[8]

By saying "you don't have to change your beliefs," Warren is
able to stretch the boundaries of his global peace plan to include
virtually every belief system and persuasion. This would be the
religious (spiritual) leg of the three-legged stool and would lead
to what Warren refers to as a "second reformation."[9] But unlike
the first reformation by those who defended the truth of God's
Word, Warren's reformation is of a different nature, which he
defines as one "about deeds" and not "about creeds." He says, "It
is not going to be about what does the church believe, but about
what is the church doing."[10] Rather than Jesus Christ being the
focal point of this ecumenical spiritual body, all that is required is
a common cause (i.e., eradicating the five global giants that Warren has identified: poverty, disease, etc.).

In the Charlie Rose interview, Warren made a remarkable statement. He mentioned having met the leader of a gay-activist group
and explained to Rose that he had found solidarity with him:

I just met with the president, the co-founder of
ACT-UP—Eric Sawyer. And I said, "Eric, how can
I help you get your message out? I know you care
about people that are dying. How can I help you
get your message out?" He said, "Use your moral
authority." I'm working with these guys.[11]

Warren's all-inclusive church includes a broad spectrum of
believers with a common cause. This inclusive church does not
just include Christian believers, but also includes all who are
like-minded (with him) and are willing to be part of the
P.E.A.C.E. Plan. In the interview, Charlie Rose asked Warren if
he was willing to work together with Catholics to establish his
plan. Warren responded:

Christianity is a global movement. In fact, Christianity was global 200 years before anybody started talking about globalism. It is the only global organization in the world. There are 2.3 billion Christians in the world.[12]

Warren identified these 2.3 billion Christians, when he told Rose:

Probably 600 million of them, I believe, are Catholic. And so when you take all of these together, it is the largest network in the world. In just the network that I'm in, I have been training leaders for 26 years. And we've trained about 400,000 pastors in 163 countries, all different denominations. Well, this network of 400,000 pastors, that's just a small, tiny network compared to Christianity around the world.[13]

In 2005, Warren spoke at the liberal think-tank, the Pew Forum on Religion. In order to clarify the ecumenical nature of the P.E.A.C.E. Plan and the global force he believes it could have, he explained:

Now when you get 25 percent of America, which is basically Catholic, and you get 28 to 29 percent of America which is evangelical together, that's called a majority. And it is a very powerful bloc, if they happen to stay together on particular issues… I would encourage you to look at this evolving alliance between evangelical Protestants and Catholics.[14]

Rick Warren's reformation, which will bring in the kingdom of God through global cooperation for a common cause, will include Catholics, Muslims, and homosexuals—a combination hardly similar to the 16th century reformation.

Warren further defined his kingdom of God aspirations in the interview with Charlie Rose, who asked him to discuss the "role of the church." Warren told Rose that "about a hundred years ago" Protestantism divided—one group focused on a social gospel ("bring in the kingdom by bringing in good social structures"), while the other focused on personal salvation for individuals. Of the two groups, Warren said to Rose, "Who is right? Well they both are ... and they need to be brought back together."*

The Kingdom of God and a Man of Peace

Most people, with any common sense and compassion, want to see a planet without poverty, disease, and illiteracy. I thank God for all the organizations working to help the suffering, the sick, and the poor. Jesus made it very clear we are to care for and reach out to those in need. However, working to bring about utopia on earth through global and religious unity is futile. My saying this might make some people angry, and they may accuse me of being fatalistic. But nowhere in Scripture is the notion supported that there will be a kingdom without tears, pain, poverty, and suffering *until* Jesus Christ physically returns and establishes it Himself.

Another question needs to be considered: Can those who don't know the King establish the kingdom of God?

Rick Warren believes that God has shown him not only the boundaries (or lack of them) of this coming global kingdom, but also the strategy to bring it about. Before Warren came up with the plan, he says he asked Jesus to show him how to reach the world. He explains:

> Then I said, "How did You do it? You wouldn't have left us without a strategy." And I found the answer in a passage in Matthew 10 and Luke 10 where Jesus sends His first followers out... He says, "When you go into a village, you find the man of

peace." Find the man of peace. There's a man of
peace in every village, in *every government*, in *every
business*, in *every church*. (emphasis added)[15]

Warren further inquired of Jesus to find out just who this
man of peace is. Here is the answer he got:

> And so I said, "What is the man of peace?" He
> said, "When you find the man of peace, if he's open
> and he's willing to work with you, you bless him
> and you start your work there. If the guy's not open
> to working with you, you dust the dust off your
> shoes and you go to the next villages, 'cause you
> can always find someone to work with." The man
> of peace is open and influential....
>
> The man of peace does not have to be a Christian
> believer. Could be Muslim. Could be Jewish.
> Because, when Jesus said, "Find the man of peace,"
> there were no Christians yet. Jesus hadn't died on
> the cross. There was no resurrection. He's just
> saying, go out and find somebody to work with.[16]

While Warren believes that a conversation with Jesus inspired his plan to establish the kingdom of God on earth, it
would be important to check out the words of Jesus written in
the Bible. Ironically, Jesus said much the opposite of what Warren is
proposing. In view of the fact that Jesus had not died and resurrected
yet, Warren suggests that Jesus sent out His disciples proclaiming
peace because there was no other message yet to proclaim; but Jesus
did send His disciples out with a Gospel of repentance in proclaiming, "The kingdom of heaven is at hand" (Matthew 10:7). This is the
same Gospel of repentance John the Baptist proclaimed in preparing
the way for the Gospel of justification by faith. Jesus did not say they
were to look for a "man of peace" in every town. Rather, He said,
"whatsoever city or town ye shall enter, enquire who in it is worthy;
and there abide till ye go thence" (Matthew 10:11).

Now Jesus did tell His disciples to use the greeting, "Peace be to this house" whenever entering a house, and if a "son of peace" is there, to remain in that house (Luke 10:5-7). However, it is important to realize that the criterion for staying in a house was not the greeting of peace itself but whether those in that house received their message:

> And whosoever shall not receive you, nor hear your
> words, when ye depart out of that house or city,
> shake off the dust of your feet." (Matthew 10:14)

In fact, Jesus makes it very clear that the disciples were sent out to proclaim a message many would reject, saying, "Think not that I am come to send peace on earth: I came not to send peace, but a sword" (Matthew 10:34). With all diligence, Jesus warns His disciples that they will be hated for preaching the Gospel. Yet Rick Warren has turned these two passages around, suggesting that Jesus sent out His disciples to proclaim peace because at that time they had no other message to proclaim.

Let me speak very boldly here: if we are going to link hands with those who believe in another gospel or no gospel at all for the sake of establishing an earthly, unified kingdom, we will not be building the kingdom of God.

Purpose Driven Ecumenism

Rick Warren's ambitious Purpose-Driven P.E.A.C.E. plan may sound good and appear to be biblically-based at first glance, but what lies beneath the surface should cause concern.

To understand Warren's new reformation program, listen to what one reporter said in an article titled "Rick Warren launches global initiative":

> Thousands of churches around the world will be setting
> out to eradicate five "giant problems" that oppress
> billions of people, Rick Warren told a crowd of 30,000

celebrating Saddleback Community Church's 25th anniversary April 17 at Angel Stadium in Anaheim, California. "Billions of people suffer each day from problems so big no government can solve them," said Warren, Saddleback's pastor. "The only thing big enough to solve the problems of spiritual emptiness, selfish leadership, poverty, disease and ignorance is the network of millions of churches all around the world."[17]

Dan Wooding (another reporter) elaborated on Warren's global initiative:

> [Rick Warren] hit a home run with a dramatic announcement on Sunday, April 17th, before 30,000 members and attendees at the church's 25th anniversary celebration in Angel Stadium, home of the Angels baseball team.... [Warren] unveiled the church's commitment to a *new reformation* in Christianity and vision for a worldwide *spiritual awakening* in the 21st Century through the PEACE Plan that he believes will mobilize one billion foot soldiers from the Christian church in missions by the year 2020. (emphasis added)[18]

According to Kelly, Warren also announced he was joining hands with Chuck Colson who would assist him in his goal to establish the kingdom of God:

> Warren also introduced Charles Colson, founder of Prison Fellowship, who announced a new partnership that will introduce Warren's Celebrate Recovery programs into prison ministries in 108 countries.[19]

While Colson's work in prisoner care is commendable, his role in bringing Protestants and Catholics together for common causes through the Evangelicals & Catholics Together document is troublesome.

The partnership agreement between Colson and Warren is significant considering they are both major influencers in the church and are both sympathetic with the Catholic Church. Warren's speech, made at the Anaheim meeting, encouraged his followers to partner with him in ushering in the kingdom of God. Warren stated:

> I stand before you confidently right now and say to you that God is going to use you to change the world. … I'm looking at a stadium full of people who are telling God they will do whatever it takes to establish God's Kingdom "on earth as it is in heaven." What will happen if the followers of Jesus say to Him, "We are yours"? What kind of spiritual awakening will occur?[20]

What does Warren mean by "whatever it takes"? Is it possible that joining together with Catholics for advancing the kingdom of God may be in Warren's agenda?

In an article titled "A Natural Alliance," the author makes some interesting observations about Warren and the reformation Warren hopes to see in his lifetime. David Brooks states:

> And when I look at the evangelical community, I see a community in the midst of a transformation—branching out beyond the traditional issues of abortion and gay marriage, and getting more involved in programs to help the needy. I see Rick Warren, who through his new PEACE initiative is sending thousands of people to Rwanda and other African nations to fight poverty and disease. I see Chuck Colson deeply involved in Sudan. I see Richard Cizik of the National Association of Evangelicals drawing up a service agenda that goes way beyond the normal turf of Christian conservatives. I see evangelicals who are more and more influenced by Catholic social teaching, with its emphasis on good works. I see the

> historical rift healing between those who emphasized
> personal and social morality. Most of all, I see a new
> sort of evangelical leader emerging.[21]

Rick Warren has stated that "a billion foot soldiers" who "have the promise of the power of God" and "have the biblical mandate and the command of God" and "the moral authority to do it"—are being called on to establish the P.E.A.C.E. Plan.[22] Time will tell whether or not Warren will be able to mobilize one billion purpose-driven foot soldiers. However, one thing is certain—in order to recruit that many committed participants, this will be an ecumenical, inter-faith army that will include more than just Bible-believing Christians.

Bible Prophecy on Trial

Many who were once looking for the return of Jesus have fallen asleep. We now live in a period of time where numerous prominent Christian leaders are telling the Christian masses that paying attention to the signs of our times in light of the Bible is a waste of time. And many of them take it a step further and accuse those who believe what Bible prophecy says about the end of the age of being negative and self-centered.

In the *Purpose Driven Life*, Warren was actually laying ground work for the emerging church's new reformation, a reformation that rejects thinking about the return of Christ and works more at convincing the multitudes that Christ is already in them as a global christ-consciousness. As you will see in the following documentation, Warren has a low regard for Bible prophecy. Perhaps this helps explain why so many who once were anticipating the return of the Lord have become occupied with worldly ambitions. Warren writes:

> When the disciples wanted to talk about prophecy,
> Jesus quickly switched the conversation to evangelism.
> He wanted them to concentrate on their mission in
> the world. He said in essence, "The details of my return

are none of your business. What is your business is the mission I have given you. Focus on that!"[23]

I find it simply astounding that a statement of this sort would be in a *New York Times* best-seller in the present-day Christian book market. Jesus was telling the disciples they could not know the day or the hour, but nowhere does Jesus ever indicate that "the details of my return are none of your business." Rather than quickly changing the subject, we find in Matthew 24 and Luke 21 two of the longest passages in Scripture quoting Jesus' own words, and what's more, where He details the signs of His coming. In essence, Jesus was saying, because you cannot know the day and hour of my return, you need to educate yourself in Bible prophecy and take heed of my words about the end times. Later on, one of those disciples, John, was given an entire book to write on the details of Jesus' coming. Jesus continually said to be alert and ready for when He returns. In both parables and straightforward talk, he spoke of this. In Luke 12:35-40, Jesus emphasized that it is essential to be prepared for His return:

> Let your loins be girded about, and your lights burning; And ye yourselves like unto men that wait for their lord, when he will return from the wedding; that when he cometh and knocketh, they may open unto him immediately. Blessed are those servants, whom the lord when he cometh shall find watching:.... And this know, that if the goodman of the house had known what hour the thief would come, he would have watched, and not have suffered his house to be broken through. Be ye therefore ready also: for the Son of man cometh at an hour when ye think not.

And Jesus frequently referred to the Old Testament prophecies. Those prophecies became the evidence that Jesus Christ was indeed whom He said He was—"Wonderful, Counsellor, The mighty

God, The everlasting Father, The Prince of Peace" (Isaiah 9:6).

But Warren tells readers to think about something other than Bible prophecy:

> If you want Jesus to come back sooner, focus on fulfilling your mission, not figuring out prophecy.[24]

What's more, Warren ends this section of his book by stating that Satan would have you "sidetracked from your mission" and by quoting Jesus out of context, saying, "Anyone who lets himself be distracted [by studying Bible prophecy] from the work I plan for him is not fit for the kingdom of God" (*Living Bible*). But Jesus was not referring to His return when He made that statement, which in the *King James Version* says: "No man, having put his hand to the plough, and looking back, is fit for the kingdom of God" (Luke 9:62). The Purpose Driven kingdom of God leaves no room for Bible prophecy, and in fact, condemns those who study it. The apostle Peter, inspired by the Holy Spirit, had a different view. He writes:

> We have also a more sure word of prophecy; whereunto ye do well that ye take heed, as unto a light that shineth in a dark place, until the day dawn, and the day star arise in your hearts. (II Peter 1:19)

Christians are called to witness and be watchmen. No Scripture exists that tells us to ignore the events that have been pointed out as signposts indicating the return of Jesus. If we do, we might be like the foolish virgins who fell asleep waiting for the bridegroom (Matthew 25:1-13).

In light of Warren's end-time views, what does he think of the emerging church? This statement he made in the foreword of Dan Kimball's book answers that question. He notes:

> Today seekers are hungry for symbols and metaphors and experiences and stories that reveal the greatness

of God. Because seekers are constantly changing, we must be sensitive to them like Jesus was; we must be willing to meet them on their own turf and speak to them in ways they understand.[25]

Rick Warren is enthusiastic about the emerging church because he believes it is the church of the future. And as you will see now, the emerging church is equally fond of Warren's view of Bible prophecy, or the omission thereof, and of his plan to usher in the kingdom of God.

The Secret Message of Jesus

It is no secret that Brian McLaren rejects the Book of Revelation's reference to a coming apocalyptic judgment in the future. McLaren's book *The Secret Message of Jesus,* reveals much of his outlook on this matter. Of the book, he says, "Everything I've written to this point has been a preparation for this book."[26] In a chapter titled "The Future of the Kingdom," he writes:

> The book of Revelation is an example of popular literary genre of ancient Judaism, known today as *Jewish apocalyptic.* Trying to read it without understanding its genre would be like watching *Star Trek* or some other science fiction show thinking it was a historical documentary, or watching a sitcom as if it were a religious parable, or reading a satire as if it were a biography—or like thinking you knew all about lions because you watched one pacing on a concrete slab one afternoon… instead of being a book about the distant future, it becomes a way of talking about the challenges of the immediate present. It becomes a book of warnings and promises.[27]

Further, discrediting the validity of the Book of Revelation as a book that provides prophetic insight, McLaren states:

If Revelation were a blueprint of the distant future, it would have been unintelligible for its original readers, as well as the readers of all succeeding generations, and would only become truly and fully relevant for one generation—the one who happened to live in one period of time it is prognosticating about. But if Revelation is instead *an example* of the literature of the oppressed, full of ever-relevant warnings and promises, it presents each generation with needed inspiration and wisdom and encouragement. In this light, Revelation becomes a powerful book about the kingdom of God here and now, available to all. (emphasis added)[28]

Not only does McLaren believe this last book of the Bible is about "the kingdom of God here and now," he claims that Jesus had nothing to say about a period of catastrophic judgment:

Other readers will be thinking of long passages in the Gospels that seem to be full of prognostication from the lips of Jesus himself—prognostications that seem to relate to the end of the world. What are we to make of these passages, such as Matthew 24-25? ...

Since Jewish apocalyptic was a popular genre in Jesus' day, we would expect him to be influenced by it and use its language and metaphors.... against the backdrop of Jewish apocalyptic, we discover that phrases that sound like they're about the destruction of the world—like "the moon will turn to blood" or "the stars will fall from the sky"—are actually rather typical stock phrases in Jewish apocalyptic. They are no more to be taken literally than phrases we might read in the paper today.[29]

Someone who might agree with McLaren is New Age leader

Barbara Marx Hubbard. But she puts a little twist in the Kingdom Now theology. She calls it *Armageddon Alternative*, which
basically means that if enough people join together and think
positively about the earth and the world, then this disastrous
end-time scenario described in the Book of Revelation doesn't
have to occur at all. She explains:

> Here we are, now poised either on the brink of
> destruction greater than the world has ever seen —
> a destruction which will cripple planet Earth forever
> and release only the few to go on—or on the
> threshold of global co-creation wherein each person
> on Earth will be attracted to participate in his or
> her own evolution to godliness.[30]

This quote is from Marx Hubbard's book she titles *Revelation*. In essence, she is describing what the New Age believes is
going to take place—that man will evolve into "godliness" and
thus prevent what the Bible has prophesied. Using language from
the Bible, she describes this time period:

> In the twinkling of an eye, we are all changed by
> this experience. It is a mass *metanoia*, a shared
> spiritual experience for the human race, a peaceful
> second coming of the divine in us *as* us.[31]

What Marx Hubbard is proposing is little different than McLaren's
message that the kingdom of God will be established here on
earth by Christians *without* King Jesus being physically present.
McLaren describes his all-inclusive kingdom:

> Sadly, for centuries at a time in too many places to
> count, the Christian religion has downplayed,
> misconstrued, or forgotten the secret message of Jesus
> entirely. Instead of being about the kingdom of God
> coming to earth, the Christian religion has too often

been preoccupied with abandoning or escaping the earth and going to heaven… We have betrayed the message that the kingdom of God is available for all, beginning with the least and last and the lost—and have instead believed and taught that the kingdom of God is available for the elite, beginning with the correct and the clean and the powerful.[32]

Barbara Marx Hubbard also speaks of this coming kingdom where all humanity will realize its divine potential and thus avoid Armageddon:

You are to prepare the way for the alternative to Armageddon, which is the Planetary Pentecost, the great Instant of Co-operation which can transform enough, en masse, to avoid the necessity of the seventh seal being broken.[33]

Christian Fundamentalists—"One of the Big Enemies"

Sounding out a warning on end-time scenarios of upheaval and the return of Christ opens the door for plenty of hostile comments. Tony Campolo says that Christians who "make a big thing of their claim that we are now living in the final stage of church history prior to the second coming of Christ"[34] have been the cause of "extremely detrimental"[35] consequences. They "discount the Sermon on the Mount,"[36] they don't care about the needy,[37] and they have had such a negative "impact on geopolitics,"[38] which Campolo says "can lead only to war."[39] Basically, according to Campolo they are the reason the world is in such a mess, and they are holding back progress of a more emerging spirituality. Rick Warren states that these types of Christians (he calls them fundamentalists) are "one of the big enemies of the 21st century," and he likens them to Islamic fundamentalists (terrorists).[40]

I often get emotional letters and e-mails expressing comments about this topic. The following is an example of one of those letters. This pastor stated:

I read your assessment of the Purpose Driven Peace Plan. Sadly you think that your version of dispensational theology is that of classic Biblical Christianity. Being that it was not at all how any Christians interpreted the Bible until about 180 years ago (and not even popular until about 75 years ago) you stand in total arrogance thinking that Rick Warren's view of the kingdom of God is un-Biblical.

This comment came shortly after I had published a commentary about the P.E.A.C.E. Plan Partners that Warren was enlisting as part of his P.E.A.C.E. Plan program. It was not my intention to be judgmental but to point out the dangers of an ecumenical plan that partners with anyone and everyone. The pastor who sent me his comments did not accept my reasoning. Instead, he claimed my comments were shaped by my *narrow-minded* theology. He said:

When we stand before Christ one day he is going to ask us if we fed the hungry, clothed the naked, visited the prisoners. How is it you can stand against a brother in the Lord who wants to do this? God will not be judging you or I by our doctrine (especially eschatology) but by our deeds.... Our salvation is through faith alone but the Bible is also clear that every believer will be judged later by their deeds.

While there is no doubt the Bible tells Christians to feed the hungry, clothe the naked, and visit the prisoners, throwing out the biblical view of the earth's last days for a paradigm that attempts to bring heaven on earth, is spiritually dangerous to say the least. Further, Paul warns Timothy that the last days will be characterized by leaders promoting the view that doctrine is not important. He says:

For the time will come when they will not endure

> sound doctrine; but after their own lusts shall they
> heap to themselves teachers, having itching ears;
> And they shall turn away their ears from the truth,
> and shall be turned unto fables. (II Timothy 4:3)

Interestingly, Peter warned that rejecting biblical truth regarding the end times would take place prior to Christ's return. Let us take heed to Peter's warning and exhort others to do the same:

> That ye may be mindful of the words which were
> spoken before by the holy prophets, and of the
> commandment of us the apostles of the Lord and
> Saviour: Knowing this first, that there shall come
> *in the last days* scoffers, walking after their own lusts,
> And saying, Where is the promise of his coming?
> for since the fathers fell asleep, all things continue
> as they were from the beginning of the creation.
> (II Peter 3:2-4)

A Utopian Kingdom and Global Healing?

The emerging church talks a lot about the kingdom of God on earth, but in language and philosophy much different than the Bible describes. One emergent writer hopes the emerging church will handle the problems of this world in a manner that is "smarter" and "more effective" than those who have gone before. With "integrative means of participating in the healing of our world," he believes:

> The Spirit of God that hovered over creation is still
> present in our world, inviting us to collaborate with
> our Maker in the fulfillment of God's reign on earth.[41]

The same writer, Mark Scandrette, expresses his communal vision for a utopian world:

> The kingdom of God is a generative people who

believe that a more beautiful and sustainable way
of life is possible.[42]

Doug Pagitt explains that the emerging church is looking
for this perfect kingdom on earth that will:

> …really be good news for the people of the world
> and not just the promise of a world to come. Many
> find good news in the call of Jesus to join the
> kingdom of God. And let me tell you "Kingdom of
> God" language is really big in the emerging church.[43]

When we think of the poor in Africa, or the homeless in
America, or a child dying of Aids, we want a world that has no
suffering like this. But is the message of the kingdom of God that
Jesus preached one that promises global healing and a world without pain and suffering? No, it isn't. Not now anyway. In our human thinking, we can't imagine that God would really want or
allow all this suffering, so we decide that the goal for humanity
should be unity, peace, no pain, or sorrow. And in an effort to
accomplish this, the most important thing is forgotten. Jesus came
to save lost sinners and give them utopia, so to speak, within their
hearts. So, while we as Christians should do what we can to help
the needy, our greatest responsibility is getting the Gospel to them.

Mark Scandrette goes so far as to say that the "interest in theologies of the kingdom of God is related" to a "sense of interconnection."[44] Leonard Sweet calls this interconnection the TOE theory
(theories of everything), in which all creation is connected together
through a spiritual force he calls New Light. Sweet states:

> If the church is to dance, however, it must first get
> its flabby self back into shape. A good place to begin
> is the stretching exercise of touching its TOEs
> [which he also refers to as Grand Unified
> Theory].… Then, and only then, will a New Light
> movement of "world-making" faith have helped

to create the world that is to, and may yet, be. Then, and only then, will earthlings have uncovered the meaning of these words, some of the last words ... Thomas Merton uttered: "We are already one. But we imagine that we are not."[45]

The Kingdom Now theology and the emerging church's utopian kingdom are all about what the natural, carnal man views as significant. Jesus came to give peace and rest to the suffering, to the poor and those in need. It's a peace that passes all earthly understanding, and it's a kingdom, as Jesus said, not of this world. In our earthly minds we cannot understand this, especially when we think about the often horrific suffering all around us.

If Rick Warren or Brian McLaren were to take their message of the kingdom of God *here and now* (and don't think about that eternal home too much) to a poor man in a hut in Africa, what will it do for him? Supposing he can never leave that hut, how will their message help him? But with Jesus Christ's message, that man can be born again and by faith, through God's grace, have Jesus living inside him every day of his remaining life. Jesus promised that of anyone invited Him in, He would come in and sup with him (Revelation 3:20).

Jesus told His disciples the world would always have suffering and there would always be poor people. He didn't say this to give allowance to ignore or avoid the poor and suffering. But He wanted His followers to know that this earth is not the final destination for those whose names are found in the Book of Life (those who belong to Christ). That is why in the Book of Revelation, the apostle John said:

> And I saw a new heaven and a new earth: for the first heaven and the first earth were passed away; and there was no more sea.... And God shall wipe away all tears from their eyes; and there shall be no more death, neither sorrow, nor crying, neither shall

there be any more pain: for the former things are passed away. (Revelation 21:1,4)

The true kingdom of God makes no sense to the unbelieving, unsaved person. The very idea of it is foolishness to him. Thus, human schemes and theologies are created to fit his way of thinking. But the Bible says what is wisdom to man is foolishness to God:

> For the preaching of the cross is to them that perish foolishness; but unto us which are saved it is the power of God. For it is written, I will destroy the wisdom of the wise, and will bring to nothing the understanding of the prudent. Where is the wise? where is the scribe? where is the disputer of this world? hath not God made foolish the wisdom of this world? For after that in the wisdom of God the world by wisdom knew not God, it pleased God by the foolishness of preaching to save them that believe. (I Corinthians 1:18-21)

10

The Undoing of Faith

> My goal is to destroy Christianity as a
> world religion and be a recatalyst for the
> movement of Jesus Christ ... Some
> people are upset with me because it
> sounds like I'm anti-Christian. I think
> they might be right.[1]—Erwin McManus

While preparing to write this book, a fellow apologist asked me if I would also discuss the good side of the emerging church in my book. Surely, there are some fruitful works coming out of this movement, a movement that has at least *some* sincere and truth-seeking people within its confines. And while I would agree there are some sincere people in the movement, I have had to examine whether the *good* that might be found outweighs the harmful, and if it doesn't, then does the harmful negate the good?

I would liken it to this: While the Mormon church teachings have some good advice (devotion to families, obeying the Ten Commandments, etc), I could never recommend this group because most of its teachings are contrary to biblical Christianity. Can you imagine if your Sunday school teacher said, "Today, we are going to study from the Book of Mormon"? The teacher then says, "While we may not agree with everything, let's not throw out the baby with the bath water. Let's glean the good."

First of all, why do that? Why would we try to filter out the cyanide from a glass of water when we have at our access pure spring water (the Word of God) *without* any poison?

I believe this scenario fits for the emerging church too. The *fruits* of the emerging church include creating a hostility towards Bible-believing Christians, no longer identifying with Christianity altogether, and restructuring missions and evangelism so that converts can remain in their own religion (just add a Christ-figure). Once the emerging church has accomplished these things, there truly will be nothing left of the Christian faith.

Christian or Christ-Follower

Emerging church leader, Erwin McManus, says his "goal is to destroy Christianity as a world religion and be a recatalyst for the movement of Jesus Christ." He says the "greatest enemy to the movement of Jesus Christ is Christianity [i.e., Christians]."[2] Just what exactly does McManus mean by these statements? *He* would say that we do not need to identify with Christianity as a religion, but we can still identify with Jesus. In his book *The Barbarian Way*, he talks about being awakened to a "primal longing that ... waits to be unleashed within everyone who is a follower of Jesus Christ."[3]

The term—follower of Jesus (or Christ-follower)—is used frequently within the scope of those promoting emerging spirituality. Rick Warren has the term throughout his pastors.com website. Lee Strobel refers to it in his book *Case for Christ* (Student Edition), and Wesleyan pastor David Drury has a Christ-Follower Pop Quiz on his website to help determine if you really are a "Christ Follower."[4]

This attitude to "destroy Christianity" but become Christ-followers is seeping through several venues. Book titles, for example, express this growing anti-Christian sentiment. One book, *Why One Can Be a Christian or a Christ-Follower (But Not Both)* by Floyd Henderson, is a case in point.

The idea behind being a Christ-follower as opposed to a Christian can be seen in the spiritual formation movement (i.e., contemplative prayer movement). That is, if you want to be like Christ, then practice certain disciplines and you can be *like* Him. Chuck Swindoll says the spiritual disciplines can help you "become like Christ."[5] Beth Moore, in the pro-contemplative film, *Be Still*, says:

> [I]f we are not still before Him [God], we will never truly know, to the depths of the marrow of our bones, that He is God. There has got to be a stillness.[6]

The one common thread woven throughout spiritual formation teachings is that the silence (induced through mantra meditation) and being a Christ-follower are practically synonymous. You can't have one without the other. But being born again, receiving Jesus Christ as Savior, Lord, and Master is not a pre-requisite to being a Christ-follower. Richard Foster teaches that anyone, not just believers, can practice these spiritual disciplines and become *like* Christ.[7]

Now here lies the difference between a Christian and an emerging Christ-follower. A person who is truly born again has Jesus Christ indwelling him—Jesus lives inside that person. And it is His life in him or her that gives the power to become progressively more like Him (sanctification), as Paul explained in his address to Corinthian Christians:

> But we all, with open face beholding as in a glass the glory of the Lord, are changed into the same image from glory to glory, even as by the Spirit of the Lord. (II Corinthians 3:18)

The believer draws his strength and power from Jesus Christ (who indwells him), and he realizes his salvation and any good thing in him is from Christ; as the Scripture says: "Not of works, lest any man should boast" (Ephesians 2:9).

But in today's progressive, emerging church, Jesus is seen as a model or an example who can be followed and mimicked. Meditation sympathizer, Ken Blanchard, says Jesus is a perfect model to follow. Blanchard's website explains:

> Ken saw Jesus as the greatest *leadership role model* and co-founded Lead Like Jesus in 1999 with the mission "to inspire and equip people to l*ead like Jesus*." (emphasis added)[8]

While Jesus *was and is* a model, that wasn't His primary mission. And when people refer to Him as a model, it is often because they see Him as a model for higher consciousness rather than the unique Son of God, Emmanuel (God with us) who came to die for us and be our Savior. In an eastern religion like Buddhism, Buddha was a model where his followers were imitators of him. But in Christianity, the Spirit of Christ indwells us through faith. So Jesus becomes more than a model; He is a living presence in us.

The reason meditation has to play such an important role in the emerging church is because without the true Gospel message being preached (faith comes by hearing the Word), so many within the movement do not have the indwelling Christ, but they sincerely long to be like Him and to feel His presence. Thus, the energy to do that has to come from somewhere. Meditation appears to be that answer. However, mantra meditation does not conjure up the presence of God, but rather demonic entities that deceptively *look* like Christ at first. So these emerging Christ-followers are learning to be *like* Christ but may not ever have received Him as Lord and Savior and thus don't have Him living inside them.

So anyone at all, from any walk of life, from any religion, can be a Christ-follower. They may come to believe they have a christ-consciousness and are Christ-like, yet they do not have the actual power of Christ within, that can only come from the indwelling presence of the Holy Spirit. The Bible is clear where the true power of God comes from:

But as many as received him, to them gave he power to become the sons of God, even to them that believe on his name. (John 1:12)

For I am not ashamed of the gospel of Christ: for it is the power of God unto salvation to every one that believeth; to the Jew first, and also to the Greek. (Romans 1:16)

For the preaching of the cross is to them that perish foolishness; but unto us which are saved it is the power of God. (I Corinthians 1:18)

"They Like Jesus but Not the Church"

In the spring of 2007, Dan Kimball's new book *They Like Jesus But Not the Church* was released. The book is a compilation of interviews Kimball conducted with several young people (one being a lesbian) who tell him they *like and respect Jesus*, but they don't want anything to do with going to church or with Christians who take the Bible literally. Kimball tells readers of one "fellow" who jokingly said, "They all should be taken out back and shot."[9] But while Kimball drives home the point that non-Christians don't like Christians, he says these are "exciting times we live in when Jesus is becoming more and more respected in our culture by non-church-going people."[10] He says we should "be out listening to what non-Christians, especially those in their late teens to thirties, are saying and thinking about the church and Christianity."[11]

Kimball believes that Christians need to be accepted by non-Christians and we need to convince the non-believers that we are not abnormal or strange. But in order to do that, Kimball says we must change the way we live and behave. He says that for Christians to do certain things that identify themselves as Christian (like using Christian bumper stickers[12] or using Christian phrases such as "food, fellowship, and fun") are "corny"[13] and might offend a non-believer or seeker. Kimball insists that "those who are rejecting faith in Jesus"[14] do so because of their views of Christians and the church. But he makes it clear throughout the book that these distorted views are not the fault of the unbeliever but are the fault of Christians—but not all Christians, just those who take the Bible literally. He says that "to them [the unbelievers], Christianity isn't normal." He adds, "This is really important to realize."[15]

Kimball's theology is flawed. The Bible makes it clear that those who belong to the Lord Jesus are *not* looked upon as normal by the world. In fact, Jesus tells us to expect this. He said to His disciples:

> If the world hates you, you know that it hated Me before it hated you. If you were of the world, the world would love its own. Yet because you are not of the world, but I chose you out of the world, therefore the world hates you. (John 15: 18, 19)

While Jesus said the world would indeed look at Christians in a negative way, Kimball believes this attitude can and should be reversed. He states:

> Christians are now the foreigners in a post-Christian culture, and we have got to wake up to this reality if we haven't … we aren't as respected by people who are growing up outside of the church as we were in the past. We aren't sought out as the ones to turn to for advice, and we aren't in the position of influence in our communities…. we need to view ourselves the way others on the outside see us.[16]

Many emerging church leaders share Kimball's sentiments. But their reasoning is faulty. Christians have always been foreigners in the world, and they have often suffered for it. Throughout the history of Christianity, countless murders and atrocities have been committed against Christians. Jesus Himself told His disciples, "I am not of this world" (John 8:23) and "My kingdom is not of this world" (John 18:36). When He prayed to the Father, He said:

> I have given them thy word; and the world hath
> hated them, because they are not of the world, even
> as I am not of the world. (John 17:14)

As do so many proponents in the emerging church movement, Kimball believes that today's generation of young people is so different from young people of any past generation ever, that special means must be applied if these young people are to see truth. But is he right in this? Isn't it the Word of God that pierces the soul and reveals truth? In the 1960s and 1970s, there was another generation of confused, searching young people, many who were looking for life's meaning. The hippies were as every bit as different as the generation of young people today. While the atmosphere was different, the sins, the questions, and the problems were not. When thousands of hippies began getting saved, what caused that? Did the pastors of the day start going barefoot and wearing their hair long? No, they gave the hippies the Word of God—straightforward, loving but uncompromised. Did they take LSD so they could better understand where the hippies were coming from? No, they gave them the Word of God. Did they apologize to the hippies for telling them they were sinners (as Kimball suggests the Church needs to do today)? No. They gave them the Word of God. And it is that Word that brought so many into God's kingdom of light. They presented the Word and gave them Jesus Christ.

In Kimball's book, he offers a description of fundamentalist Christians:

> [P]eople who are always saying negative things about
> the world, are anti-gay, take the whole Bible literally,
> are card-carrying Republicans, are pro-Israel, read end-
> times novels, and endorse snake handling and fire-
> and-brimstone preaching. They think of King-James,
> finger-pointing, teetotaling, vengeful people who credit
> God for using natural disasters to punish people for

sin, and who use Christian jargon and are arrogant
and unloving toward anyone but themselves.[17]

Telling readers that this is how non-Christians view "conservative" Christians, he assures them "this caricature doesn't fit all fundamentalists." Kimball masterfully condemns Christians who are pro-Israel, take the Bible literally, study end-time Bible prophecy, and talk about hell—he likens them to negative, arrogant, unloving, and vengeful people.

When Kimball says that unbelievers like Jesus (but not Christians), who is this Jesus they like? Is it the Jesus of the Bible, or is it a Jesus the world has formulated to fit its mold? The biblical Jesus told the Pharisees that if they did not believe He was God in the flesh and Christ, they would die in their sins. That is the very essence of dogmatism. Jesus didn't dialogue with them and say, "I can understand why you don't think I am the Messiah, and I can respect that." He *was* dogmatic! As Paul says in Scripture, it is another Jesus they preach; for if it were the *real* Jesus, they would not like or respect Him until the day they bow down before Him, worship Him as God, and give their lives 100 percent to Him, denying all other gods and belief systems: "Whoever transgresses and does not abide in the doctrine of Christ does not have God" (II John 9).

Emergent Missiology

> I must add, though, that I don't believe making disciples must equal making adherents to the Christian religion. It may be advisable in many (not all!) circumstances to help people become followers of Jesus and remain within their Buddhist, Hindu, or Jewish contexts.[18]—Brian McLaren

Emerging spirituality is changing the way missions is being conducted. The idea is that you can go for Jesus, but you don't have to identify yourself as a Christian or part of the Christian church. This concept spills over into some mission-

ary societies too, where they teach people from other religions
they can keep their religion, just add Jesus to the equation. They
don't have to embrace the term *Christian*. At the 2005 United
Nations Interfaith Prayer Breakfast, Rick Warren made the following comments to 100 delegates who represented various
different religions:

> I'm not talking about a religion this morning. You
> may be Catholic or Protestant or Buddhist or
> Baptist or Muslim or Mormon or Jewish or you
> may have no religion at all. I'm not interested in
> your religious background. Because God did not
> create the universe for us to have religion.[19]

While he did go on afterwards and say he believed that Jesus
was God, the implication was that your religion doesn't matter
to God, and being Buddhist, Mormon, or whatever will not in-
terfere with having Jesus in your life. Donald Miller, author of
the popular *Blue Like Jazz*, puts it this way:

> For me, the beginning of sharing my faith with people
> began by throwing out Christianity and embracing
> Christian spirituality, a nonpolitical mysterious system
> that can be experienced but not explained.[20]

In Erwin McManus' book *The Barbarian Way*, he refers to
"Barbarians" in a positive light and says that this is how *Christ-
followers* should be:

> They [Barbarians] see Christianity as a world
> religion, in many ways no different from any other
> religious system. Whether Buddhism, Hinduism,
> Islam, or Christianity, they're not about religion;
> they're about advancing the revolution Jesus started
> two thousand years ago.[21]

A May/June 2000 issue of *Watchman's Trumpet* magazine explains what this new missiology really entails:

> Several international missions organizations, including Youth With a Mission (YWAM), are testing a new approach to missionary work in areas where Christianity is unwelcome. A March 24, 2000, Charisma News Service report said some missionaries are now making converts but are allowing them to "hold on to many of their traditional religious beliefs and practices" so as to refrain from offending others within their culture.[22]

The *Charisma* article in which *Watchman's Trumpet* reports elaborates:

> "Messianic Muslims" who continue to read the Koran, visit the mosque and say their daily prayers but accept Christ as their Savior, are the products of the strategy, which is being tried in several countries, according to Youth With a Mission (YWAM), one of the organizations involved.[23]

The *Charisma* story reports that a YWAM staff newsletter notes the new converts' lifestyle changes (or lack thereof):

> They [the new converts] continued a life of following the Islamic requirements, including mosque attendance, fasting and Koranic reading, besides getting together as a fellowship of Muslims who acknowledge Christ as the source of God's mercy for them.[24]

When one of the largest missionary societies (YWAM) becomes a proponent of the new missiology, telling converts they can remain in their own religious traditions, the disastrous results should be quite sobering for any discerning Christian.

"Churchless" Christianity

In an article titled "Christ-Followers in India Flourishing Outside the Church," the following statement is made regarding the research of Herbert Hoefer, author of *Churchless Christianity*:

> In striking research undertaken in the mid-eighties and published in 1991, Herbert E. Hoefer found that the people of Madras City are far closer to historic Christianity than the populace of any cities in the western Christian world could ever claim to be. Yet these are not Christians, but rather Hindus and Muslims. In their midst is a significant number of true believers in Christ who openly confess to faith in fundamental Biblical doctrines, yet remain outside the institutional church.[25]

The article expands this idea that one does not need to become a Christian or to change his religious practices; he just needs to add Jesus to his spiritual equation:

> However, some might argue that this [the "smothering embrace of Hinduism"] is the danger with the *ishta devata* strategy I am proposing. It will lead not to an indigenous Christianity but to a Christianized Hinduism. Perhaps more accurately we should say a Christ-ized Hinduism. I would suggest that really both are the same, and therefore we should not worry about it. We do not want to change the culture *or the religious genius* of India. We simply want to bring Christ and His Gospel into the center of it. (emphasis added)[26]

Herbert Hoefer's research is quite interesting. His idea that rather than "changing or rejecting" the Hindu and Muslim culture missionaries should be "Christ-izing" it.[27] He says there are thousands of believers in India whom he refers to as "non-baptized believers." Reasons for the believers not becoming baptized vary, but usually it is because they will suffer financial or social loss and status. Hoefer admits that these non-baptized believers are not Christians, and usually they do not choose to call themselves that. In many of his examples, these non-baptized believers continue practicing their religious rituals so as not to draw suspicion or ridicule from family and friends. Hoefer explains one story:

> [There is] a young man of lower caste who earns his livelihood by playing the drum at Hindu festivals and functions. "All this is what I must do," he said, "but my faith is in Christ. Outside I am a Hindu, but inside I am a Christian."[28]

Another family of the Nayar caste consisted of a wife, her husband and one son. Hoefer describes their situation:

> [H]er husband and son have been believers in Christ for eight years. They both had studied in Christian schools and learned of Christ. The husband's father had a vision of Christ, and one brother also is a non-baptised believer. The husband does not join his wife in coming to Church, but he occasionally joins her for the big public meetings. They do not have family devotions, but worship Jesus along with the Hindu gods in their home. Their approach to the Hindu festivals is to carry them out but to think of God, not Jesus specifically.[29]

I am not here to judge whether these non-baptized believers are truly born again. That is for the Lord to decide. My concern lies with the way missions is changing and how the Gospel is being presented. To say that someone does not have to leave their pagan religion behind, and in fact they don't have to even stop calling themselves Hindu or Muslim, is not presenting the teachings of the Bible.

And the apostle Paul, who ended up dying for his faith, exhorted believers to be willing to give up all for the sake of having Christ:

> I count *all things but loss* for the excellency of the knowledge of Christ Jesus my Lord: for whom I have suffered the loss of all things, and do count them but dung, that I may win Christ. (Philippians 3:8, emphasis added)

The implications of this new missiology are serious and, what's more very unbiblical. Mike Oppenheimer of Let Us Reason ministries has done extensive research and analysis on the new missiology. In his article, "A 'New Evangelism' for the 21st Century," Oppenheimer states:

> Can a Christian now call himself a Muslim? The word Muslim is made up of two words, Islam and Mu. Muslim does not just mean submission; it means submission to the God Allah; not the Lord Jesus Christ or Yahweh. Can a Muslim be called a Christian and walk with Allah? This seems to make no doctrinal or practical sense, unless they change the names and the meaning. This only brings confusion. Why do this when you can introduce Yahweh as the true God without any baggage and shuffling around in names, nature or descriptions? The answer is that you may not see the same results. This is what this is all about isn't it, results; pragmatism, the end justifies the means.[30]

In a book by Oppenheimer and Sandy Simpson titled *Idolatry in Their Hearts*, they show how widespread this new missiology has become. Listen to some of the comments made by a few new missiology proponents:

New Light embodiment means to be "in

connection" and "information" with other faiths....
One can be a faithful disciple of Jesus Christ without
denying the flickers of the sacred in followers of
Yahweh, or Kali, or Krishna."[31]—Leonard Sweet
I happen to know people who are followers of
Christ in other religions.[32]—Rick Warren
I see no contradiction between Buddhism and
Christianity. . . . I intend to become as good a
Buddhist as I can.[33]—Thomas Merton

Allah is not another God...we worship the same
God.... The same God! The very same God we
worship in Christ is the God the Jews—and the
Muslims—worship.[34]—Peter Kreeft

Oppenheimer and Simpson present page after page of documentation showing this paradigm shift in Christian missions. They ask the question, "Can one be a Hindu or a Muslim and follow Jesus?" They explain why the answer is no:

One cannot be in relationship with Jesus within the
confines of a false religion. One must leave his or
her religion to follow Jesus, not just add Him on....

This broadens Jesus' statement of the road being
narrow into a wide, all encompassing concept. What
is concerning is that these same kinds of statements
are also made by those who are New Agers that
hold a universal view. Alice Bailey* said, "I would
point out that when I use the phrase 'followers of
the Christ' I refer to all those who love their
fellowmen, irrespective of creed or religion."[35]

With Rick Warren saying your religion should have no bearing on your spiritual life, Erwin McManus saying he would like to

---

*Alice Bailey was an occultist who coined the term New Age.

destroy Christianity, and missionary societies telling new converts they can have Jesus without Christianity (or baptism), the results could be devastating and will very likely undo the tireless efforts of many dedicated missionaries around the world. These Bible-believing missionaries have risked their lives and given up comforts and ease to travel around the world sharing the good news that becoming a Christian (having Jesus Christ come into your heart and life) is the way to eternal life. Now, right behind them, come emerging church *missionaries* who say Christianity is a terrible religion, and Christians are out to lunch—so just become a Christ-follower, and you don't even have to tell anyone about it. In fact, you can still live like you always have.

To the many who have suffered persecution and martyrdom over the centuries for being Christians and being courageous enough to call themselves that, we now must believe they suffered and died unnecessarily—after all, they did not need to confess Jesus as the only way. And they didn't need to renounce their pagan religions. We also find that the following words of Jesus do not fit into this emerging church paradigm:

> Whosoever therefore shall confess me before men, him will I confess also before my Father which is in heaven. But whosoever shall deny me before men, him will I also deny before my Father which is in heaven. (Matthew 10:32-33)

There is a powerful story in the Book of Acts, in which the apostle Paul had been arrested for preaching the Gospel. He was brought before King Agrippa and given the opportunity to share his testimony of how he became a Christian. He told Agrippa that the Lord had commissioned him to preach the Gospel and:

> To open their eyes, and to turn them from darkness to light, and from the power of Satan unto God, that they may receive forgiveness of sins, and

inheritance among them which are sanctified by faith that is in me. (Acts 26:18)

Agrippa continued listening and then said to Paul, "Almost thou persuadest me to be a Christian (vs. 28)." Paul answered him:

I would to God, that not only thou, but also all that hear me this day, were both almost, and altogether such as I am, except these bonds. (vs. 29)

If Paul had been following the emerging mentality, he would have told Agrippa, "No need to become a Christian. You can remain just as you are; keep all your rituals and practices, just say you like Jesus." In actuality, if Paul had been practicing emerging spirituality, he wouldn't have been arrested in the first place. He would not have stood out, would not have preached boldly and without reservation, and he would not have called himself a Christian, which eventually became a death sentence for Paul and countless others.

The Inclusive Gospel

Eddie Gibbs and Ryan K. Bolger are the co-authors of *Emerging Churches: Creating Christian Community in Postmodern Cultures*. A claim that sits on the back cover states: "The Best Book Yet on the Emerging Church." Brian McLaren agrees with this assessment, when he states:

If you want to be truly conversant with emerging churches, this is the book to read... It recognizes the essential theological emphases of emerging churches, and it is based on actual conversations with over 50 people.[36]

Gibbs, author and Professor of Church Growth at Fuller Theological Seminary, and Bolger, Academic Director of Arts in Global Leadership at Fuller Theological Seminary, have teamed up to provide an overview of the nine patterns they see unfolding in emerging churches. Their research took place over a period of almost five years.[37]

One of the trends the authors examine in detail is evangelism in the emerging church, which they say, "involves sharing the deep experiences of life with those outside the faith."[38] They found that emerging church leaders are not impressed with Christians who defend the faith by offering *definitive* answers to those who doubt the faith.[39]

Gibbs and Bolger substantiate this thought by quoting emerging church leader Pip Piper from Birmingham, UK:

> Evangelism or mission for me is no longer persuading people to believe what I believe, no matter how edgy or creative I get. It is more about shared experiences and encounters. It is about walking the journey of life and faith together, each distinct to his or her own tradition and culture but with the possibility of encountering God and truth from one another.[40]

However, Piper's definition of evangelization contradicts Scripture. The apostle Peter states:

> But sanctify the Lord God in your hearts: and be ready always to give an answer to every man that asketh you a reason of the hope that is in you with meekness and fear. (I Peter 3:15)

Where in the Bible are we instructed to join hands with pagans and consider their beliefs as a means of evangelism? Gibbs and Bolger believe the advantages of this style of evangelism outweigh the negatives. They write:

> Christians can not truly evangelize unless they are prepared to be evangelized in the process. In sharing the good news, people are enriched by the spiritual

insights, honest questions and depth of devotion demonstrated by those of other faiths. Including others involves listening to them, learning from them. Much of what exists in other faiths may not necessarily be hostile to the kingdom. Christians can learn a lot from other walks of life.[41]

What if someone who *had* a Bible-based faith, in an attempt to reach someone who did *not* have faith, in their endeavor to reach this person, is drawn away from the faith? Wouldn't this be evangelism in reverse? Nowhere in the Bible is there any precedent for this kind of evangelism. The Old Testament prophets warned the children of Israel not to join hands with pagans—yet they ignored God's warning as Jeremiah proclaimed:

> And the LORD said unto me, a conspiracy is found among the men of Judah, and among the inhabitants of Jerusalem. They are turned back to the iniquities of their forefathers, which refused to hear my words; and they went after other gods to serve them: the house of Israel and the house of Judah have broken my covenant which I made with their fathers. Therefore thus saith the LORD, behold, I will bring evil upon them, which they shall not be able to escape; and though they shall cry unto me, I will not hearken unto them. (Jeremiah 11:9-11)

In spite of such clear warnings from Scripture, Gibbs and Bolger provide another example of *successful* emerging church evangelism. This one is Spencer Burke (from The Ooze) whose community "visits different Christian traditions every few weeks." Burke explains:

> [T]he Christian tradition could hold to *an inclusive model*, not an exclusive one. We have a community

hermeneutic. We read other sacred writings, then get back to the Scripture and decide together how to interpret what we have read from the literature that other religions hold to be sacred. (emphasis added)[42]

But the scope of Burke's "inclusive model" goes outside "Christian tradition." Gibbs and Bolger describe this emergent community that "reads other sacred writings." They state:

Burke's community is prepared to learn from faith traditions outside the Christian fold. There is a Buddhist family in their church. As a community, the church visited a Buddhist temple. They participated in a guided meditation with this family. Burke celebrates the many ways God is revealed. He recognizes that the Spirit has been with these people all along. The community celebrates other traditions. They reach out to other traditions, and see them as beloved children of God. With a focus on kingdom rather than on church, people find that their relationship with other faiths changes.[43]

In the name of emergent and vintage faith, the very idolatry the children of Israel were guilty of is being repeated. But this pathway to deception is not only being repeated, it is being applauded. As emerging church evangelization unfolds, walls that once separated biblical Christianity from pagan religious belief systems are being demolished. Instead of proclaiming the Gospel of Jesus Christ that saves sinners from hell, a new gospel is being preached, and its preachers are wearing interspiritual robes of deception. Jesus proclaimed it is a narrow pathway that leads to heaven, and He is the only door through which to enter—but on the contrary, the emergent message forsakes the narrow pathway to God for the sake of *establishing the kingdom*.

Worse yet, Jesus' command that we are to be His witnesses has been reinterpreted to mean the very opposite of what He said. Gibbs and Bolger quote another emergent leader to drive home their point. Karen Ward, Abess of Apostles Church in Washington, says she "no longer believes in evangelism." Resonating with Gibbs, Bolger, and Burke, Ward states:

> We do not do evangelism or have a mission. The Holy Spirit is the evangelist, and the mission belongs to God. What we do is simply live our lives publicly as a community in the way of Jesus Christ, and when people inquire why we live this way, we share with them the account of the hope within us. We are to love one another, and that creates its own attraction. Taking care of the sick and the needy—creates all the evangelism we need.[44]

While taking care of the sick and needy does create opportunities to share the Gospel, emerging spirituality *evangelists* would silence those who preach Christ openly, calling them too obtrusive. The new evangelization of the emerging church, while it may be in the name of Christ, is against Christ. A bridge has been established that has the potential to unite all religious beliefs in the name of Christ, by circumventing the Gospel of Jesus Christ.

Bridging the Gap between Good and Evil

The serpent's temptation of Eve in the Garden of Eden, that we can be like God, remains with mankind to this very day. Satan's plan is to lessen or eliminate (he hopes) the gap between himself and God. The following explanation puts it well:

> It is important to understand that Satan is not simply trying to draw people to the dark side of a good versus evil conflict. Actually, he is trying to eradicate the gap between himself and God, between good and evil, altogether. When we understand this approach it helps us see why Thomas Merton said everyone is already united with God or why Jack Canfield said he felt God flowing through all things. All means all—nothing left out. Such reasoning

implies that God has given His glory to all of creation;
since Satan is part of creation, then he too shares in
this glory, and thus is "like the Most High."[45]

When those in the emerging church try to persuade people
that we need to bridge the gap between Christians (or Christ-
followers as they put it) and non-Christians, they aren't really
talking about reaching out to the unsaved in order to share the
Gospel with them. They are talking about coming to a consensus, a common ground. Leonard Sweet explains:

> The key to navigating postmodernity's choppy, crazy
> waters is not to seek some balance or "safe middle
> ground," but to ride the waves and *bridge the opposites*,
> especially where they *converge in reconciliation* and
> illumination.[46]

It takes a little thinking to figure out what Sweet is saying by
this statement, but when he talks about bridging the opposites, he's
referring to a chasm that exists between good and evil. This tension
between the two is called dualism, and at the heart of occultism is
the effort to eradicate it. If that gap could truly be closed, then
Satan and God would be equal. The Bible clearly states this will
never happen, but it also says that it is Satan's desire:

> How art thou fallen from heaven, O Lucifer, son of
> the morning! how art thou cut down to the ground,
> which didst weaken the nations! For thou hast said in
> thine heart, I will ascend into heaven, I will exalt my
> throne above the stars of God: I will sit also upon the
> mount of the congregation, in the sides of the north:
> I will ascend above the heights of the clouds; I will be
> like the most High. Yet thou shalt be brought down
> to hell, to the sides of the pit. (Isaiah 14:12-15)

This misguided effort to unite all things, to give people the
option of maintaining their own religious practices, suggesting they

do not have to call themselves Christians is a slippery slope and an undoing of the Christian faith.

Samir Selmanovic was raised in a European Muslim home, then served as a Seventh Day Adventist pastor in the US. Today, he helps to develop the emerging church through his role in the Coordinating Group at Emergent Village and his leadership in Re-church Network. Selmanovic has some interesting and alarming views on Christianity. He states:

> The emerging church movement has come to believe that the ultimate context of the spiritual aspirations of a follower of Jesus Christ is not Christianity but rather the kingdom of God. …to believe that God is limited to it [Christianity] would be an attempt to manage God. If one holds that Christ is confined to Christianity, one has chosen a god that is not sovereign. Soren Kierkegaard argued that the moment one decides to become a Christian, one is liable to idolatry.[47]

On Selmanovic's website, Faith House project, he presents an interfaith vision that will:

> …seek to bring progressive Jews, Christians, Muslims, and spiritual seekers of no faith to become an interfaith community for the good of the world. We have one world and one God.[48]

While Selmanovic says he includes Christians in this inter-spiritual dream for the world, he makes it clear that while they might be included, they are in no way beholders of an exclusive truth. He states:

> Is our religion [Christianity] the only one that understands the true meaning of life? Or does God place his truth in others too? Well, God decides, and not us. The gospel is not our gospel, but the

gospel of the kingdom of God, and what belongs
to the kingdom of God cannot be hijacked by
Christianity.[49]

While it is true that God is the One who decides where He
is going to place truth, He has already made that decision. And
the answer to that is found in the Bible. When Selmanovic asks
if Christianity is the only religion that understands the true meaning of life, the answer is yes. How can a Buddhist or a Hindu or
a Muslim fully understand truth when their religions omit a Savior who died for their sins?

Though world religions may share some moral precepts
(don't lie, steal, etc), the core essence (redemption) of Christianity is radically different from all of them. Interspirituality may
sound noble on the surface, but in actuality, Selmanovic and the
other emerging church leaders are facilitating occultist Alice
Bailey's rejuvenation of the churches. In her rejuvenation everyone remains diverse (staying in their own religion), yet united in
perspective, with no one religion claiming a unique corner on
the truth. In others words all religions lead to the same destination and emanate from the same source. And of course, Bailey
believed that a "coming one"[50] whom she called Christ would
appear on the scene in order to lead united humanity into an era
of global peace. However, you can be sure that if such a scenario were to take place as Bailey predicted, there would be no
room for those who cling to biblical truth.

As is the case with so many emergent leaders, Selmanovic's
confusing language dances obscurely around his theology,
whether he realizes it or not. Sadly, for those who are lost and
who are trying to find the way, the emerging church movement
offers confusion in place of clarity. It blurs if not obliterates the
walls of distinction between good and evil, truth and falsehood,
leaving people to stumble along a broken path, hoping to find
light. In sharp contrast, Jesus commanded believers to stand out
as beacon lights in this dark world, bearing the Word of God to

a lost and dying generation. In such times we live in, let us not be quickly deceived, but let us heed the words that give life and true peace:

> Ye are the light of the world. A city that is set on an hill cannot be hid. Neither do men light a candle, and put it under a bushel, but on a candlestick; and it giveth light unto all that are in the house. (Matthew 5:14-15)

11

A Slaughterhouse Religion?

In whom we have redemption through his blood, the forgiveness of sins, according to the riches of his grace. (Ephesians 1:7)

For he hath made him to be sin for us, who knew no sin; that we might be made the righteousness of God in him. (II Corinthians 5:21)

The heart and core of the Christian faith is based upon Jesus Christ's shed blood at Calvary as the only acceptable substitutionary atonement for mankind's sins. The Gospel message requires this foundation. The Bible says the wages of sin is death— thus every person alive should receive the penalty of spiritual death because none of us is without sin, since we are born with our sin nature intact. Satan hates the Gospel message. He understands what the Gospel means, and his agenda is to deceive mankind from understanding and believing so they can suffer eternally with him. While Scripture is very clear about the necessity of Christ's death in order for us to be saved, some believe this would make God a blood-thirsty barbarian. Embedded within the structure of the emerging church is just such a belief.

Precivilized Barbarity

Many in the emerging church movement would vehemently object if someone told them that emerging church leaders don't like the Cross. They would jump up and say, "Yes, they do. I've heard them talk about Jesus and His going to the Cross. They say they love the Cross."

Some emerging church leaders *do* say they love the Cross, but an underlying theme is gaining momentum among them. It says Jesus' going to the Cross was an example of sacrifice and servanthood that we should follow; but the idea that God would send His Son to a violent death for the sins of mankind—well, that is not who God is. A loving God would never do that! Such a violent act would make Christianity a "slaughterhouse religion."[1]

Liberal theologian and pastor of the Riverside Church in New York City, Harry Emerson Fosdick (1878-1969), believed that the doctrine of the atonement, where "Jesus suffered as a substitute for us" because of our sins, is a "precivilized barbarity."[2]

In his book, *The Modern Use of the Bible*, Fosdick says that Jesus going to the Cross should be seen as an example of a life of service and sacrifice and not compared with "old animal sacrifices" and "made 'a pious fraud' played by God upon the devil."[3] In Fosdick's book *Dear Mr. Brown*, he states:

> Too many theories of the atonement assume that by one single high priestly act of self-sacrifice Christ saved the world.[4]

Fosdick ends that statement with a pronounced—"No!" He insists, "These legalistic theories of the atonement are in my judgment a theological disgrace."[5]

Fosdick considered the idea that God would actually send His Son to die on a Cross *to take our place* to be the basis for a violent and bloody religion. He rejected the biblical message of an atonement and substitutionary sacrifice.

Fosdick was the pastor of Riverside Church of New York City from 1925 to 1946. While he has been long gone, his ideologies have remained intact and have drifted right into the emerging church. In October 2006, Riverside Church held the 5th Fosdick Convocation in honor of their former pastor. Two of the emerging church's most influential teachers were there as speakers in honor of Fosdick—Brian McLaren and Tony Campolo.[6] As I will show you, McLaren resonates with Fosdick's view of the Cross.

False Advertising for God

In an interview, Brian McLaren questioned the idea of God sending His Son to a violent death, calling it "false advertising for God":

> [O]ne of the huge problems is the traditional understanding of hell. Because if the cross is in line with Jesus' teaching then—I won't say, the only, and I certainly won't say even the primary—but a primary meaning of the cross is that the kingdom of God doesn't come like the kingdoms of this world, by inflicting violence and coercing people. But that the kingdom of God comes through suffering and willing, voluntary sacrifice. But in an ironic way, the doctrine of hell basically says, no, that's not really true. That in the end, God gets His way through coercion and violence and intimidation and domination, just like every other kingdom does. The cross isn't the center then. The cross is almost a distraction and *false advertising for God*. (emphasis added)[7]

What an extraordinary example of faith under attack and the consequences of thinking *outside of the box*. If McLaren is right, all those who have ever lived and believed in Christ's atonement have been misled and wrong. McLaren has taken the freedom to reconstruct what faith means by distorting the Scriptures, or worse yet, saying the very opposite of what the inspired

Word of God says. This is blasphemy! McLaren also states:

> And I heard one well-known Christian leader, who—
> I won't mention his name, just to protect his reputation.
> 'Cause some people would use this against him. But I
> heard him say it like this: The traditional understanding
> says that God asks of us something that God is
> incapable of Himself. God asks us to forgive people.
> But God is incapable of forgiving. God can't forgive
> unless He punishes somebody in place of the person
> He was going to forgive. God doesn't say things to
> you—Forgive your wife, and then go kick the dog to
> vent your anger. God asks you to actually forgive. And
> there's a certain sense that, a common understanding
> of the atonement presents a God who is incapable of
> forgiving. Unless He kicks somebody else.[8]

To further back up McLaren's rejection of the message of Christ's atonement through His blood, we look to Episcopal priest Alan Jones. In his book *Reimagining Christianity*, Jones carries through with this idea that God never intended Jesus' sacrifice on the Cross to be considered a payment for our sins:

> The Church's fixation on the death of Jesus as the
> universal saving act must end, and the place of the
> cross must be reimagined in Christian faith. Why?
> Because of the cult of suffering and the vindictive
> God behind it.[9]

> The other thread of just criticism addresses the
> suggestion implicit in the cross that Jesus' sacrifice
> was to appease an angry God. Penal substitution [the
> Cross] was the name of this vile doctrine.[10]

Brian McLaren has endorsed *Reimagining Christianity* and says of the book:

Jones is a pioneer in reimagining a Christian faith
that emerges from authentic spirituality. His work
stimulates and encourages me deeply.[11]

"*That* God Does Not Exist"

This idea of rejecting God's judgment placed on Jesus Christ
instead of us is not exclusive with Fosdick or McLaren. In
fact, such rejection is integrated into the teachings of many others. In 1991, William Shannon (biographer of Catholic monk
and mystic Thomas Merton) said:

> This is a typical patriarchal notion of God. He is the
> God of Noah who sees people deep in sin, repents
> that He made them and resolves to destroy them.
> He is the God of the desert who sends snakes to
> bite His people because they murmured against Him.
> He is the God of David who practically decimates a
> people ... He is the God who exacts the last drop of
> blood from His Son, so that His just anger, evoked
> by sin, may be appeased. This God whose moods
> alternate between graciousness and fierce anger ...
> *This God does not exist.* (emphasis added)[12]

So in other words, according to Fosdick, McLaren, and Shannon,
Jesus should be seen as a *model of sacrifice* to follow in our own lives,
but to view God the Father as a judge against sin is not a proper view
of God. Those who reject the atonement realize the greatest threat
to their heretical views is those who take the Scriptures literally and
seriously. Fosdick explains:

> Were you to talk to that fundamentalist preacher,
> he doubtless would insist that you must believe in
> the "substitutionary" theory of atonement—
> namely, that Jesus suffered as a substitute for us the
> punishment due us for our sins. But can you imagine
> a modern courtroom in a civilized country where
> an innocent man would be deliberately punished

for another man's crime? … [S]ubstitutionary atonement … came a long way down in history in many a penal system. But now it is a precivilized barbarity; no secular court would tolerate the idea for a moment; only in certain belated theologies is it retained as an explanation of our Lord's death … Christ's sacrificial life and death are too sacred to be so misrepresented.[13]

This is another perfect example of how the emerging church turns doctrine it doesn't understand into a mockery against Scripture and God's plan of salvation. God's ways are not our ways and to expect them to line up with our own human reasoning is ludicrous:

For my thoughts are not your thoughts, neither are your ways my ways, saith the LORD. For as the heavens are higher than the earth, so are my ways higher than your ways, and my thoughts than your thoughts. (Isaiah 55: 8-9)

Former Catholic priest Brennan Manning has been a major influence in emerging spirituality. In his 2003 book *Above All*, he quotes William Shannon almost word for word, regarding the atonement:

[T]he god whose moods alternate between graciousness and fierce anger … the god who exacts the last drop of blood from his Son so that his just anger, evoked by sin, may be appeased, is not the God revealed by and in Jesus Christ. And if he is not the God of Jesus, *he does not exist*. (emphasis added) [14]

Dying for the Sins of the World

Marcus Borg is Distinguished Professor in Religion and Culture and Hundere Endowed Chair in Religious Studies at Oregon State University. He is a lecturer and the author of several books, some of which are *Jesus and Buddha*, *The God We Never Knew*, and *Reading the Bible Again for the First Time: Taking the Bible Seriously But not Literally*. While most would not consider him an emerging church leader, his thinking has greatly influenced the movement and its leaders. Brian McLaren says he has "high regard"[15] for Borg; the two of them participated in a summer seminar series at an interspiritual center in Portland, Oregon in 2006.[16] Rob Bell references and praises him in Bell's popular book *Velvet Elvis*.[17] Walter Brueggemann, a professor at Columbia Theological Seminary and one of the contributors for Richard Foster's *Renovare Spiritual Formation Study Bible*, considers Borg an essential part of the emerging spirituality. Brueggemann states:

> Marcus Borg is a key force in the emerging "new paradigm" of Christian faith.[18]

Borg explains in his book *The God We Never Knew* that his views on God, the Bible, and Christianity were transformed while he was in seminary:

> I let go of the notion that the Bible is a divine product. I learned that it is a human cultural product, the product of two ancient communities, biblical Israel and early Christianity. As such, it contained their understandings and affirmations, not statements coming directly or somewhat directly from God.... I realized that whatever "divine revelation" and the "inspiration of the Bible" meant (if they meant anything), they did not mean that the Bible was a divine product with divine authority.[19]

This attitude would certainly explain how Borg could say:

> Jesus almost certainly was not born of a virgin, did not think of himself as the Son of God, and did not see his purpose as dying for the sins of the world.[20]

If what Borg is saying is true, then we would have to throw out John 3:16 which says God so loved the world He gave His only Son, and we would have to dismiss the theme of a blood offering that is prevalent throughout all of Scripture. In the Old Testament, it is clear:

> For the life of the flesh is in the blood: and I have given it to you upon the altar to make an atonement for your souls: for it is the blood that maketh an atonement for the soul. (Leviticus 17:11)

But Borg rejects this emphasis:

> To think that the central meaning of Easter [resurrection] depends upon something spectacular happening to Jesus' corpse misses the point of the Easter message and risks trivializing the story. To link Easter primarily to our hope for an afterlife, as if our post-death existence depends upon God having transformed the corpse of Jesus, is to reduce the story to a politically-domesticated yearning for our survival beyond death.[21]

What is behind this mindset? Listen to one New Ager describe what underlies this line of thought:

> Jesus was an historical person, a human becoming Christ, the Christos, is an eternal transpersonal condition of being. Jesus did not say that this higher state of consciousness realized in him was his alone for all time. Nor did he call us to worship him. Rather, he called us to follow him, to follow in his steps, to learn from him, from his example.[22]

Fosdick would resonate with this. When he says, "Christ's sacrificial life and death are too sacred to be so misrepresented," he means that Christ is an example to be followed, not an innocent sacrifice for our guilt and thus worthy of praise and worship. Satan wants desperately to be worshiped and adored as God. He hates all that Jesus' death stands for. Jesus Christ, God in the flesh, purchased with his own blood the lives of those written in the Book of Life.

The Bible says, "without the shedding of blood is no remission" (Hebrews 9:22), and also, "He appeared to put away sin by the sacrifice of Himself" (Hebrews 9:26). Are we to reject these Scriptures and other ones as well that speak of the atonement because it doesn't sound logical? Scripture tells us that the carnal mind is at enmity against God. We need to recognize that the Bible is God's revelation of Himself to man. It is our final authority, and we must adhere to the truth of its teachings:

> Herein is love, not that we loved God, but that he loved us, and sent his Son to be the propitiation for our sins.... And we have seen and do testify that the Father sent the Son to be the Saviour of the world. (I John 4:10, 14)

12

A New Reformation?

A sea change of transitions and transformations is birthing a whole new world and a whole new set of ways of making our way in the world.... It is time for a Postmodern Reformation ... Reinvent yourself for the 21st century or die. Some would rather die than change.[1]—Leonard Sweet

A new reformation. Most likely, you have heard the term *by some of today's prolific leaders*. Rick Warren talks about it, emerging church leaders discuss it, and New Agers for a long time have been saying, We need a *new* reformation. Referring to the reformation that took place in the 16th century, these emerging reformation advocates believe that something as radically different as that previous reformation must happen again. In fact, they believe that the church, and the world, will not survive without it. Statements like "whatever it takes,"[2] or "reinvent or die" often leave the lips of the new reformation *evangelists*.

What is the *nature* of this paradigm shift that many say we are on the brink of experiencing? Is it a biblical reformation? Does it truly have the best interest of humanity in mind? Or is this "change of transitions and transformations" actually going to lead to massive spiritual deception? Before we can answer that last question, we need to examine the underlying makeup of this new reformation. And when we have done so, let us ask ourselves, is this indeed a reformation inspired by the same Lord who is the Author and Finisher of our faith:

> Looking unto Jesus the author and finisher of our faith; who for the joy that was set before him endured the cross, despising the shame, and is set down at the right hand of the throne of God. (Hebrews 12:2)

Where is this new reformation headed? One thing is for sure, when Leonard Sweet states, "It *is* a whole new world out there,"[3] when it comes to the postmodern reformation, his words are very accurate. He says:

> More and more are admitting it. Of the five coping mechanisms for relating to any transition ("hold out," "keep out," "move out," "close out," "reach out"), fewer and fewer are able to "hold out" and deny the changes that are taking place.[4]

These changes, discussed in this book, are going to produce not just "a whole new world," but a whole new Christianity. Traditional Christian attitudes toward those who take the Bible literally, toward the Catholic Church and other religions, toward sexuality, toward biblical eschatology (study of the last days), and toward Israel and the role this tiny nation plays in God's sovereign plan—all are being redefined through the emerging church.

Apocalyptic Millennialists

If you haven't already noticed, anti-Christian sentiment is growing toward those who believe in a biblical *last days*/Book of Revelation scenario prior to Christ's return. A 2005 article titled "Lutheran leader calls for an ecumenical council to address growing biblical fundamentalism" should help convince you.

The article shows not only this growing resentment towards Bible-believing Christians but also the interspiritual path this change in attitude is taking:

> The leader of the nation's largest Lutheran denomination has called for a global Christian council to address an "identity crisis" on how churches interpret and understand the Bible. Presiding Bishop Mark Hanson of the Evangelical Lutheran Church in America ... called for Catholics, Eastern Orthodox, Anglican and Lutheran churches to come together to combat a fundamentalist-millenialist-apocalypticist reading of Scripture.[5]

Hanson's request for a group to monitor and expose anti-ecumenists who take the Bible literally carries some weight! His message contains other statements showing his concern about Bible literalists—particularly those who take Bible prophecy seriously and see Israel and the Middle East crisis as an end-times sign post. The article continues:

> [M]ainline churches traditionally are uneasy with literal readings of Scripture, particularly in fundamentalist churches, regarding the end of the world and political unrest in the Middle East. In addition, mainline churches have been divided over what the Bible says about hot-button issues such as homosexuality and women's ordination.[6]

Bishop Hanson believes that a global ecumenical group made up of Catholics, Eastern Orthodox, Anglicans, and Lutherans is the answer to the crisis he sees. Hanson calls this effort a "ministry of reconciliation," that will "result of Christ breaking down the dividing walls," and "reconcil[ing] the whole creation to God's self."[7] But Hanson says that those who believe in a biblical end times and a literal Bible interpretation are counterproductive to and holding back the cause of Christ, which he suggests is to unite all of creation and produce a planetary utopia.

Incredibly, Hanson would like to reverse the outcome of the first reformation, join hands with the Catholic Church, and embrace the Eucharistic Jesus in order to bring about an ecumenical unity and the kingdom of God here on earth. He explains:

> How do we as LWF [Lutheran World Federation] member churches continue to express our commitment to Eucharistic hospitality and sharing with the Roman Catholic Church without minimizing the theological issues that remain? Will 2017 and the 500th anniversary of the Lutheran Reformation provide an opportunity for shared reflection with the Roman Catholics on our contributions and commitment to the unity of Christ's church and to the work for justice and peace in all the earth.[8]

In this goal to bring about the kingdom of God on earth through an ecumenical, inter-faith movement, Reverend Munib Younan, bishop of the Evangelical Lutheran Church in Jerusalem, believes that those who adhere to an apocalyptic end-time scenario (with a focus on Israel) are spreading "heresy." He says they "pretend to love the Jewish people" but are "actually anti-Jewish" with teachings that are "racist." He has requested that Lutherans "alert all Christians everywhere to its dangers and false teachings."[9]

As I mentioned earlier in the book, Rick Warren tells his followers that the details of Christ's return are none of our business. Tony Campolo says Christians that focus on end-time scenarios have been the cause of "extremely detrimental" consequences (see chapter 9). One thing you will notice in the writings of most emerging church leaders is an absence of discussion on a catastrophic apocalyptic atmosphere before Christ's literal return to earth. What you *will* see though is lots of discussion about establishing the kingdom now and never mind thinking about life after our earthly deaths. Brian McLaren gives an example:

> The church has been preoccupied with the question, "What happens to your soul after you die?" As if the reason for Jesus coming can be summed up in, "Jesus is trying to help get more souls into heaven, as opposed to hell, after they die." I just think a fair reading of the Gospels blows that out of the water. I don't think that the entire message and life of Jesus can be boiled down to that bottom line.[10]

In an interview on Planet Preterist website, McLaren discusses his dilemma over eschatological-thinking believers:

> I didn't start with any interest in rethinking eschatology ... I think many of us are in this kind of rethinking process—some starting from the beginning part by rethinking, perhaps, the relation of faith and science in relation to evolution and young-earth creationism ... some starting from the middle, as they re-examine what the gospel of the kingdom of God is supposed to mean, or the idea of integral or holistic mission ... and some starting from the end, re-examining eschatology....
>
> Sometimes I think that people who are *thoroughly indoctrinated* and habituated into this kind of system will not be able to break free from it without experiencing both *psychological and social dislocation and disorientation.* (emphasis added)[11]

McLaren also says that such Christians are really going to hurt our world. He continues:

> An eschatology of abandonment, which is how I would characterize certain streams of the left-behind approach, has disastrous social

consequences.... Any project geared toward improving the world long term is seen as unfaithful, since we're supposed to assume that the world is getting worse and worse.[12]

In the interview, McLaren is asked what he thinks about a "preterist book"* that was being released. McLaren states:

A lot is at stake in these conversations—and very literally, the lives of thousands of people hang in the balance because if the dominant religious group in the country with the most weapons of mass destruction embraces an eschatology that legitimates escalating violence ... well, I hate to think about it.[13]

In essence, McLaren is saying if you believe the Book of Revelation and Matthew 24 are yet to take place, you are a dangerous psychological misfit and are assumed to have no compassion for the suffering, no concerns for the environment or the world in which we live, and have the potential to blow up the world with "weapons of mass destruction." If McLaren was talking about big governments and political parties, that would be one thing, but he is clear—he is referring to Christians who believe what the Bible says about the last days.

Resisters—"Leave or Die"

In an article written by Rick Warren, "What Do You Do When Your Church Hits a Plateau?" Warren told pastors and church leaders not to be discouraged about slow change in their churches. He told them it would take time ... and in many cases, it would take these resisters either leaving the church or simply dying. Warren exhorts:

---

*Preterism: The belief that biblical prophecies, such as in Matthew 24, took place before 70 AD, thus preterists do not wait for a second coming of Christ.

If your church has been plateaued for six months, it might take six months to get it going again. If it's been plateaued a year, it might take a year. If it's been plateaued for 20 years, you've got to set in for the duration! I'm saying some people are going to have to die or leave. Moses had to wander around the desert for 40 years while God killed off a million people before he let them go into the Promised Land. That may be brutally blunt, but it's true. There may be people in your church who love God sincerely, but who will never, ever change.[14]

By making statements like this, Rick Warren marginalizes those who won't go along with the new reformation that he is hoping for. While Warren doesn't say that people should kill them, he does say that God may have to end their lives, just like when "God killed off a million people before he let them go into the Promised Land."

One of the tools Rick Warren uses to help churches make the transformation into the new paradigm is a book called *Transitioning: Leading Your Church Through Change*. Written by Dan Southerland, a Saddleback pastor and the director of Church Transitions Inc., an organization that "trains pastors and church leaders to effectively manage major transitions,"[15] Southerland states in a chapter titled "Dealing with Opposition":

> We have experienced two major sources of criticism during our transitions. The first is Christians from more traditional backgrounds.... Not all of our traditional backgrounded Christians have been critical—just the ornery ones. Our second source of criticism is traditional church pastors. Again, not all traditional church pastors—just the meaner ones.[16]

Southerland tells readers that "some folks are going to get very angry." He likens these opposers to "leader[s] from hell." He says:

If you have read Nehemiah recently, you will remember that Sanballat is Nehemiah's greatest critic and number one enemy. Let me put it plainer than that. Sanballat is a leader from hell.... We all have some Sanballats in our churches. This is the guy who opposes whatever you propose.... You cannot call this guy a leader from hell to his face—but you could call him Sanballat.[17]

The concept of *get with the program, change, or die* is very common in New Age and emerging circles as well—those who don't get on board (or ride the wave as Leonard Sweet puts it), will have to die. Listen to the words of New Age activist Barbara Marx Hubbard. She states:

Christ-consciousness and Christ-abilities are the natural inheritance of every human being on Earth. When the word of this hope has reached the nations, the end of this phase of evolution shall come. All will know their choice. All will be required to choose.... All who choose not to evolve will die off.[18]

This sounds much like Leonard Sweet when he says, "Reinvent yourself for the 21st century or die. Some would rather die than change."[19]

It is quite ironic that one of the biggest complaints by New Agers and emerging church proponents alike is the black and white, either/or mindset of their critics, but in actuality, this is what they are doing themselves—telling believers to "reinvent or die."

The Barbarian Way

In a *Relevant* magazine interview, Erwin McManus, pastor of a church called Mosaic and a popular author and speaker, states the following:

Because people don't know where to put our community [Mosaic] they put us in the "emergent" category, and we really are a different animal than emergent. We're not against emergent, but we are not like them.[20]

In the interview, McManus says, "Our dilemma is that we are trying to create *an entire new category* and people keep trying to put us in different ones."[21] While McManus may not be part of the *emergent* team, he *is* helping to propel emerging spirituality. Of Dan Kimball's book, *The Emerging Church*, he states:

> The future of the church in North America hinges on innovators like Dan Kimball and the ideas presented in *The Emerging Church*. Vintage Christianity can be applied to new and existing congregations to help reach the next generation.[22]

In 2003, McManus was one of five authors in the book, *Church in the Emerging Culture*. Two of the other authors were Brian McLaren and Leonard Sweet. McManus' disclaimer that he is not part of the emerging church does not line up with his words and actions.

In McManus' book *The Barbarian Way*, he tells readers they have been "recreated to live in a raw and primal spirituality" and that "Barbarians are not welcome among the civilized and are feared among the domesticated."[23] The theme of *The Barbarian Way* is a comparison of the "refined and civilized"[24] and the barbarian, who McManus says we should become like. Christianity is something that stands in the way though. McManus explains:

> The way of Jesus is far too savage for their sensibilities [those who are "civilized"]... Why a reckless call to awaken the barbarian faith within us at the risk of endangering this great civilization we have come to know as Christianity? ... It is time to hear the barbarian call, to form a barbarian tribe, and to unleash the barbarian revolt. Let the invasion begin.[25]

When, as I mentioned earlier, McManus said it was his "goal to destroy Christianity," the previous statement reiterates those convictions, and the following statement shows that McManus includes not just Christianity in this upheaval but Israel as well. McManus says that Jesus doesn't like Israel[26] (although in fact the Bible says He wept for her). He says that since God decided to destroy Israel, we should not think He wouldn't destroy Christianity too:

> Two thousand years ago, God started a revolt against the religion He started. So don't ever put it past God to cause a groundswell movement against churches and Christian institutions that bear His name.[27]

McManus erroneously states that God revolted against Judaism, which simply isn't true. In reality, God established the Law and the Prophets through the Jew whom He refers to as the "apple of His eye":

> When the Most High divided to the nations their inheritance, when he separated the sons of Adam, he set the bounds of the people according to the number of the children of Israel. For the LORD's portion is his people; Jacob is the lot of his inheritance. He found him in a desert land, and in the waste howling wilderness; he led him about, he instructed him, he kept him as the apple of his eye. (Deuteronomy 32: 8-10)

Jesus came as a sacrificial Lamb to save, and He informed His followers that the time is fulfilled—he wasn't overthrowing a religion—He came to *fulfill* prophecy. And now McManus' thinking extends to Christianity, suggesting now God will revolt against it as well.

McManus' use of words like barbarian, savage, and other warlike terms belittle and mock anything that calls itself Christian. He exhorts readers by saying:

When an opponent beheads one barbarian, he better be prepared, for we will return in force.... We need to move together as God's people, a barbarian tribe .... There's a future to be created.[28]

The Barbarian Way tries to show that to be a barbarian is to live radically for Jesus. But explaining the barbarian life in terms of beheadings, mysticism, and rejection of Christianity will at best, give a confusing message to many young readers.

McManus' "new category" of spiritual quest sounds very much like the emergent quest. By his own admission, McManus resonates with the one element consistent throughout the emerging church—mysticism. For example, at Bethel Theological Seminary where McManus is a professor for the Doctor of Ministry of Emerging Leaders program, he teaches with his brother Alex McManus, author of *Into the Mystic* (a promotion of mysticism). McManus sees mysticism as an integral part of the "barbarian's" spiritual walk. He explains:

> [W]e have to learn how to see the invisible and hear the inaudible. We are called to join the barbarian tribe and to embrace our call as mystical warriors.[29]

In another interview with *Relevant* magazine, McManus explains what is the "core" of his book. He states:

> *The Barbarian Way* was, in some sense, trying to create a volatile fuel to get people to step out and act. It's pretty hard to get a whole group of people moving together as individuals who are stepping into a more mystical, faith-oriented, dynamic kind of experience with Christ. So, I think *Barbarian Way* was my attempt to say, "Look, underneath what looks like invention, innovation and creativity is really *a core mysticism* that hears from God, and what is fueling this is something really ancient." That's what was really the core of *The Barbarian Way*. (emphasis added)[30]

On McManus' website, Mosaic Alliance, he includes a section called "Awaken Humanity," which "serves the purpose of history by maximizing the divine potential in every human being."[31]

Sexuality in the New Reformation

It may seem out of place to include a section on sexuality in this chapter on the postmodern reformation. However, one aspect of the topic cannot be ignored, and it has become an earmark in the emerging church—that aspect is related to homosexuality.

In this section, I am merely going to present certain statements made by those in the emerging church for the purpose of showing you this paradigm shift in attitude toward sexuality. How you interpret these statements is up to you, but it is my prayer you will look at them through the eyes of Scripture. One thing is for sure, after reading this section, I think you will agree that emerging spirituality is attempting to redefine how Christians view and think about sexuality. I begin first with the Word of God:

> I beseech you therefore, brethren, by the mercies of God, that ye present your bodies a living sacrifice, holy, acceptable unto God, which is your reasonable service. And be not conformed to this world: but be ye transformed by the renewing of your mind, that ye may prove what is that good, and acceptable, and perfect, will of God. (Romans 12:1-2)

One example of this new reformation mindset on sexuality can be found in Dan Kimball's book, *They Like Jesus but Not the Church*. Kimball devotes an entire chapter (called "The Church is Homophobic") to homosexuality and says that Christians need to re-interpret what we thought the Bible says about homosexuality. He states:

> Because this is such a huge issue in our culture, and because all of the tension and discussion on this issue is over what the Bible says about it, we can no longer

just regurgitate what we have been taught about homosexuality.... We cannot do that any longer ... We must approach the Bible with humility, prayer, and sensitivity, taking into consideration the original meaning of Greek and Hebrew words and looking into the historical contexts in which passages were written.... we can no longer with integrity merely quote a few isolated verses and say "case closed."[32]

Kimball elaborates:

Quite honestly, and some people might get mad at me for saying this, I sometimes wish this [homosexuality] weren't a sin issue, because I have met gay people who are the most kind, loving, solid, and supportive people I have ever met. As I talk to them and hear their stories and get to know them, I come to understand that their sexual orientation isn't something they can just turn off. Homosexual attraction is not something people simply choose to have, as is quite often erroneously taught from many pulpits.[33]

Kimball does not stand alone within the ranks of the emerging church in his permissive, accepting view of homosexuality. Someone else in this camp is Jay Bakker, son of Jim Bakker of the former PTL Club. In an interview with *Radar* magazine, Bakker says, "I felt like God spoke to my heart and said '[homosexuality] is not a sin (brackets in original)."[34] On Bakker's website, he upholds this view.[35] And in a December 15th, 2006 interview with Larry King, the following conversation took place:

KING: Would you say that you're part of the liberal sect of Christianity?
JAY BAKKER: Well, I definitely say I'm a little bit more liberal than probably most, yes.
KING: You, for example, in your church would you marry gays?

JAY BAKKER: If the laws passed, yes.
KING: You favor there being a law, though?
JAY BAKKER: Yes, I do.[36]

Brian McLaren expressed his views (or lack of them) over the subject and stated:

> Most of the emerging leaders I know share my agony over this question [on homosexuality].... Frankly, many of us don't know what we should think about homosexuality. We've heard all sides but no position has yet won our confidence so that we can say "it seems good to the Holy Spirit and us." ... Perhaps we need a five-year moratorium on making pronouncements.[37]

One pastor who runs a ministry that helps homosexuals leave the lifestyle, can help us see the extent of these changing attitudes toward homosexuality. He explains:

> They call themselves new-evangelicals. Philip Yancey devoted a whole chapter to homosexuality in his book *What's So Amazing About Grace?* He thinks we need to extend grace to people who can't change their homosexuality.... Tony Campolo thinks people who can't change their homosexuality should live in celibate homosexual partnerships. His wife thinks gays should just get married to each other. Lewis Smedes agrees with Richard Foster. They all seem to agree there are some gay people who cannot change their homosexuality, are not able to live celibately and therefore exceptions should be made for them.[38]

The pastor, an ex-homosexual, disputes those in the church who publicly embrace homosexuality, and he believes there is an answer to these postmodern views. He states:

Since when are Richard Foster, Philip Yancey, Tony Campolo and Lewis Smedes experts on the changeability of homosexuality? ... I have lived this issue for most of my 42 years. For seventeen years I've helped hundreds, maybe thousands, of people come out of homosexuality. I've never seen two healings alike. And I've never seen someone who by the grace of God could not be healed. Now *that's* what's so amazing about grace! It empowers us to live a moral and transformed life in Christ.[39]

In 2004, Philip Yancey (author and editor for *Christianity Today*) accepted an interview with Candace Chellew-Hodge for *Whosoever*, "an online magazine for Gay, Lesbian, Bi-Sexual, and Transgendered Christians." When Chellew-Hodge asked Yancey about his views on gays and lesbians in the church, Yancey answered:

When it gets to particular matters of policy, like ordaining gay and lesbian ministers, I'm confused, like a lot of people. There are a few—not many, but a few—passages of Scripture that give me pause. Frankly, I don't know the answer to those questions.[40]

My question to Yancey and other proclaiming Christian leaders is why don't you know the answer? The Bible is clear on this matter. We may not always understand but part of being a Christian is accepting God's Word and trusting that it is truly just that. Yancey may not be an emergent leader, but his beliefs certainly fit with emerging spirituality. The following statement he makes shows he shares a similar disregard for biblical doctrine:

Perhaps our day calls for a new kind of ecumenical movement: not of doctrine, nor even of religious unity, but one that builds on what Jews, Christians, and Muslims hold in common.... Indeed, Jews, Christians, and Muslims have much in common.[41]

The Great Emergence

Phyllis Tickle is a best-selling author and the founding editor of the religion department at *Publishers Weekly*. She is also a friend of the emerging church. Doug Pagitt says of her:

> Phyllis Tickle is the best friend the emergent movement could ever have.[42]

In the fall of 2008, Baker Books (through their partnership with Emergent Village—Emersion Books) will release Tickle's book called *The Great Emergence*. The following description of the book confirms Tickle's allegiance to emerging spirituality:

> [I]ntended to provide a practical, positive vision of the church as it steps into the future. Tickle says the book will discuss the development of the emerging church, what she calls the "Great Emergence," placing it among the other great phenomena in the history of Christianity, including the Great Schism and the Great Reformation. "Every 500 years," Tickle said, "the empowered structures of institutionalized Christianity, whatever they may be, become an intolerable carapace that must be shattered so that renewal and growth may occur. Now is such a time."[43]

In a PBS interview, Tickle referred to this "[e]very 500 years" theory and said, "the church has a giant rummage sale." She said, "Christianity is in the midst of a new reformation that will radically remake the faith."[44] At the Joint Annual Meeting of the Society of Biblical Literature (SBL) where Tickle and McLaren shared a platform, one participant noted that, "[Tickle said] Brian McLaren is to this new reformation what Martin Luther was to the Protestant Reformation."[45]

If indeed Brian McLaren, or any of the emergent leaders or upstarts, lead and direct this new reformation, it will do as Tickle says—"radically remake the faith." Emergent proponent Troy Bronsink reveals that this remaking will include all of humanity and all of creation. In *An Emergent Manifesto of Hope*, Bronsink, a minister in the Presbyterian Church (USA), states:

> Emergent ... is a gift given to all the church that is placing us in tension with things as they are.... we will discover courage to let go of the old orientations, see creation expanding.[46]

He continues:

> If the Emergent conversation is to have a "next chapter," it will need to learn from other sketches outside of Western Christendom as well as from within the depths of other traditions (denominations and communions) once dismissed on rational-political grounds, and it must continue, all the more, to seek ways of sketching that benefit the rest of creation.[47]

Bronsink says that Emergent is "a guild of prophets" that will lead the way for "existing practitioners of Christianity."[48] He says they will create an "environment" that will equip "any and all for the process of emergence."[49] He adds that "practices of meditation" are necessary to "sustain" the emergent hope[50] but gives a word of caution to emerging seekers:

> [M]erely seeing ourselves as a creative agent within the domain of the Christian church will domesticate Emergent into what one critic has already claimed is an "asterisk on the landscape of American church growth." On the other hand, seeing the integrated whole of the church (emerging and otherwise) as a creative agent within creation, Emergent can be a place where practitioners embody the church's creative agency *for all of emerging society*. (emphasis added)[51]

Bronsink says the emerging church must not become confined within the structure of Christianity, and this is perhaps where we can understand the theological limits of the emerging church. Those limits? There are none! The sky is the limit for the all-encompassing emerging church that includes all faiths, and all creation. Atonement is not part of this new reformation because all creation is already being saved and unified with God. It's no wonder emerging prophets over the past several decades from Fosdick to Alan Jones to Brian McLaren reject penal substitution—in their grand emergence, it just isn't needed.

A poem from *An Emergent Manifesto of Hope* illustrates what the emerging church calls *expanded redemption*. I think you will see how such a theology has no room for atonement through Jesus Christ. The poem reads:

> Not only *soul*, whole body!
> Not only *whole body*, all of the faithful community!
> Not only all of the *faithful community*, all of humanity!
> Not only *all of humanity*, all of God's creation![52]

This is very contradictory to what Jesus said,

> Many will say to me in that day, Lord, Lord, have we not prophesied in thy name? and in thy name have cast out devils? and in thy name done many wonderful works? And then will I profess unto them, I never knew you: depart from me, ye that work iniquity. (Matthew 7:22-23)

It's a noble and comforting notion that all humanity and creation are redeemed, but it doesn't square with biblical spiritual reality.

Emergent leader Karen Ward asks the question, "Is there an 'emerging' theology of the atonement?"[53] She answers, "I think not." Calling it "the mystery we're in," she refers to the atonement as *at-one-ment*,[54] which occultist and New Age prophet Alice Bailey refers to as our (all humanity) oneness and equality with God.[55]

Ward explains her views:

> We are being moved, as a community, beyond
> theories about atonement, to enter into atonement
> itself, or at-one-ment—the new reality and new
> relationship of oneness with God which Christ
> incarnated (in life, cross, and resurrection) and into
> which we are all invited "for all time."[56]

The emergent reformation, when it comes to fruition, will stand
on the side of the line drawn in the sand that says all humanity is
One—regardless of religion, beliefs—we are all One. That Oneness will mean one with all creation too, and inevitably with God.
This is what the New Age movement is striving for—a time when
all of mankind will *realize* both their unity and divinity—and the
Gospel as we know it, according to Scripture, will be no more.

Many people, even many Christians, do not believe in a last
days, apocalyptic time period. Some think talk of an anti-Christ,
a mark of the beast, and a great falling away are nothing but silly
and nonsensical myths. Others believe that the biblical prophecies talking about such ideas have already come to pass. But if
an end-time apostasy where Satan will deceive the whole world
(Revelation 12:9) is going to occur (which I believe it will), what
would such an apostasy look like? Is it possible it would resemble the emergent, new reformation that is even today capti-
vating the hearts and minds of a growing number of people,
many who once believed the Bible to be the Word of God?

Is this postmodern reformation a move of God … or could
it indeed be part of a great and horrible end-time deception?
The apostle Paul writing under the inspiration of the Holy Spirit
stated the following:

> Now we beseech you, brethren, by the coming of
> our Lord Jesus Christ, and by our gathering together
> unto him, That ye be not soon shaken in mind, or be
> troubled, neither by spirit, nor by word, nor by letter

as from us, as that the day of Christ is at hand. Let no man deceive you by any means: for that day shall not come, except there come a falling away first, and that man of sin be revealed, the son of perdition; Who opposeth and exalteth himself above all that is called God, or that is worshipped; so that he as God sitteth in the temple of God, shewing himself that he is God. (II Thessalonians 2:1-4)

Are we living at this very time in history that Paul was warning about?

13

Or An End-Time Deception

Is Christianity the Reason the World is in Trouble?

As the world continues to plunge into further darkness and despair, emerging church leaders say it is the church's fault, particularly in rigid Christians who won't bend their beliefs or convictions. While certainly Christians are not without sin, true believers are not causing the world to fall apart. It is happening for one reason alone … man's sinful condition. We are each responsible for the sin in our own lives. The Bible is clear that the penalty for sin is death. We all, each, and every one of us, have had a death sentence meted to us. But we have also been offered a free gift of salvation.

As Christians, God expects us to reach out to those suffering and in need. When Jesus dwells in a human being, He convicts and He communes with that individual. He has saved us from destruction, and He desires to live in us and fellowship with us. And He compels us to live righteously and care about those less fortunate than ourselves.

The world is in trouble because of sin. And Jesus commissioned us as believers to go out into the world and preach the wonderful Good News of His free gift of salvation to all who come to Him by faith. Satan hates this Gospel message, and he hates the messengers, the church. Is it any wonder that as this new, self-deifying reformation takes form, its followers will increasingly grow hostile to those who preach the biblical Gospel of Jesus Christ?

Ironically, the emerging church who says its main goal is to help the suffering and to help eradicate the world's problems, is not pointing the world to Jesus Christ and His body. Rather it is rejecting the atonement, locking arms with a religion (Catholicism) that teaches we are justified by works rather than by grace alone, embracing mystical practices and altered states of consciousness, and pulling these suffering lost souls further and further away from the only thing that will ever help them—a personal one-on-one relationship with Jesus Christ, who explains very clearly who He is:

> Verily, verily, I say unto you, I am the door of the sheep. All that ever came before me are thieves and robbers: but the sheep did not hear them. I am the door: by me if any man enter in, he shall be saved, and shall go in and out, and find pasture. The thief cometh not, but for to steal, and to kill, and to destroy: I am come that they might have life, and that they might have it more abundantly. I am the good shepherd: the good shepherd giveth his life for the sheep. (John 10: 7-11)

A Glorious Destiny?

There is no question about it, the world is in serious chaos, with poverty, sickness, and disease inflicting millions and millions of people. Suffering seems to be at an all time high level. Understandably, the world is looking for answers. Many religious leaders (including New Agers) believe we need a new reformation. Neale Donald Walsch, a prominent leader in the New Age, is one of those with new reformation on his mind. He states:

> We are suggesting that people become modern day Martin Luther's and take the five steps to peace and

tack them up on church house doors, as Martin
Luther did with his 95 theses in 1517 in Wittenburg,
Germany, which started of course, the first
Reformation. Our intention is to stimulate the
second great Reformation of world religion. That
is our intention, our goal and our purpose. We
intend to, in fact, inspire the second great
Reformation of world religion.[1]

Comments like the one above are quite interesting because Walsch
is not a Christian, but he speaks of a religious reformation he is
hoping to witness. But Walsch's reformation does not include Jesus
Christ. On his website Group of 1000, a statement explains what
Walsch calls "the new spirituality":

The New Spirituality is a global movement to create
the space for humanity to experience its *natural impulse
toward the divine* in a way which makes no one else
wrong for the way in which they are doing it.
(emphasis added)[2]

Walsch's reformation is one that will fulfill Thomas Merton's
vision (and Leonard Sweet's):

We are already one. But we imagine that we are not.
And what we have to recover is our original unity.[3]

Merton believed that God dwells in all humans, and what's
more, that we are part of the Divine—or to say it more succinctly, that we are all God.[4]

Thus, the new reformation on the horizon is not one that
points to Jesus Christ as the single Savior who shed His blood to
redeem sinners heading to hell. The new reformation *gospel* says
that God is in everybody, and humanity just needs to come to
this enlightened understanding. When mankind comes into full
unity, the global giants of poverty, disease, sickness, etc. will be

eradicated. It is the perfect ploy of Satan to keep souls from true salvation and eternal life. It is a grand deception that will seduce the masses—a deception the Bible has warned about, and it *will* come to pass. And yet, as the Lord is slow to anger and quick to forgive, He continues to draw and beckon while there is still time. The apostle Paul expresses the heart of the Lord:

> Take heed, brethren, lest there be in any of you an evil heart of unbelief, in departing from the living God. But exhort one another daily, while it is called To day; lest any of you be hardened through the deceitfulness of sin. For we are made partakers of Christ, if we hold the beginning of our confidence stedfast unto the end; While it is said, To day if ye will hear his voice, harden not your hearts, as in the provocation. (Hebrews 3:12-15)

We must ask ourselves: Is the emergent reformation truly a new and God-given reformation that we are witnessing? Or is it no different from Neale Donald Walsch's or Thomas Merton's, in which man is lifted up and deified? While it appears the world is crumbling before our very eyes, despite continued efforts to help the poor and suffering and to stop crime and terrorism, governments, nations, and the people within them have decided that Jesus Christ is not the answer. The emerging church has solidified this position by placing such emphasis on ushering in the kingdom of God now and minimizing the true Gospel message.

I realize that most Christians would probably laugh incredulously if someone told them they were heading toward the spirituality of Neale Donald Walsch. Most of them would see themselves as orthodox and biblically-based and certainly not as New Agers entering some kind of new reformation that says everyone is God. But I have tried to document in this book how the emerging church bridges Christianity and this "new spirituality." And the question we Christians must ask ourselves is, is this a bridge I am willing to walk on and eventually cross?

I watch prominent Christian leaders today, embracing and promoting many of the individuals I have discussed in this book. They seem to be following these new reformation evangelists blindly, without question. And right behind them comes the majority of the church in general following these leaders.

I Timothy 4:1 says: "Now the Spirit speaketh expressly, that in the latter times some shall depart from the faith, giving heed to seducing spirits, and doctrines of devils." I exhort every believer to consider this: once the departure from faith begins, it is difficult to turn back. I challenge you to carefully and prayerfully consider what the emerging church is really presenting.

We have seen the actions and heard the words of those who are attempting to undo the very tenants of the Christian faith; they have now come to the point of saying they wish to destroy Christianity. Listen to the words of Alice Bailey as she describes her *prophesied* "Coming One," whom she calls "the Christ":

> The reason He has not come again is that the needed work has not been done by His followers in all countries. His coming is largely dependent, as we shall later see, upon the establishing of right human relations. [T]he church has hindered … and has not helped because of its fanatical zeal to make "Christians" of all peoples and not followers of Christ. It has emphasized theological doctrine, and not love.[5]

A Global Community

Over 400,000 churches have now participated in Rick Warren's Purpose Driven program. Quite obviously, millions of Christians have bought into the idea that the details of Christ's return are none of our business, and we must help usher in a new reformation to eradicate the global problems facing the earth. According to Rick Warren, we accomplish this only if we all work together.

This togetherness/community mindset is the same message that Alice Bailey referred to as "right human relations" and the same one the emerging church hopes to convey to the people of the world. Personal, individual relationships with Christ are considered self-centeredness,[6] because they don't focus on the global, common good. Communal spirituality is seen as the only path to the world's survival. Listen to today's new reformation thinkers:

> The church is only an anticipation of the full, promised community of the whole world ... the church itself is not a goal of God's creation.[7]—Walter Brueggemann, *An Emergent Manifesto of Hope*

> The Church, in all its expressions—Catholic, Evangelical, Pentecostal, Protestant and many others—has 2.3 billion followers.... Let's use the grassroots network that is already on the ground. It's time to lay aside our prejudices and work together.[8]—Rick Warren, *Forbes* magazine

> We are emerging into a new era of Christian faith as a "living color" global community. ... It is immediately clear that this kind of emergence must lead to a convergence ... a kind of relationship that has never before existed.[9]—Brian McLaren

Unfortunately, the "global community" so often spoken of in the emerging church camp is disguised language for a worldwide religious body that incorporates all belief systems. As Neale Donald Walsch said, It's a "global movement ... which makes no one else wrong for the way in which they are doing it."

"The Sign of Thy Coming"

The rate at which this global unity is occurring should tell us that the return of Christ could very well be near. But not everyone who professes the name of Christ is going to be ready. Jesus Himself asked, "[W]hen the Son of man cometh, shall he find faith on the earth?" (Luke 18:8). As in the parable of the ten virgins (Matthew 25:1-13), many will not be ready when the Lord returns. Many will have fallen asleep.

Do you remember what Jesus told the disciples when they asked Him, "what shall be the sign of thy coming, and of the end of the world?" (Matthew 24:3) He did not tell them the whole world would be experiencing a spiritual revival, turning to the Gospel. Rather he said:

> Take heed that no man deceive you. For many shall come in my name, saying, I am Christ; and shall deceive many. (Matthew 24: 4-5)

Jesus warned that in the days before He came back, there would be such a great falling away that "many" would be deceived. The word *many* in Greek means *a vast amount* or *multitudes*. In fact, the majority of the signs Jesus said to expect dealt with spiritual deception. He even forewarned there would be false appearances or manifestations of false Christs that would be associated with lying signs and wonders (Matthew 24: 23-25).

The apostle Paul also issued Jesus' warning about a time of deception that would dupe the whole world:

> For the mystery of iniquity doth already work: only he who now letteth will let, until he be taken out of the way. And then shall that Wicked be revealed, whom the Lord shall consume with the spirit of his mouth, and shall destroy with the brightness of his coming: Even him whose coming is after the working of Satan with all power and signs and lying wonders, And with all deceivableness of unrighteousness in them that perish; because they received not the love of the truth, that they might be saved. And for this cause God shall send them strong delusion, that they should believe a lie. (II Thessalonians 2:7-11)

Notice how Satan's deceptive plan operates. As with the temptation of Eve in the garden, he will first call into question what God has said, influencing many to reject the Bible as the inerrant Word of God, or they will get lost in strange interpretations pulled out of context. Next, he will undermine the Word of God as taking second place to experience. After all, doesn't God want everyone to be happy and to "love" all? This love typically translates into accepting everyone and their strange beliefs as well. Ultimately, deception means rejecting the truth of God's Word for a lie all the while thinking that God is being served.

Certainly, the words of warning Paul wrote to the church at Corinth regarding Satan's seductive plans are very relevant today:

> But I fear, lest by any means, as the serpent beguiled Eve through his subtlety, so your minds should be corrupted from the simplicity that is in Christ. For if he that cometh preacheth another Jesus, whom we have not preached, or if ye receive another spirit, which ye have not received, or another gospel, which ye have not accepted, ye might well bear with him. (II Corinthians 11: 3-4)

Many have forgotten these basic warnings found in Scripture regarding the last days when another gospel and another Jesus will be presented to a deceived world.

Emergent Reformation—What Should We Expect?

The emerging church movement cannot be ignored. It has the potential to reshape or redefine Christianity, as many of its leaders claim it will.

While some say these changes are comparable to those that took place during the 16th century reformation, the emerging church reformation is actually a reversal of what occurred in the past. Rather than pointing the lost to the Word of God and out of an apostate church, many are being led to dogmas, traditions, and extrabiblical experiences.

While there will be a remnant that will hold true to the Scriptures, these Bible-believing Christians will be a minority. As has always been the case throughout the history of the body of Christ, persecution and ridicule await those who refuse to accept Kingdom Now and utopian theologies. As the world prepares for the *man of peace*, those who hold fast to a biblical view of the end times will be seen as trouble-making oddballs and a menace to society and world government.

As the world becomes more and more resentful toward Israel, the view that the church takes the place of Israel, leaving Israel no prophetic significance (replacement theology), will become increasingly accepted within Christianity at large. Those who believe the Book of Revelation predicts an apocalyptic future will be considered a danger to society and the wellbeing of this new kingdom of God.

The ecumenical nature of the emerging church indicates the process to reunite with Rome has already begun. As many embrace experience-based spirituality through the promotion of contemplative/mystical prayer, what we know right now as the Christian faith (based upon God's Word) will transform to a faith based on subjective experiences.

Manifestations of the spiritual dimension will appear, and deceptive signs and wonders will abound. More attention will be paid to *Mary*, the Mother of the Eucharistic Jesus. Appearances of this *Jesus* will manifest around the world accompanied with healings and other miraculous phenomenon.

Finally, these lying signs and wonders will be so effective, and the majority of the world's people so seduced through meditative states, that the world's religions will come together for the cause of peace. The new Christ, or as Alice Bailey calls him the "Coming One"[10] will be established in the name of God and he will expect all to bow down to him and worship him.

While we live in spiritually dark times, and it appears the majority of people do not discern the signs of the times or the magnitude of the deception, the Lord is faithful to His church. Though what is happening may seem overwhelming, we have the Bible and the Holy Spirit to guide us in all wisdom and truth. The light of God's Word penetrates the darkness, and those who are being delivered from deception see what is taking place. Those of us who see must continue to proclaim the truth in strength and with love. As Paul instructed Timothy:

> And the servant of the Lord must not strive; but be gentle unto all men, apt to teach, patient, In meekness instructing those that oppose themselves; if God peradventure will give them repentance to the acknowledging of the truth; And that they may recover themselves out of the snare of the devil, who are taken captive by him at his will. (II Timothy 2: 24-26)

There are still pastors and churches dedicated to proclaiming the truth. Find out where they are and support them. If you are in a location where this does not seem to be possible, seek out materials that are available from solid Bible-based Christian ministries and hold Bible studies in your homes.

When Jesus returns, He will not find a utopian world filled with peace but one in shambles, unrest, violence, and war for having forsaken the Word of God, the true Gospel, and the One true God. Rather than being a time when He will praise the world for discovering its christ-consciousness, He will come as a judge and powerful King.

In concluding, may I leave you with the words Paul wrote to Timothy regarding these difficult times in which we live:

> I charge thee therefore before God, and the Lord Jesus Christ, who shall judge the quick and the dead at his appearing and his kingdom; Preach the word; be instant in season, out of season; reprove, rebuke, exhort with all long suffering and doctrine.
>
> For the time will come when they will not endure sound

doctrine; but after their own lusts shall they heap to themselves teachers, having itching ears; And they shall turn away their ears from the truth, and shall be turned unto fables. But watch thou in all things, endure afflictions, do the work of an evangelist, make full proof of thy ministry. (II Timothy 4: 1-5)

The Lord through His Word warned us that perilous times *would* come. But He also made it clear that the church of Jesus Christ would survive in the midst of great deception and attack on the Christian faith. In a profound discourse between Jesus and His disciples, Jesus assured them of this very thing:

When Jesus came into the coasts of Caesarea Philippi, he asked his disciples, saying, Whom do men say that I the Son of man am?

And they said, Some say that thou art John the Baptist: some, Elias; and others, Jeremias, or one of the prophets.

He saith unto them, But whom say ye that I am?

And Simon Peter answered and said, Thou art the Christ, the Son of the living God.

And Jesus answered and said unto him, Blessed art thou, Simon Barjona: for flesh and blood hath not revealed it unto thee, but my Father which is in heaven. And I say also unto thee, That thou art Peter, and upon this rock I will build my church; and the gates of hell shall not prevail against it. (Matthew 16:13-18)

The Lord is faithful to uphold His church. Keep looking to Him—He is coming soon!

Endnotes

1/A New Kind of Church

1. Brian McLaren, *A New Kind of Christian* (San Francisco, CA: Jossey-Bass, 2001), p. xvi, citing from McLaren's 1st book, *Reinventing Your Church* (Grand Rapids, MI: Zondervan, 1998), pp. 13, 35-36.

2. Antonio Mora, "New Faithful Practice Away From Churches" (*Chicago News*, CBS Broadcasting, July 10, 2006).

3. Ibid.

4. Ibid.

5. Ibid.

6. Brian McLaren, *A is for Abductive*, (Grand Rapids, MI: Zondervan, 2003), p. 239.

7. Robert Wright, Professor Corban College, "The Emerging (Emergent) Church" (http://www.lighthousetrailsresearch.com/The Emerging Church.doc).

8. Brian McLaren, *Church on the Other Side* (Grand Rapids, MI: Zondervan, 2000 edition, formerly titled *Reinventing Your Church*), pp. 7-8).

9. Dan Kimball, *The Emerging Church* (Grand Rapids, MI: Zondervan, 2003), p. 60.

10. Ibid.

11. Ibid.

12. Mark Driscoll, "A Pastoral Perspective on the Emergent Church" (*Criswell Theological Review*, Spring 2006), p. 88.

13. Ibid.

14. Spencer Burke, *Making Sense of Church* (El Cajon, CA: Emergent YS, 2003), p. 25.

15. Ibid., p. 19.

2/The Birth of the Emerging Church

1. Mark Driscoll, "A Pastoral Perspective on the Emergent Church," op. cit., pp. 87-89.

Note: Because of the ever-changing nature of the Internet, websites listed in this section may not remain active. However, all links were checked and accessed just prior to *Faith Undone* going to press.

2. Bob Buford, *Game Plan* (Grand Rapids, MI: Zondervan, 1997), pp. 169-170.

3. "Drucker's Impact on Leadership Network" (Leadership Network Advance, November 14, 2005, http://www.pursuantgroup.com/leadnet/advance/nov05o.htm).

4. Bob Buford from his website, Active Energy, http://www.active energy .net/templates/cusactiveenergy/details. asp?id= 29646 &PID = 207602.

5. Bob Buford, *Halftime* (Grand Rapids, MI: Zondervan, 1994), dedication page.

6. Peter Drucker, "The Unfashionable Kierkegaard" (1933: http://www.peterdrucker.at/en/texts/p_drucker_kierkeg_en.pdf).

7. Peter Steinfels, "A Man's Spiritual Journey from Kierkegaard to General Motors" (*New York Times*, November 19, 2005).

8. Peter Drucker, "The Unfashionable Kierkegaard," op cit.

9. Jack E. Mulder, Jr., "Faith and nothingness in Kierkegaard: A mystical reading of the God-relationship (Soren Kierkegaard) (Dissertation at Purdue University, 2004, http://docs.lib.purdue.edu/dissertations/AAI3150807/).

10. Peter Drucker, "The Unfashionable Kierkegaard" op. cit.

11. Bob Buford endorsement of Jim Collins at http://www.activeenergy.net/templates/cusactiveenergy/details.asp?id=29646&PID=308743&Style=.

12. Michael Ray and Rochelle Myers, *Creativity in Business* (New York, NY: Broadway Books, 1986), back flap.

13. Ibid., pp. 37, 142.

14. Jim Collins endorsement of *Creativity in Business*, from Creativity in Business website: http://www.creativityinbusiness.org.

15. Michael Ray, *The Highest Goal*, (San Francisco, CA: Berrett-Koehler Publishers, Inc, 2004), p. 92.

16. Ibid.

17. Ibid.

18. Bob Buford's website, http://www.activeenergy.net/templates/cusactiveenergy/details.asp?id=29646&PID=313434.

19. Peter Drucker, *Landmarks of Tomorrow* (New York, NY: Harper & Brothers, 1959), p. ix.

20. Ibid., p. x.

21. Ibid.

22. Ibid., p. 21.

23. Ibid., back cover flap.

24. Several of Martin Buber's writings and books reflect his embracing of both Hasidism and mysticism in general. A few of those are: *Ecstatic Confessions: The Heart of Mysticism, Tales of the Hasidim, Hasidism and Modern Man.*

25. Martin Buber, *The Way of Man* (New York, NY: Kensington Publishing Corporation, 1964, 1994 Citadel Press edition), p. 5.

26. Frederic and Mary Ann Brussat, "Birthday of Martin Buber (*Spirituality and Practice*, http://www .spirituality and practice.com/days/features.php?id=16577).

27. Martin Buber, *Between Man and Man* (New York, NY: Routledge Classics, 2002, first published in 1947), p. 219.

28. Drucker, *Landmarks of Tomorrow*, op. cit., pp. 264-265.

29. John E. Flaherty, *Peter Drucker: Shaping the Managerial Mind* (San Francisco, CA: Jossey-Bass, 1999), p. 258.

30. Michael Schwarz, "Early Influences upon Peter Drucker's Perception of 'the Public Interest'" (Royal Melbourne Institute of Technology, 2002, http://www.iipe.org/conference2002/papers/Schwartz.pdf).

31. Leader to Leader Institute, *Thought Leaders Forum*: http://www.leadertoleader.org/knowledgecenter/thoughtleaders/booklist.html.

32. Peter Steinfels, "A Man's Spiritual Journey from Kierkegaard to General Motors," op. cit. ("The future was with 'pastoral churches,' he argued, ones that put a higher priority on answering people's needs than perpetuating some specific doctrine or ritual or institutional structure.")

33. Leith Anderson, *A Church for the 21st Century* (Minneapolis, MN: Bethany House Publishers, 1992), p. 17.

34. Webster's Dictionary: http://www.m-w.com/dictionary/paradigm.

35. Rick Warren's endorsement of Bob Buford's book *Halftime*, 2nd page of endorsements in front of book.

36. Rick Warren, "Myths of the Modern Mega-Church" (Event hosted by the Pew Forum on Religion, 2005), see transcript: http://pewforum.org/events/index.php?EventID=80.

37. Bob Buford, information gathered at http://www.activeenergy.net/templates/cusactiveenergy/details.asp?id=29646&PID=207455.

38. The Foundation Conferences: http://activeenergy.org/templates/cusactiveenergy/details.asp?id=29646&PID=208258&Style=.

39. Quote from Rick Warren's e-newsletter, issue 46, April 3, 2002, http://www.pastors.com/RWMT/?ID=46.

40. Leonard Sweet, Rick Warren, *Tides of Change* audio series (Abingdon Press, 2005).

41. *Church Report*, "The 50 Most Influential Christians" (2006, http://www.thechurchreport.com/mag_article.php?mid= 875& mname =January).

42. Peter Drucker, *Landmarks of Tomorrow*, op. cit., pp. x, 2.

43. Ibid., p. 21.

44. Leonard Sweet, *Quantum Spirituality: A Postmodern Apologetic* (Dayton, OH: Whaleprints, First Edition, 1991), p. viii.

45. Ibid.

46. Ibid., p. 7.

47. Ibid., p. viii.

48. Ibid., pp. viii-ix.

49. Ibid., p. ix.

50. Matthew Fox, *The Coming of the Cosmic Christ* (San Francisco, CA: HarperCollins, 1988), p. 5.

51. Ibid., pp. 234-235.

52. Leonard Sweet, *Quantum Spirituality*, op. cit., p. 76.

53. Bob Buford, endorsement on Leonard Sweet's website at http://www.leonardsweet.com/sweetened/books.asp.

54. Dan Kimball, *The Emerging Church*, op. cit., citing Rick Warren in the foreword, p. 7.

55. Youth Specialties' 30th Anniversary: http://www.youth specialties .com/about/30th.

56. Ibid.

57. Malcolm Gladwell, "How Rick Warren Built His Ministry" (*New Yorker*, September 12, 2005, http://www.pastors.com/RWMT/article.asp?ArtID=9636).

58. "News Corporation: Earnings Release for the Quarter and Fiscal Year Ended June 30th 2004," accessed online at http://www.newscorp.com/Report2004/2004_annual_report.pdf.

59. Steve Boggan, "Catholic anger at Murdoch's papal knighthood (The (London) Independent, February 17, 1998).

60. From the Youth Ministry & Spirituality Project website: http://www.ymsp.org/about/history.html.

61. "Youth Ministry and Spirituality Project Receives Major Grant," (*Youth Specialties News*, January 11, 2001).

62. Press release from Zondervan, Tara Powers, "Leading Christian Publisher Zondervan Acquires Ministry Organization Youth Specialties" (May

2, 2006).

63. "Leadership Network's Top-Selling Books and Why" (Leadership Network Advance, November 2005, http://www.pursuant group.com/leadnet/advance/nov05s2a.htm).

64. "25 Most Influential Evangelicals" (*Time*, February 7, 2005).

65. Lori Leibovich, "Generation: A look inside fundamentalism's answer to MTV: the postmodern church" (*Mother Jones*, July/August 1998).

66. From Bob Buford's website: http://www.activeenergy.net/templates/cusactiveenergy/details.asp?id=29646&PID=207455.

3/A "New" Faith for the 21st Century

1. Doug Pagitt, *Church Re-Imagined* (Grand Rapids, MI: Zondervan, 2005), pp. 17, 19.

2. Ibid., p. 41.

3. Ibid.

4. Ibid., pp. 27, 29.

5. Brian McLaren, *A Generous Orthodoxy* (Grand Rapids, MI: Zondervan, 2004).

6. Pagitt, *Church Re-Imagined*, op. cit., pp. 17, 19.

7. Ibid., p. 166.

8. Doug Pagitt, *Church Re-Imagined*, op. cit., p. 167.

9. Stephen B. Bevans, *Models of Contextual Theology* (Maryknoll, NY: Orbis Books, Seventh Printing, November 2000, http://www.cca.orghk/resources/ctc/ctc94-02/1.Yuzon.html), p. 1.

10. Paul L. Lehmann, "Contextual Theology" (Theology Today, Princeton Theological Seminary, 1972, http://theologytoday.ptsem.edu/apr1972/v29-1-editorial2.htm).

11. Dean Flemming, *Contextualization in the New Testament* (Downers Grove, IL: InterVarsity Press, 2005), p. 14.

12. Ibid, pp. 14-15.

13. Brian McLaren, *Church on the Other Side*, op. cit., p. 68.

14. Dan Kimball, *They Like Jesus but Not the Church* (Grand Rapids, MI: Zondervan, 2007), p. 167.

15. Doug Pagitt and Tony Jones, *An Emergent Manifesto of Hope* (Grand Rapids, MI: Baker Publishing Group, 2007), Will Sampson section, "The End of Reinvention," pp. 155-156.

16. Ibid., p. 157.

17. Ibid., p. 158.

18. Ibid.

19. Ibid., p. 159.

20. Ibid.

21. Interview by David Kuo with Rick Warren, "Pastor Rick Warren of Purpose-Driven Life talks to Beliefnet about Africa" (Belief net.com, http://www.beliefnet.com/story/177/story_17718.html).

22. Brian McLaren, *A Generous Orthodoxy*, op. cit., p. 22.

23. Doug Pagitt, *Church Re-Imagined*, op. cit., p. 102.

4/Riding the Emerging Church Wave

1. Leonard Sweet, *Quantum Spirituality*, op. cit., p. 218.

2. Leonard Sweet, *Soul Tsunami* (*Grand Rapids, MI:* Zondervan Publishing House: Grand Rapids, MI, p. 34.

3. Ibid., 420.

4. Leonard Sweet, *Quantum Spirituality*, op. cit., p. 69.

5. Leith Anderson, *A Church for the 21st Century*, op. cit., p. 21.

6. Dan Kimball, *The Emerging Church*, op. cit., pp. 13-14.

7. Jim L. Wilson, *Future Church* (Nashville, TN: Broadman & Holman, 2004), pp. 38-39.

8. Dan Kimball, *The Emerging Church*, op. cit., p. 127.

9. Ibid., p. 133.

10. Ibid., p. 143.

11. Ibid., p. 155.

12. Ibid., p. 116.

13. Robb Redman, *The Great Worship Awakening* (San Francisco, CA: Jossey-Bass, 2002), p. 129.

14. Ibid., p. 197.

15. Julie B. Sevig, *The Lutheran*, "Ancient New" (*The Lutheran*, September, 2001).

16. Ibid., Sevig citing Leonard Sweet from *Soul Tsunami*.

17. Ibid., citing Karen Ward.

18. Leonard Sweet, *Postmodern Pilgrims* (Nashville, TN: Broadman & Holman Publishers, 2000), p. 28.

19. Chuck Fromm, "The Impact of the Image" (*Worship Leader Magazine*, January-February 2005).

20. Ibid.

21. Ibid.

5/ Ancient Future Worship

1. Dan Kimball, *The Emerging Church*, op. cit., p. 136.

2. "The National Reevaluation Forum: The Story of the Gathering" (Youth Leader Networks -NEXT Special Edition, 1999, http://web.archive.org/web/19991007223358/www.youngleader.org/specialedition/index.html), pp. 1-2.

3. Ibid.

4. Ibid.

5. Robert Webber, "Wanted: Ancient-Future Talent" (*Worship Leader*, May/June 2005), p. 10.

6. Ibid.

7. Robert Webber, *Ancient-Future Faith* (Grand Rapids, MI: Baker Books, 1999), p. 135.

8. Ibid.

9. Ibid.

10. Ibid.

11. Ibid., p. 85.

12. Raphael Brown, *Saints Who Saw Mary* (Rockford, IL: Tan Books and Publishing, Inc., 1994 edition), p. 25.

13. Ibid., p. 71.

14. Ibid., p. 119.

15. Ibid., p. 126.

16. Ibid., p. 108.

17. Ibid., p. 21.

18. "The National Reevaluation Forum: The Story of the Gathering," op. cit., pp. 3-8, citing Mark Driscoll, "Themes of the Emerging Church."

19. Dan Kimball, *The Emerging Church*, op. cit., p. 127.

20. Ibid., p. 136.

21. Ibid., p. 169.

22. Kimball, "A-Maze-ing Prayer" (*Christianity Today*, October 1, 2001, http://ctlibrary.com/9665).

23. Ibid.

24. Ibid.

25. Mark Tooley, "Labyrinths are Latest Fad for Spiritual Seekers" (The Institute for Religion and Democracy, Ecumenical News, November 21, 2001, http://www.ird-renew.org/site/apps/nl/content2.asp?c=fvKVLfMVIsG&b=470197&ct=416271).

26. Ibid.

27. Doug Pagitt, *Church Re-imagined*, op. cit., p. 103.

28. Zachary Reid, "Feeling the beat: The spiritual side of drum circles" (*Richmond Times Dispatch*, Mar 10, 2007).

29. Ibid.

30. "World wide Drumming event, Heartfelt Arena" (One World Beat 2006 event, May 6, 2006, http://www.christians.co.za/news/newsarticle.asp?nid=117#).

31. Zachary Reid, "Feeling the beat: The spiritual side of drum circles" op. cit.

32. Ibid.

33. Johan Malan, University of Limpopo, South Africa, "African Drumming Becomes a World-wide Phenomenon" (http://www.lighthousetrailsresearch.com/drummingjohan.htm).

34. Ibid.

35. Asher Mains "Drumming in Intergenerational Worship" (Calvin Institute of Christian Worship, March 2005, http://www.calvin.edu/worship/lit_arts/music/intergen_drumming.php).

36. Johan Malan, "African African Drumming Becomes a World-wide Phenomenon," op. cit.

37. Dale Dirksen, "Old is 'New' Again" (*Passport Magazine*, Fall 2005, Vol. 64. No. 2, http://www.briercrest.ca/passport/online/articles/default.asp?id=497&cat=top_story), p. 6.

38. Ibid., pp. 6-7.

39. Ibid., p. 7.

40. Ibid.

41. Ibid.

42. Robert Webber, *Ancient-Future Faith*, op. cit., pp. 88-89, italics in original.

43. Ibid., p. 89.

44. Ibid.

45. Douglas Mosey, "Importance of Studying the Church Fathers" (International Catholic University, http://home.comcast.net/~icuweb/c01701.htm).

46. Ibid.

47. Marcus Grodi, *Journeys Home* (Goleta, CA: Queenship Publishing Company, 1997), p. xvi.

48. Ibid., p. 88.

49. Ibid. p. 89.

6/When West Meets East

1. Thomas Keating, *Open Mind, Open Heart* (New York, NY: The Continuum International Publishing Group, 2006 Twentieth Anniversary Edition), pp. 18, 21, 23.

2. Marilyn Norquist Gustin, *Inward Journey* © 1991 p. 29.

3. Jacquelyn Small, *Awakening in Time*, New York: Bantam Books, 1991, p. 261.

4. Thomas Keating, *Open Mind, Open Heart*, op. cit. (online edition (http://www.centeringprayer.com/OpenHeart/open02.htm), chapter 1.

5. Ray Yungen, *A Time of Departing*, (Silverton, OR: Lighthouse Trails Publishing, 2nd edition, 2006), p. 15.

6. Brian Flynn, *Running Against The Wind* (Silverton, OR: Lighthouse Trails Publishing, 2005, 2nd ed.), p. 137.

7. Carol Zimmermann, citing Pope John Paul II, "Priests say new mysteries of rosary are welcome addition" (*Catholic News Service* October 24, 2002, http://web.archive.org/web/20030520221531/http://www.nccatholic.org/news.php?ArtID=655).

8. *St. John of the Cross on Contemplation* (http://www.inner explora tions.com/catchspmys/fromp1.htm).

9. Rob Baker and Gray Henry, Editors, *Merton and Sufism* (Louisville, KY: Fons Vitae, 1999), p. 69.

10. Ibid., p. 41.

11. Henri Nouwen, *Thomas Merton, Contemplative Critic* (San Francisco, CA: Harper & Row Publishers, 1981 edition), p. 28.

12. Ibid., p. 29.

13. William Shannon, *Silent Lamp, The Thomas Merton Story* (New York, NY: Crossroad Publishing Company, 1992), p. 276.

14. Thomas Merton, *Conjectures of a Guilty Bystander* (Garden City, NY: Doubleday Publishers, 1989), pp. 157-158.

15. Statistic on Barclay Press website, www.barclaypress.com, where Richard Foster is a featured article writer.

16. "The Top 50 Books That Have Shaped Evangelicals" (*Christianity Today*, October 2006, http://www.christianitytoday.com/ct/2006/october/23.51.html).

17. Richard Foster, *Celebration of Discipline* (San Francisco, CA: Harper & Row, 1978 edition), p. 13.

18. Tilden Edwards, *Spiritual Friend* (New York, NY: Paulist Press, 1980), p. 18.

19. Ibid., p. 19.

20. Richard Foster and James Bryan Smith, *Devotional Classics* (San Francisco, CA: HarperCollins, 1993 edition), p. 61.

21. Ibid., p. 66.

22. Richard Foster and Emilie Griffin, *Spiritual Classics* (San Francisco, CA: HarperCollins, 2000, First Edition), p. 17.

23. Ibid.

24. Richard Foster, *Devotional Classics*, op. cit., p. 61.

25. Ray Yungen, *A Time of Departing*, 2nd ed., op. cit., p. 74.

26. Paul T. Harris: "Silent Teaching: The Life of Dom John Main" (*Spirituality Today*, Winter 1988, Vol. 40, #4, http://www.spiritualitytoday.org/spir2day/884043harris.html#6), pp. 320-332.

27. Richard Foster, *Spiritual Classics*, op. cit., p. 155.

28. Paul T. Harris: "Silent Teaching: The Life of Dom John Main," op. cit.

29. Kay Warren on the Ministry Toolbox (Issue #54, 6/5/2002, http://www.pastors.com/RWMT/?ID=54).

30. Henri Nouwen, *In the Name of Jesus* (New York, NY: Crossroad Publishing Company, 2000), pp. 31-32.

31. Henri Nouwen, *The Way of the Heart* (New York, NY: The Ballantine Publishing Group, First Ballantine Books/Epiphany Edition, 1983, 15th Printing, July 1991), p. 64.

32. Henri Nouwen, *Sabbatical Journey* (New York, NY: Crossroad Publishing, 1998), p. 149.

33. Ibid., p. 51.

34. Henri Nouwen, *Here and Now* (The Crossroad Publishing Company, Inc., August 25, 1994), p. 22.

35. Richard Foster, "Spiritual Formation: A Pastoral Letter" (January 18, 2004, http://www.theooze.com/articles/article.cfm?id=744).

36. Richard Foster, *Be Still* DVD (Fox Home Entertainment, 2006), section titled "Contemplative Prayer."

37. Agnieszka Tennant, "Yes to Yoga" (*Christianity Today*, May 2005, http://www.christianity today.com/ct/2005/120/42.0.html).

38. Ibid.

39. Ibid.

40. Ibid.

41. Ibid.

42. Yogi Baba Prem, Vedavisharada, CYI, C.ay, C.va, "There is No Christian Yoga" (October 2006, http://yogibabaprem.sulekha.com/blog/post/

2006/10/there-is-no-christian-yoga.htm).

43. Brian Flynn, *Running Against the Wind*, op. cit. p. 132.

44. Ibid., pp. 132-133.

45. Ibid., pp. 195-196.

46. Richard Foster, *Prayer: Finding the Heart's True Home* (Harper: San Francisco, 1992, First Edition), p. 157.

47. Ibid., p. 156.

48. Ibid.

49. Richard Foster, *Celebration of Discipline* (San Francisco, CA: Harper & Row, 1978 edition), p. 13.

7/Monks, Mystics, and the Ancient Wisdom

1. Spencer Burke, "From the Third Floor to the Garage," online chapter from *Stories of Emergence* published by Zondervan/Youth Specialties, 2003, http://www.theooze.com/etrek/spencerburke.cfm.

2. Max Lucado, *Cure for the Common Life* (Nashville, TN: Thomas Nelson, 2005), pp. 3, 215.

3. Martin Buber, *The Way of Man*, op. cit., p. 17.

4. Ibid.

5. Martin Buber, *Ecstatic Confessions: The Heart of Mysticism* (New York, NY: Harper & Row, Publishers, Inc, 1985), p xv.

6. Ibid., xvi.

7. Tony Jones, *The Sacred Way* (Grand Rapids, MI: Zondervan, 2005), quote by Phyllis Tickle in foreword, pp. 7-8.

8. Generation X monastery, see "24-7 Prayer" by Anne McCarthy for some background information on the Reading Boiler Room (*Relevant Magazine*, http://www.bananie.com/archives/24-7%20article(2).doc).

9. Tony Jones, *The Sacred Way*, op. cit., p. 16.

10. Ibid., p. 17.

11. Ibid., p. 65.

12. Ibid., pp. 70, 71.

13. Ibid., p. 71.

14. Ibid., pp. 17-18.

15. Mike Perschon, "Desert Youth Worker: Disciplines, Mystics and the Contemplative Life," (Youth Specialties, http://www.youth specialties.com/articles/topics/spirituality/desert.php).

16. Ibid.

17. Ibid.

18. Ibid.

19. Ray Yungen, *A Time of Departing*, op. cit., p. 176.

20. Laurie Cabot, *The Power of the Witch* (New York, NY: Bantam Doubleday Dell Publishing, 1989), p. 173.

21. Ibid.

22. Ron Miller citing Aldous Huxley, *As Above, So Below* (New York, NY: G. P. Putnam's Sons, 1992), p. 2.

23. Tony Campolo, *Speaking My Mind* (Nashville, TN: Thomas Nelson, 2004), pp. 149-150.

24. Cathleen Falsani, citing Brian McLaren in "Maverick minister taps new generation" (*Chicago Sun Times*, June 4, 2006, http://findarticles.com/p/articles/mi_qn4155/is_20060604/ai_n16455238/pg_1).

25. "The 50 Most Influential Christians" (*The Church Report*, January 2007, http://www.thechurchreport.com/mag_ article. php? mid =875&mname=January).

26. Cathleen Falsani citing Rob Bell, "Maverick minister taps new generation" op. cit.

27. Andy Crouch citing Rob Bell, "Emergent Mystique" (*Christianity Today*, November 2004).

28. Rob Bell, *Velvet Elvis* (Grand Rapids, MI: Zondervan, 2005), p. 192.

29. From Ken Wilber's website, http://www.kenwilber.com/personal/ILP/MyILP.html.

30. Leonard Sweet, *Quantum Spirituality*, op. cit., p. 11.

31. Rob Bell, *Velvet Elvis*, op. cit., p. 157.

32. Quote from the March 19, 2006 service at Mars Hill. Audio file of this service was available on Mars Hill website: http://www.marshill.org/teaching.

33. See Dominican Center at Marywood: http://www.dominicancenter.com/Bodywork/432.

34. William Lee Rand, "Developing Your Reiki Practice" (International Center for Reiki Training, http://www.reiki.org/ReikiPractice/PracticeHomepage.html).

35. Ray Yungen, *A Time of Departing*, 2nd ed., op. cit., p. 13.

36. Tony Campolo, *Letters to a Young Evangelical* (New York, NY: Perseus Books Group (Basic Books), 2006), p. 20.

37. Ibid., p. 25.

38. Ibid., p. 26.

39. Ibid.

40. Carol and Rick Weber, "Journeying Together" (*Thin Places*, April/May 2007, Year Eight, Issue Four, Number 46), p. 1.

41. Chris Baker, "A Positive Articulation of Marcus Borg's Theology" (Sandlestraps Sanctuary blog, April 5, 2007, http://sandalstraps.blog spot.com/2007/04/positive-articulation-of-marcus-borgs_05.html.

42. Marcus Borg, *The Heart of Christianity* (New York, NY: HarperCollins, First HarperCollins Paperback Edition, 2004), p. 155.

43. Ibid.

44. Mike Perschon, "Desert Youth Worker: Disciplines, Mystics and the Contemplative Life,", op. cit.

45. Tony Campolo, *Letters to a Young Evangelical*, op. cit., p. 30.

46. Ignatius of Loyola (1491-1556), founder of the Society of Jesus (Jesuits), known also for his mystical experiences, now called The Spiritual Exercises of Ignatius of Loyola. These are becoming increasingly popular within the evangelical spiritual formation movement.

47. Tony Campolo, *Speaking My Mind*, op. cit., p. 72.

48. Tony Campolo, *Letters to a Young Evangelical*, op. cit., p. 31.

49. Brian McLaren, *A Generous Orthodoxy*, op. cit., p. 246.

50. J.P. Moreland and Klaus Issler, *The Lost Virtue of Happiness* (Colorado Springs, CO: NavPress, 2006), back page.

51. Ibid., p. 51.

52. Ibid.

53. Henri Nouwen, *Reaching Out* (New York, NY: Doubleday, Image Book edition, 1986), p. 38.

54. J.P. Moreland and Klaus Issler, *The Lost Virtue of Happiness*, op. cit. pp. 54-55.

55. Ibid., p. 90.

56. Ibid., p. 92.

57. Ibid., p. 93.

58. Ibid., p. 90.

59. Brian McLaren, *A Generous Orthodoxy*, op. cit., p. 59.

60. Ibid., p. 62.

61. Ibid., p. 59.

62. Ibid., p. 62.

8/The Second Coming of the Eucharistic Christ

1. According to Catholic teaching, the Eucharist is the central compo-

nent of the Mass. It is believed that when a priest consecrates the Communion bread, the wafer is no longer bread, but the actual body, blood, soul, and divinity of Jesus Christ. For a better understanding of the Eucharist and the Catholic's New Evangelization plan , read Roger Oakland's book, *Another Jesus*, Lighthouse Trails Edition, Summer 2007. Also for extensive research on Catholicism, see the website of former Catholic priest, Richard Bennett (Berean Beacon): http://www.berean beacon.org.

2. *Catechism of the Catholic Church*, para. 1374, page 383.6

3. H. J. Schroeder, *The Canons and Decrees of The Council of Trent* (Rockford, IL: Tan Books and Publishers, 1978), page 79, Canon 1.

4. Joseph Cardinal Ratzinger, "The New Evangelization" (http://www.ewtn.com/new_evangelization/Ratzinger.htm).

5. H. J. Schroeder, *The Canons and Decrees of The Council of Trent*, op. cit., p. 79. Canon 1.

6. Ibid., page 80, Canon 8.

7. *Zenit: The World Seen From Rome*, "Why the Pope Would Write an Encyclical on the Eucharist: To Rekindle Amazement," cited April 17, 2003, http://www.zenit.org.

8. "Pope Benedict calls on faithful to intensify devotion to Eucharistic Jesus," http://www.catholicnewsagency.com/new.php?n=3686.

9. Ibid.

10. "Pope Benedict on Corpus Christi" (*Zenit News*, June 2006).

11. "Exploring a Catholic Rite" (*Newsday*, Long Island, NY, June 19, 2006).

12. Ibid.

13. Ibid.

14. Thomas W. Petrisko, *Mother of the Secret* (Santa Barbara, CA: Queenship Publishing Company, 1997), back cover.

15. Ibid, page xiii.

16. Ibid., page xxiv.

17. Ted and Maureen Flynn, *Thunder of Justice* (Sterling, VA: MaxKol Communications, 1993), p. 12.

18. Ibid.

19. From Dwight Longenecker's website: http://www.dwight longe neck er.com/Content/Pages/Bio.

20. Lockenecker, *The Path to Rome* (Herefordshire, UK: Gracewing, Reprinted 2000), back cover.

21. Interview with Scott Hahn, "Eucharist in the Pontificate of Benedict XVI" (*Pontifications*, June 12, 2005, http:// catholica.pontifications.net/

?p=940).

22. "Evangelicals & Catholics Together," http://www.leaderu.com/ ftissues/ft9405/articles/mission.html.

23. Ibid.

24. The complete Evangelicals & Catholics Together document can be viewed at http://www.leaderu.com/ftissues/ft9405/articles/mission.html.

25. Rick Warren, speaking at the Pew Forum on Religion, "Myths of the Modern Mega-Church" (May 23, 2005, Key West, Florida, see transcript at: http://pewforum.org/events/index.php?EventID=R80).

26. Ibid.

27. Ibid.

28. Catholic Purpose Driven Life program: http://www.purposedriven.com /en-US/40DayCampaigns/PurposeDrivenChurches/Catholics/ PDCatholics.htm.

29. Larry Osborne, "Sharing the Pulpit" (Ministry ToolBox, Issue #17, July 25, 2001, http://www.pastors.com/RWMT/?ID= 17& artid=556&expand=1).

30. Keith Howard McIlwain "The Eucharist as a Key to Pastoral Care and Renewal in the Church" (http://www.geocities.com/Heartland/ Ranch/9925/do_this.html).

31. *Alpha News*, Alpha International, Holy Trinity Brompton, UK, March/June 2004.

32. There are numerous such occasions where Raniero Cantalamessa addressed an Alpha audience, such as is documented in the following article: "Papal Preacher gives Alpha follow-up talks" (from the Alpha website: http://alpha.org/runningacourse/news/1999/08/papel preach er.htm, 1999). For more information on Alpha's connections to Catholicism, see Bayith Ministries, http://www.users.globalnet.co.uk/~emcd/ index.htm.

33. Matthew Hay Brown, "Returning to the rituals: Some evangelicals are exploring high liturgy," (*Baltimore Sun*, March 2, 2006), p. 4.

34. Ibid.

35. Doug Pagitt, *Church Re-Imagined*, op. cit., p. 103.

36. Scot McKnight, "Five Streams of the Emerging Church" (*Christianity Today*, February 2007, http://www.christianitytoday.com/40534).

37. Scot McKnight, "An Anglican Service" (Jesus Creed blog, http:// www.jesuscreed.org/?p=2258).

38. Scot McKnight, *Turning to Jesus*, (Louisville, KY: Westminister John Knox Press, 2002 edition), p. 7.

39. Robert Webber, "A Call to an Ancient Evangelical Future" (Online at: http://www.aefcall.org/read.html.

40 . Brian McLaren, "The AEF Document as a Preaching Resource" (From the AEF Call website: http://www.aefcall.org/documents/TheAEFDocumentasaPreachingResource_000.doc).

41. Matthew Hay Brown citing Robert Webber, "Returning to the rituals," op. cit.

42. Interview by Jordan Cooper with Robert Webber, "An Interview with Robert Webber, author of The Younger Evangelicals" (The Ooze, December 11, 2002, http://www.theooze.com/articles/article.c fm ?id =385).

43. Robert Webber, *Signs of Wonder* (Nashville, TN: Star Song Publishing Group, 1992), p. 3.

44. Ibid.

45. Ibid.

46. Ibid. pp. 3-4.

47. Ibid., p. 4.

48. Ibid., p. 5.

49. Father Raniero Cantalamessa, "Father Cantalamessa on Corpus Christi" (*Catholic Online*, June 17, 2006, http://www.catholic.org/featured/headline.php?ID=3402).

50. Peter Kreeft, *Ecumenical Jihad* (San Francisco, CA: Ignatius Press, 1996), p. 164.

9/The Kingdom of God on Earth

1. Doug Pagitt, "Unraveling Emergent" (*Relevant Magazine*, http://www.relevantmagazine.com/god_article.php?id =6365).

2. Brian McLaren, *A Generous Orthodoxy*, op. cit., p. 267.

3. Ibid., p. 268.

4. Ibid.

5. Ibid.

6. The term *partnering (or partners) with churches* is sometimes added to Rick Warren's P in P.E.A.C.E. Plan as in this example: http://www.purposedriven.com/en-US/Events/SG_Conference/FillInAnswers.htm.

7. Interview with Rick Warren, (*Philippine Daily Inquirer*, July 30, 2006, http://showbizandstyle.inquirer.net/lifestyle/lifestyle/view_ article.php ?article_id=12466).

8. Interview by Charlie Rose with Rick Warren (August 17, 2006, http://video.google.com/videoplay?docid=-5555324196046364882).

9. Rick Warren, "Myths of the Modern Mega-Church," op. cit.

10. Interview by David Kuo with Rick Warren, "Rick Warren's Second Reformation" (http://www.beliefnet.com/story/177/story_17718_1.html.

11. Interview by Charlie Rose with Rick Warren , op. cit.

12. Ibid.

13. Ibid.

14. Rick Warren, "Myths of the Modern Mega-Church," op. cit.

15. Interview by Charlie Rose with Rick Warren , op. cit.

16. Ibid.

17. Mark Kelly, "Rick Warren launches global initiative" (Baptist Press, http://www.bpnews.net/bpnews.asp?ID=20603, April 19, 2005).

18. Dan Wooding, "Rick Warren Hits Home Run with Announcement of Global Peace Plan to Battle Giants of Our World" (Assist News Service, http://www.assistnews.net).

19. Mark Kelly, "Rick Warren launches global initiative," op. cit.

20. Ibid.

21. David Brooks, "A Natural Alliance" (New York Times, May 26, 2005).

22. "Rick Warren Says Church Best Equipped to Solve Africa's Problems" (Assist News Service, can be read at: http://jmm.aaa.net.au/articles/15452.htm).

23. Rick Warren, Purpose Driven Life (Grand Rapids, MI: Zondervan, 2002), p. 285.

24. Ibid., p. 286.

25. Rick Warren in foreword of Dan Kimball's The Emerging Church, op. cit., p. 8.

26. From biography on Brian McLaren's website: http://www.brianmclaren.net/biography.html.

27. Brian McLaren, The Secret Message of Jesus (Nashville, TN: W. Publishing Group, A division of Thomas Nelson, 2006), pp. 175-176.

28. Ibid., pp. 176-177.

29. Ibid., pp. 177-178.

30. Barbara Marx Hubbard, The Revelation (Mill Valley, CA: Nataraj Publishing, 1995), p. 174.

31. Ibid., p. 324.

32. Brian McLaren, The Secret Message of Jesus, op. cit. pp. 78-79.

33. Barbara Marx Hubbard, The Revelation, op. cit., pp. 172, (for more

information, this topic, see *Reinventing Jesus Christ* by Warren Smith, http://www.reinventingjesuschrist.com).

34. Tony Campolo, *Speaking My Mind*, op. cit., p. 209.

35. Ibid., p. 211.

36. Ibid., p. 217.

37. Ibid., pp. 212-213.

38. Ibid., p. 215.

39. Ibid.

40. Paul Nussbaum, "The Purpose Driven Pastor" (*Philadelphia Enquirer*, January 8, 2006, http://www.freerepublic.com/focus/f-religion/1555425/posts).

41. Doug Pagitt and Tony Jones, *An Emergent Manifesto of Hope*, op. cit., Mark Scandrette section, "Growing Pains, p. 30.

42. Doug Pagitt, "Unraveling Emergent," op. cit.

43. Ibid.

44. Mark Scandrette, *An Emergent Manifesto of Hope*, op., cit., p. 27.

45. Leonard Sweet, *Quantum Spirituality*, op., cit., p. 13.

10/The Undoing of Faith

1. CE Staff Reporter citing, Erwin McManus, "Pastor, noted author takes uncivil approach in new offering" (*Christian Examiner*, http://www.christianexaminer.com/Articles/Articles%20Mar05/Art_Mar05_09.html).

2. Statement from Mosaic website: http://www.mosaic.org/internship.

3. Erwin McManus, *The Barbarian Way* (Nashville, TN: Thomas Nelson, 2005) p. 4.

4. David Drury, *The Christ-Follower Pop Quiz*, "Am I a True Follower of Jesus Christ?" (http://www.drurywriting.com/david/05-PopQuizFollower.htm).

5. Charles Swindoll, *So You Want To Be Like Christ?* (Nashville, TN: W Publishing Group, Thomas Nelson, 2005), pp. xvi and 12.

6. Beth Moore in *Be Still* DVD, op. cit., "Contemplative Prayer" segment.

7. Richard Foster, *Be Still* DVD, op. cit., "Contemplative Prayer" segment.

8. From Ken Blanchard's website, Lead Like Jesus: http://www.leadlikejesus.com/templates/System/details.asp?id=36749&PID=422009.

9. Dan Kimball, *They Like Jesus but Not the Church*, op. cit., p. 37.

10. Ibid., pp. 11-12.

11. Ibid., p. 12.

12. Ibid., p. 40.

13. Ibid., p. 41.

14. Ibid., p. 19.

15. Ibid., p. 29.

16. Ibid., pp. 30, 32.

17. Ibid., p. 191.

18. Brian McLaren, *A Generous Orthodoxy*, op. cit., p. 293.

19. Rick Warren at the 2005 United Nations Prayer Breakfast, September 2005. For more information about the prayer breakfast, see "Rick Warren Speaks about Purpose at United Nations" by Rhonda Tse (Christian Post, September 14, 2005, http://www.christianpost.com/article/20050914/21340_ Rick_ Warren_Speaks_about_ Purpose_at_ United_ Nations.htm); quote in this book is from transcript of Warren's talk that was provided to Lighthouse Trails Publishing.

20. Donald Miller, *Blue Like Jazz* (Nashville, TN: Zondervan, 2003), p. 115.

21. Erwin McManus, *The Barbarian Way*, op. cit., p. 6.

22. "Youth with a Mission Experiments with New, Unscriptural Missions Strategy" (Foundation, Watchman's Trumpet, May - June 2000, http://www.feasite.org/WTrumpet/fbcwt004.htm#Youth%20With), p. 39.

23. Andy Butcher, "Radical Missionary Approach Produces 'Messianic Muslims' Retaining Islamic Identity" (*Charisma News Service*, March 24, 2000, http://web.archive.org/web/20010818051517/www.charismanew s.com/news.cgi?a=285&t=news.html).

24. Ibid., quoting from a report in "The International YWAMer," YWAM's staff newsletter..

25. H. L. Richard, "Christ-Followers in India Flourishing Outside the Church, a review of *Churchless Christianity* by Herbert Hoefer (Mission Frontiers, March/April 1999, http://www.missionfrontiers.org/1999/0304/articles/04f.htm).

26. Ibid.

27. Herbert Hoefer, *Churchless Christianity* (Pasadena, CA: William Carey Library, 2001 edition), p. xii.

28. Ibid., p. 17.

29. Ibid., p. 16.

30. Mike Oppenheimer, "A 'New Evangelism' for the 21st Century" (Let Us Reason ministries, 2006, http://www.letusreason.org/Curren 33. htm).

31. Leonard Sweet, *Quantum Spirituality*, op. cit., p. 130.

32. Rick Warren, "Discussion: Religion and Leadership," with David Gergen and Rick Warren (Aspen Ideas Festival, The Aspen Institute, July 6, 2005, http:/

/www.aspeninstitute.org); for more information: http://www. lighthouse trailsresearch.com/newsletternovember05.htm.

33. David Steindl-Rast, "Recollection of Thomas Merton's Last Days in the West" (*Monastic Studies,* 7:10, 1969).

34. Peter Kreeft, *Ecumenical Jihad,* op. cit., pp. 30, 160.

35. Sandy Simpson and Mike Oppenheimer, *Idolatry in Their Hearts* (Pearl City, HI: Apologetics Coordination Team, 2007, 1st Edition), p. 358.

36. Eddie Gibbs and Ryan K. Bolger, *Emerging Churches: Creating Christian Community in Postmodern Cultures* (Grand Rapids, MI: Baker Academic of Baker Publishing Group, 2005), citing Brian McLaren on back cover.

37. Ibid., p. 235.

38. Ibid., p. 130.

39. Ibid.., p. 126.

40. Ibid., p. 131.

41. Ibid.

42. Ibid., p. 132.

43. Ibid.

44. Ibid., p. 135.

45. Ray Yungen, *A Time of Departing,* op. cit., p. 108.

46. Leonard Sweet, *Soul Tsunami,* op. cit., p. 163.

47. Doug Pagitt and Tony Jones, *An Emergent Manifesto of Hope,* op cit., Samir Selmanovic section, "The Sweet Problem of Inclusiveness," pp. 192-193.

48. From Faith House Project website: http://samirselmanovic. typepad.com/faith_house/2.WhatisFaithHouseProject.pdf.

49. Doug Pagitt and Tony Jones, *An Emergent Manifesto of Hope,* op. cit., p. 194.

11/A Slaughterhouse Religion

1. Beka Horton, *Church History and Things to Come* (Pensacola, FL: Pensacola Christian College, 1997 printing), p. 156.

2. Harry Emerson Fosdick, *Dear Mr. Brown* (New York, NY: Harper & Row, Publishers, 1961), p. 136.

3. Harry Emerson Fosdick, *The Modern Use of the Bible* (New York NY: The Macmillan Company, 1924), p. 230.

4. Harry Emerson Fosdick, *Dear Mr. Brown,* op. cit., p. 135.

5. Ibid., p. 134-135.

6. Riverside City Church, New York City, http://www.the riversidechurchny.org/getinvolved/?fosdick-speakers.

7. Interview by Leif Hansen (The Bleeding Purple Podcast) with Brian McLaren, January 8th, 2006); Part 1: http://bleeding purple podcast .blog spot.com/2006/01/brian-mclaren-interview-part-i.html; Part II: http:// bleeding purple pod cast. blog spot.com/2006/01/interview-with-brian-mclaren-part-ii.html).

8. Ibid., part II.

9. Alan Jones, *Reimagining Christianity* (Hoboken, NJ: Wiley and Sons, 2005), p. 132.

10. Ibid., p. 168.

11. Ibid., Brian McLaren on back cover.

12. William Shannon, *Silence on Fire* (New York, NY: The Crossroad Publishing Company, 1995 edition), pp. 109-110.

13. Harry Emerson Fosdick, *Dear Mr. Brown*, op. cit., p. 136.

14. Brennan Manning, *Above All* (Brentwood, TN: Integrity Publishers, 2003), pp. 58-59.

15. Statement by Brian McLaren on McLaren's website: http:// www.brianmclaren.net/archives/000201.html, "What about other websites?"

16. The Center for Spiritual Development, 2006 Summer Seminar called "The Church in the 21st Century" where Brian McLaren and Marcus Borg were two of the speakers, http://www.center-for-spiritual-develop ment.org/DVDCatalog.html.

17. Rob Bell, *Velvet Elvis*, op. cit., pp. 180, 184.

18. Walter Brueggemann cited on United Theological Seminary web-site: http://www.united.edu/portrait/borg.shtml in reference to Marcus Borg's book, *The Heart of Christianity*.

19. Marcus Borg, *The God We Never Knew* (New York, NY: HarperCollins, First HarperCollins Paperback Edition, 1998), p. 25.

20. Ibid.

21. Marcus Borg, "Easter About Life, Not Death" (*Washington Post/ Newsweek* "On Faith" column, April 7, 2004, http://newsweek.wash ington post.com/onfaith).

22. John White, (*Science of Mind*, September 1981), p. 15.

12/A New Reformation?

1. Leonard Sweet, *Soul Tsunami*, op. cit., pp. 17, 75.

2. Rick Warren, "The Angel Stadium Declaration" (from pastors.com website: http://www.pastors.com/RWMT/?ID= 203& artid =8205&exp and=1, April 17, 2005).

3. Leonard Sweet, *Postmodern Pilgrims*, op. cit., p. xiv.

4. Ibid.

5. Kevin Eckstrom, "Lutheran leader calls for an ecumenical council to address growing biblical fundamentalism" (*Religious News Service*, August 11, 2005).

6. Ibid.

7. Bishop Mark S. Hanson, Lutheran World Federation President and presiding Bishop of the ELCA, "The Church: Called to a Ministry of Reconciliation," Address to the LWF Council in Jerusalem (*Lutheran World*, September 2005, http://www.lutheranworld.org/LWF_Documents/2005-Council/President_Address-2005_EN.pdf), p. 1.

8. Ibid., p. 8.

9. "Younan: Christian Zionism is heresy" (*The Lutheran*, March 2003, http://findarticles.com/p/articles/mi_qa3942/is_200303/ai_n9221870). Note: According to one online encyclopedia, Christian Zionism is defined as: a belief among some Christians that the return of the Jews to the Holy Land, and the establishment of the State of Israel in 1948, is in accordance with Biblical prophecy, http://en.wikipedia.org/wiki/Christian _ Zionism).

10. Brian McLaren cited on "PBS Special on the Emerging Church" (*Religion and Ethics Weekly*, July 15, 2005, http://www.pbs.org/wnet/religionandethics/week846/cover.html), part 2.

11. Interview by Planet Preterist with Brian McLaren (http://planet prete rist.com/news-2774.html).

12. Ibid.

13. Ibid.

14. Rick Warren, "What Do You Do When Your Church Hits a Plateau?" (Rick Warren June 16, 2006 e-newsletter, Issue 263, http://www.pastors.com/RWMT/default.asp?id=263& artide=4533&expand=1).

15. From Church Transitions website: http://www.church transitions.com/about_cti.htm.

16. Dan Southerland, *Transitioning* (Grand Rapids, MI: Zondervan, First Zondervan Edition, 2000), p. 116.

17. Ibid., p. 115.

18. Mike Oppenheimer, "The Plan" (Let Us Reason ministries, citing Barbara Marx Hubbard, *Happy Birthday Planet Earth*, Ocean Tree Books, 1986), p. 17, http://www.letusreason.org/NAM20.htm).

19. Leonard Sweet, *Soul Tsunami*, op. cit., p. 75.

20. Interview by Al Sergel with Erwin McManus, "Soul Cravings, Q&A (*Relevant Magazine*, http://www.relevantmagazine.com/god_ article .php ?id=7241).

21. Ibid.

22. Erwin McManus endorsement of Dan Kimball's book, *The Emerging Church* (Vintage Faith website: http://www.vintagefaith.com/endorsements.html.

23. Erwin McManus, *The Barbarian Way*, op. cit., pp. 14-15.

24. Ibid., p. 32.

25. Ibid., pp. 15, 17.

26. Ibid., p. 110.

27. Ibid., p. 114.

28. Ibid., pp. 134, 138.

29. Ibid., p. 63.

30. Interview by *Relevant Magazine* with Erwin McManus, "In That Smoky Room" (*Relevant Magazine*, http://www.relevant magazine .com/god_article.php?id=6989).

31. Erwin McManus "Bio" (http://erwinmcmanus.com/bio).

32. Dan Kimball, *They Like Jesus but Not the Church,* op. cit., p. 137.

33. Ibid., p. 138.

34. Interview with Jay Bakker, "Empire of the Son" (*Radar*, http://radaronline.com/features/2006/12/empire _of_the _son _par t_iii.php).

35. Bakker's website: http://www.revolutionnyc.com/links.htm.

36. Interview by Larry King with Jay Bakker; see transcript: http://transcripts.cnn.com/TRANSCRIPTS/0612/15/lkl.01.html.

37. Brian McLaren, "Leader's Insight: No Cowardly Flip-Flop: How should pastors respond to "the Homosexual Question"?(*Christianity Today*, January 23, 2006, http://www.christianitytoday.com/leadersnewsletter/2006/cln60123.html).

38. Mario Bergner, "Conversations with Jason about Homosexuality" (*Redeemed Lives News*, Spring/Summer 2001, http://www.redeemedlives.org).

39. Ibid.

40. Interview by Candace Chellew-Hodge with Philip Yancey, "Amazed by Grace" (*Whosoever* online magazine, http://www.whosoever.org/v8i6/yancey.shtml).

41. Philip Yancey, "Hope for Abraham's Sons" (*Christianity Today*, November 1, 2004).

42. Steve Knight citing Doug Pagitt, "Phyllis Tickle to Write Book for Baker Books/Emersion"(Emergent Village, May 30, 2007, http://www.emergentvillage.com/weblog/phyllis-tickle-to-write-book-for-baker-booksemersion).

43. Ibid.

44. Fred Plumer, "What is Progressive Christianity Anyway?" (The Center for Progressive Christianity, http://www.tcpc.org/library/article.cfm?library_id=377).

45. Citing from Emergent Village Weblog, http://www.emergent village.com/weblog/emergent-and-the-new-reformation).

46. Doug Pagitt and Tony Jones, *An Emergent Manifesto of Hope*, op. cit., Troy Bronsink section: "The Art of Emergence," p. 68.

47. Ibid., pp. 68-69.

48. Ibid., p. 69.

49. Ibid., p. 70.

50. Ibid., p. 71.

51. Ibid., pp. 72-73.

52. Ibid., p. 83.

53. Robert Webber (editor), *Listening to the Beliefs of the Emerging Churches* (Grand Rapids, MI: Zondervan, 2007), Karen Ward chapter: "The Emerging Church and Communal Theology," p. 163.

54. Ibid., pp. 163-164.

55. Throughout Alice Bailey's writings is the concept of humanity's at-one-ment (oneness) with God.

56. Robert Webber (editor), *Listening to the Beliefs of the Emerging Churches*, Karen Ward, op. cit., p. 164.

13/ Or An End-Time Deception

1. Interview by Debbie Smoker with Neale Donald Walsch (Edge Life Expo, 2004, http://edgelifeexpo.com/interviews/walsch.html).

2. Neale Donald Waslch, "What is the New Spirituality?" (Group of 1000 website: http://www.thegroupof1000.com/newspirituality.cfm).

3. Leonard Sweet, *Quantum Spirituality*, op. cit., p. 13, citing Thomas Merton from "Thomas Merton's View of Monasticism" [delivered in Calcutta, October 1968], in *The Asian Journal of Thomas Merton*, ed. Naomi Burton, Patrick Hart, and James Laughlin (New York: New Directions, 1973), p. 308.

4. See footnote #14 of chapter 6.

5. Alice Bailey, *The Reappearance of the Christ* (London, UK: Lucis Publishing Company, 1948, fourth printing, 1962), p. 12.

6. The term *self-centeredness* is used by New Agers to indicate those who will not work together for the larger common good. Barbara Marx Hubbard stated: "[T]here's something of a deeper nature happening among the … "Emergence" … like a shift of identity, from the separated *self-centered* stage to a more unified stage. … I think we're becoming homo universalis, a universal humanity." (Interview with Barbara Marx Hubbard from Share Guide, http://www.shareguide.com/Hubbard.html). See also: "The Plan," by Mike Oppenheimer for more information: http://www.letusreason.org/NAM20.htm.

7. Walter Brueggemann, cited in *An Emergent Manifesto of Hope*, op. cit., p. 311.

8. Rick Warren, "The Power of Parishioners" (*Forbes* magazine, May 7, 2007, http://www.forbes.com).

9. Doug Pagitt and Tony Jones, *An Emergent Manifesto of Hope*, op. cit., Brian McLaren section, "Church Emerging," p. 149.

10. Alice Bailey, *The Reappearance of the Christ*, op. cit., p. 5.

Index

A

Alpha course 132
An Emergent Manifesto of Hope 47, 215, 216, 224
ancient wisdom 101, 102, 104, 106, 115, 120
Anderson, Leith 28, 55
Artress, Lauren 68, 69
        also see labyrinth
atonement, the
        92, 104, 190, 191, 192, 193, 194, 195, 197, 198, 216, 217, 220

B

Bailey, Alice 179, 181, 188, 216, 223, 227
Be Still DVD 91, 158
Bell, Rob 109, 110, 111, 112, 196
Benedict XVI, Pope 124, 125, 126
Bible prophecy 154, 155, 156, 157, 173, 201
Blanchard, Ken 169
Blue Like Jazz 174
Bolger, Ryan 181, 182, 183, 184, 185
Borg, Marcus 115, 116, 195, 196, 197
Bronsink, Troy 215, 216
Brueggemann, Walter 196, 224
Buber , Martin 27, 103
Buddhism 14, 84, 85, 86, 93, 110, 120, 169, 174, 179
Buford, Bob 23, 24, 25, 26, 28, 29, 34, 37, 38, 104
Burke, Spencer 102, 183, 184, 185

C

Calvin Institute 71, 237
Campolo, Tony 108, 112, 113, 114, 116, 120, 160, 192, 202
Cantalamessa, Raniero 133, 139
Catholicism 50, 51, 59, 62, 64, 65, 67, 74, 75, 76, 77, 78,
        105, 107, 134, 174, 201
Catholic Church
        50, 74, 75, 76, 77, 78, 116, 122, 123, 126, 127, 129, 139, 140, 153, 200, 202
Celebration of Discipline 86, 87, 107

Christian yoga 94, 95, 96
Collins, Jim 25, 26, 231
Colson, Chuck 130, 152, 153
contemplative 58, 67, 81, 82, 83, 84, 85, 86, 87, 88, 89, 90,
    91, 97, 98, 99, 100, 101, 102, 105, 106, 107, 108, 111,
    112, 114, 117, 121, 139, 168, 227
contextual theology 42, 43, 47, 48

D

Dirksen, Dale 71, 72, 73
Driscoll, Mark 22, 23, 37, 65
Drucker, Peter 22, 23, 24, 25, 26, 27, 28, 29, 30, 31, 37,
    38, 103, 146
drumming 69, 70, 71

E

Eastern religion 25, 83, 86, 87, 93, 94, 95, 109, 112, 169
Eckhart, Meister 25, 27, 64, 107
ecumenism 13, 40, 70, 105, 137, 140, 147, 148, 154, 161, 200,
    202, 213, 227
Edwards, Tilden 86
EFCA 131
Emergent Village 47, 134, 187, 214
emerging spirituality 19, 20, 26, 30, 36, 106, 160, 167, 173,
    181, 185, 195, 196, 207, 210, 213, 214
end times 143, 201
eschatology 136, 143, 144, 161, 204
Eucharist, the 63, 78, 122, 123, 124, 125, 126, 127, 128, 129,
    130, 131, 132, 133, 134, 135, 136, 137, 139, 140, 202, 227
Evangelicals & Catholics Together 130
evangelism 30, 60, 132, 154, 167, 178, 182, 183, 185

F

Flemming, Dean 43, 44
Flynn, Brian 97, 98, 99
Fosdick, Harry Emerson 191, 192, 194, 197, 216
Foster, Richard 64, 86, 87, 88, 89, 90, 91, 99, 100, 107, 168,
    196, 212, 213
Fox, Matthew 32, 33, 83
Fromm, Chuck 60

N

O

P

R

S

T

V

W

Other Books by Lighthouse Trails Publishing

A Time of Departing
by Ray Yungen
$12.95, ISBN: 978-0-9721512-7-6

Another Jesus, 2nd Ed.
by Roger Oakland
$12.95, ISBN: 978-0-9791315-2-3, *Released Summer 2007*

For Many Shall Come in My Name, 2nd Ed.
by Ray Yungen
$12.95, ISBN: 978-0-9721512-9-0

Laughter Calls Me
by Catherine Brown
$12.95, ISBN: 978-0-9721512-6-9

Running Against the Wind
by Brian Flynn
$12.95, ISBN: 0-9721512-5-7

Tapestry: The Journey of Laurel Lee
by Laurel Lee (author of *Walking Through the Fire*)
$15.95, ISBN: 0-9721512-3-0

The Other Side of the River
by Kevin Reeves
$12.95, ISBN: 978-0-9791315-0-2

Trapped in Hitler's Hell
by Anita Dittman with Jan Markell
$12.95, ISBN: 978-0-9721512-8-3

To Order Additional copies of:
FAITH UNDONE

send $12.95 plus $3.75 (for 1 book) to:
Lighthouse Trails Publishing
P.O. Box 958
Silverton, Oregon 97381

Call or go online for information about quantity discounts.

You may order online at
www.lighthousetrails.com
or
Call our toll-free number:
866/876-3910
[ORDER LINE]

For all other calls: 503/873-9092
Fax: 503/873-3879

Faith Undone, as well as all books by Lighthouse Trails Publishing, can be ordered through all major outlet stores, bookstores, online bookstores, and Christian bookstores.

Bookstores may order through
Ingram, Spring Arbor, or Send the Light.
Libraries may order through Baker and Taylor.

Quantity discounts available for most of our books.
International orders may be placed either online, through e-mail or by faxing or mailing order form.

For more information:
Lighthouse Trails Research Project
www.lighthousetrailsresearch.com
or visit the author's website at:
www.understandthetimes.org